101
SCHOOLING EXERCISES
FOR HORSE & RIDER

CELEBRITY EXERCISES CONTRIBUTED BY
Richard Davison, Pippa Funnell,
Tim Stockdale, Lizzie Murray, Sylvia Loch,
John Lassetter, Jennie Loriston-Clarke,
Karen Dixon, Mary King, Lee Pearson

Compiled by
JAKI BELL
in consultation with
ANDREW DAY

D&C
David and Charles

To all my long-suffering and patient instructors who have, over the years, shared their knowledge and expertise with me:

- ❏ Andrew Day
- ❏ Helen Anderson
- ❏ Meryl Doran
- ❏ Claire Lilley
- ❏ Psyche Dell
- ❏ Karen Foster

A DAVID & CHARLES BOOK
David & Charles is a subsidiary of F+W (UK) Ltd.,an F+W Publications Inc. company

First published in the UK in 2005
Reprinted 2005, 2006

Copyright © Jaki Bell 2005

Distributed in North America
by F+W Publications, Inc.
4700 East Galbraith Road
Cincinnati, OH 45236
1-800-289-0963

A catalogue record for this book is available from the British Library.

ISBN 0 7153 1950 7

Printed in Singapore by KHL Printing Co Pte Ltd
for David & Charles
Brunel House   Newton Abbot   Devon

All line illustrations by Ethan Danielson except p41 Maggie Raynor and p54–5 Dianne Breeze
Photographs on pp 22, 52–52 Matthew Roberst

Commissioning Editor: Jane Trollope
Desk Editor: Louise Crathorne
Art Editor: Sue Cleave
Project Editor: Anne Plume
Production: Beverley Richardson

Visit our website at www.davidandcharles.co.uk

David & Charles books are available from all good bookshops; alternatively you can contact our Orderline on (0)1626 334555 or write to us at FREEPOST EX2 110, David & Charles Direct, Newton Abbot, TQ12 4ZZ (no stamp required UK mainland).

Contents

Introduction

I am absolutely passionate about schooling.

Some people love to hack, others love to compete, but whilst I enjoy both, I find a real buzz in a lesson that stretches both me and my horse. During my 'career' as a rider – spanning some twenty years, with the exception of a couple of gaps when I was without horse – I have had a lesson almost every week. If you conclude from this information that I must be a pretty good rider, then think again. I'm great on the theory, but Mother Nature didn't provide me with what is necessary, mentally and physically, to be a talented sportsman or woman: hence the regular lessons. However, this book is not about my athletic prowess.

Have you ever ridden into wherever it is that you school your horse and thought: 'What shall I do today?' That's where this book comes in: its aim is to give you an exercise, or a series of exercises to work on in order to solve a problem, or simply to move your horse's training forward. It is a collection of exercises that my equestrian friends and acquaintances, and I myself, have found useful, and that celebrity trainers have shared with me. I am a journalist, not a qualified instructor or trainer, and so I have worked in collaboration with one of my trainers, Andrew Day, to check the validity of these exercises in an arena and as part of a training programme. Andrew was an international event rider who turned his focus of attention to dressage and now conducts clinics across the country, training riders from beginner to Prix St Georges level. He is also senior lecturer at the Training the Teachers of Tomorrow Trust.

In compiling this book, some assumptions and generalizations have had to be made: firstly that you, the reader, have a basic knowledge of what we are trying to achieve with our horses, and are capable of the rudiments of riding. Riders are referred to as female – it's a sad fact for the sport that the majority of riders up to international professional level are female – and horses as male: my sincere apologies if these generalizations cause anyone offence. All the exercises are intended to be ridden in a rectangular arena or area with 90-degree corners, measuring 20m by 40m, and are graded by 'star rating' according to the ability of and appropriateness to the horse and rider.

This book is not intended to teach you how to ride, or to present a progressive training programme; if either of these is your goal you will need the help and advice of a good trainer – and it is at this point that I have to say that there is no replacement for a good trainer. As Lizzie Murray says: 'Everybody needs lessons and help. And everybody needs somebody on the ground. You can't train a horse totally on your own, you still need somebody else to say, "That looks good".'

Every trainer that I've worked with over the years, including during my time as editor of *Horse* magazine, and all the celebrity trainers whom I have consulted whilst preparing this book, have their favourite exercises and style of training – and I'm quite sure that yours is the same. Maybe, however, this book will bring something new, controversial or helpful into your work together; or perhaps you'll use it on those cold, dark winter mornings when schooling your horse is the last thing you really want to do, and you need some inspiration.

Think of me when you're there, because I bet I'll be out schooling, too......

Why School Your Horse?

The work done in the arena is only one part of the overall training programme that a rider should be involved with, and aware of, in connection with the horse(s) for which they are responsible. It is the area where, potentially, the most dramatic successes can be achieved – but where the most damage can be done, too. In my opinion there are three objectives to schooling a horse:

1 To gain his trust and respect

As most riders are aware, horses are flight animals. In a successful schooling session the horse, in theory, hands over to his rider the control of his ability to flee from anything that threatens him. If you ride with sympathy and consistency, making the most of his abilities, he will understand that you are there to help him.

2 To establish a method of communication via the aids

Horses and humans speak different languages. The aids are our means of communication, which is why it is so important to be consistent in your aids. A successful partnership with your horse is the result of good communication.

3 To build up and develop his fitness

Horses were not intended to carry humans, so our weight on their back disrupts their natural balance and can cause all sorts of physical and muscular problems. The first aim of schooling is to help your horse work through his back, to hopefully prevent any of these problems, and to develop his balance in such a way that he can carry our weight and move forwards in a co-ordinated and lively manner. Once a horse is working through his back he has the ability to 'work on the bit' or 'on the aids' in a 'correct' and therefore more comfortable fashion.

The Aims of Schooling

- ❏ Rhythm
- ❏ Straightness
- ❏ Balance
- ❏ Acceptance of the bit
- ❏ Suppleness
- ❏ Impulsion
- ❏ Development of the gaits

Structuring Your Schooling

Having a plan for what you intend to achieve is just that – a plan; and quite often plans have to be changed. Horses have good and bad days just as we do, so whilst on some days you will be able to work on the finer points of your horse's schooling, on others all you may be able to do is just work on persuading him to stand still. So whilst it is best to go into the arena with an idea of what you intend to achieve that day, it is essential that you are flexible.

It is just as well to have a long- and a short-term goal. Your long-term objective can range from being fit enough for a three-hour pleasure ride, to wanting to compete in whatever your chosen discipline may be. Short-term goals, such as working on the quality of your horse's canter, are the building blocks on which the long-term plan can rest.

Envisage these aims as a pyramid, and break down your long-term goal as much as you possibly can. For example, your horse's canter may be affected by your inability to keep your heel down and in the stirrup, so one brick in the wall of your training programme may be a schooling session working on your position and how to re-train that wayward heel.

Allow yourself time to achieve your goals. There are very few riders out there who are not guilty of working on a particular dressage test a week before the competition, for example. Write some extra contingency time into your training programme and put it to good use if you don't need to spend it in the school.

Be realistic about your own and your horse's abilities: for example, most horses and riders can be identified as 'preferring' or favouring jumping or flatwork. Whilst a comprehensive training programme should ideally allow the horse to experience as much as possible, working according to your natural talents and preferences will set you off on the right foot.

This same approach to positive attributes should be applied to your pre-school thinking wherever possible. Rather than starting off in the school with the intention of correcting a particular fault, begin by working on movements that your horse is good at to gain his confidence and trust, progress through related exercises, and only then tackle the problem.

Try not to become involved in a battle of wills. Of course your horse has to understand that his job is to do what you ask of him, but you must ask yourself whether what you are asking is too much, or whether you've asked the question clearly. This is one of many occasions when the assistance of a trainer, or somebody on the ground with a knowing eye, is invaluable. You are the one with the smarter brain, and you should use it to find another way of tackling the problem and achieving the result – remember that, at the end of the day, your horse will always be stronger than you are.

Always begin your schooling session by warming up. The most favoured way of doing this is to allow your horse to stretch and work in a long and low outline. A young or lively horse, however, may need to let off excess energy when he first comes into the arena, and if safety is an issue, in this case it may be wise to lunge before schooling. Others may benefit from a short hack before they go into the school – for example, an older horse may take longer to loosen up than he once did. It is up to you to work out which is the best method to warm up the horse you are riding.

SCHOOLING TIP FROM SYLVIA LOCH

Working long and low does not mean hollow. 'If I give [a horse] a long rein when his back is hollow, I'm actually encouraging him to hollow more. A horse shouldn't be stretching with a hollow back, he should be stretching with a more rounded back. (Exercise 23)

Reprimanding your horse when he ignores your aids or misbehaves must be done immediately, but should not be accompanied by anger. This is a vital part of your communication with your horse. But don't forget to reward him when he makes the breakthrough and understands what you are asking of him, or does any manoeuvre particularly well. In fact, use every opportunity to praise your horse with a pat, or by using whichever words work for you, or by relaxing the reins, or even by concluding the schooling session: in the right circumstances the horse will understand any of these gestures as his reward. As Karen Dixon puts it: 'It's all a confidence thing. As the horse grows in confidence, you've got to reward it and pat it, even if it only gives you a little bit.'

Have one objective in mind and an idea of how you will reach it; think of all aspects of your schooling as building blocks. Sometimes you will need to go back to the basics that you have already laid down. And once you are in working mode, remember to take frequent rest periods: Sylvia Loch advises: 'Don't do anything for too long – that's how you keep your horse listening.' Whatever happens in the arena, it is important for both you and your horse that you end on a positive note, even if at the end of the session this is as simple an exercise as riding a great circle, or a movement that you know your horse does well.

Once you have achieved something that you can leave the arena with, and can notch up as a success, allow your horse to 'wind down' at a slower pace before dismounting and leaving the school.

Training programmes vary according to horse, rider and objective, but as a rough guideline, most of our celebrity contributors recommend working in the school or arena at least twice a week in a seven-day training programme that includes one day off. The length of time spent schooling varies not only from trainer to trainer, but also from day to day, as on some occasions your horse will go into the arena and perform brilliantly, whilst on others more work is needed.

In summary

❏ Identify your long-term goal.

❏ Build up your training progressively 'brick by brick'. Identify a series of short-term aims that relate to the long-term goal. This may need to be broken down even further, depending on how much you have to achieve.

❏ Include breaks and cooling-down periods in your schooling.

❏ Be sure that your aims and aids are clear and consistent.

❏ Discover the best way to warm up your horse.

❏ Be aware of your own and your horse's strengths, and don't forget to re-appraise your successes.

❏ Finally, in the words of Jennie Loriston-Clarke: 'Never lose your temper. If things aren't going right, take a back seat and look at what you are doing, or seek advice.'

The Horse's Way of Going

The most important thing when schooling your horse is that he works towards a correct outline. A young or unschooled horse will put about two-thirds of his weight on his forehand: this is his most natural position, that enables him to forage successfully and to move as economically as possible in the wild. If, however, you watch a colt or a gelding in a field showing off to a passing mare or to his fieldmates, you will see that he elevates himself from the front end, and it is this natural showmanship that has influenced our perception of the way a horse is seen to his best advantage. This is not, however, just an aesthetic issue, because in this position his body muscle is braced to carry his weight, which relieves the skeleton of its supportive function and reduces shock on the limbs.

At the other end of the scale, with his weight on his forehand a horse is difficult to steer and to stop, more likely to stumble, and uncomfortable to ride. So, to enable him to move in an uphill fashion with this lightness and elevation, the emphasis of balance needs to be transferred to the hindquarters. As your horse becomes accustomed to carrying himself in this way, it becomes easier for him, and he is better able to maintain this position. Thus he will become physically better developed, healthier, nicer to look at, and a pleasure to ride.

This transfer of weight and balance is referred to as 'engaging the back and hindquarters', and it develops gradually throughout a horse's training. It is part of a complex bio-mechanical chain that engages what is known as the horse's 'postural ring': this is a ring of muscle that runs from the poll, down the neck, over the back, round the haunches, under the stomach and through the front legs to the throat.

When you ask your horse to work actively and he is balanced, he will engage this ring of muscle. This engagement begins with his stomach and abdominal muscles and as he contracts these, his back lifts and he is able to take your weight. At the same time this contraction helps close the ribcage and draw in the muscles on the underside of the neck, thereby arching the neck. His shoulders are able to reach forward and he can accept the bridle. At the more advanced levels of training, when a horse can maintain the uphill position, the poll is deemed to be the highest point and his nose should be vertical – but this should only be the result of training, and not of manipulation by the rider's hands. It is acceptable for a horse developing his musculature to work in a lower outline.

This is what we are looking for when the horse is working in an outline:
- ❏ the abdominal muscles contract;
- ❏ the back is raised;
- ❏ the quarters lower and the hind legs step further under the horse;
- ❏ the underside of the neck contracts and draws the upper neck into the correct arch.

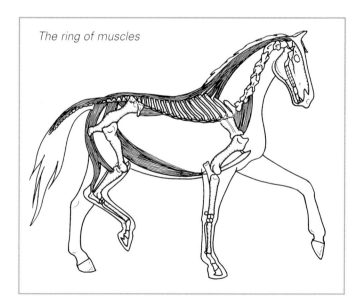

The ring of muscles

The Rider's Position

As previously stated, in preparing this book a certain level of competence has been assumed. However, it never does any harm to check on your position, since working in the correct position makes it easier for you to apply the aids to best effect. In schooling work, the dressage seat is the normal position, and the old adage 'a straight line through ear, shoulder, hip and ankle' should be ingrained in every rider's mind.

Head:	Your head should be held with the chin up, so your eyes are looking through the horse's ears.
Shoulders:	Your shoulders should be carried naturally, but slightly back to support your chest.
Elbows:	Your elbows should be relaxed and touching your sides.
Hands:	A straight line should run from the bit ring, through your forearm to your elbows. On this line, the position of your hands is established by the need to keep your thumbs on top.
Seat:	Your seat should be in the lowest point of your saddle. Your weight should be equal in each hip bone and inside thigh muscle. Both your seat and thigh muscle should be relaxed. A balanced seat is essential to the correct application of your aids.
Thighs:	Your thighs should be turned slightly inwards in order that your knees can rest against the saddle and be as near the vertical as possible.
Knees:	Your knee should be bent.
Calfs:	The inside of your calf should rest softly against your horse's body, just behind the girth strap.
Feet, heels and toes:	Your feet should rest in the stirrups, parallel to the horse's sides. Your toes should not turn in or out. Your heels should be the lowest point of your body.
Upper body and back:	Your upper body should be 'tall' and evenly balanced above the saddle and your hips; collapsing on one side is a common fault. It should be supple enough to move with the movement of the horse's back, but at the same time should support your shoulders, neck and head. Your back should retain its natural curve and remain relaxed.

RIDER'S TIP

If your stirrups are too long, your weight will fall on to your thighs and raise you out of the saddle. This will also prevent you using your legs properly.

The Rider's Problem Solver

Throughout any horse's training it is inevitable that you will encounter problems. During my time at *Horse* answering readers' enquiries, there were several questions that kept coming up. To give you an idea of just one of the ways in which this book may be used, we have identified what appear to be the most common difficulties that riders encounter and have collected together the exercises that may help resolve the particular issue.

'My horse is stiff on one side.'
5 9 25 41 53 61 66 72 84

'How do I train an older horse?'
3 7 16 18 22 25 33 40 51 55 81 90

'My horse is a youngster, I'm just beginning his training. Where do I start?'
1 3 4 9 13 18 22 40 51

'My horse tends to rush, what exercises will help?'
1 4 13 17 28 35 43 71 72

'Help, my horse is ignoring my leg aids. Is there anything I can do?'
1 6 10 11 13 15 21 34 38 57 62 66 71 75 76 80 97 98 99 100

'Can you help with my canter transitions?'
9 10 13 21 25 35 69 71 72

'Can you suggest some exercises to warm up my novice horse?'
3 4 9 15 18 22 23 24 25 40 44 49 50 51 54 58

'My horse really worries when we go into the arena.
How should I work him so that I avoid winding him up?'
1 3 4 7 9 13 15 22 25 26 29 31 40 49 50 51 56 57 61 80 90

'My horse is really lazy. How do I get him going?'
1 10 14 15 17 18 19 20 21 22 35 40 44 52 59 65 67 68 69 83 90 97 98

'What exercises should I work on to supple my horse's back?'
4 9 12 13 15 16 18 19 20 22 23 25 29 33 35 40 43 51 54 56 58 62 69

'I'm struggling to lengthen my horse's stride. Which exercises will help?'
16 18 19 20 22 23 24 35 62 64 65 67 68

'What exercises can I work on to generally improve my test scores?'
2 5 7 13 21 22 23 26 33 34 35 36 37 53 70 84

'How do I lighten my horse's forehand?'
1 4 9 12 13 14 15 16 19 22 23 30 35 36 38 44 52 53 57 60 62 67 68 69 79
90 96 98

Making Things Work
by Andrew Day

Everyone who cares for and rides the same horse regularly will, in a short time, develop a relationship with him. Horses, as herd animals, are governed by a fairly strict social order based on personal space, territory and frontiers. They are subject to hierarchy according to pecking order. When we stable and ride a horse we become the other member of the herd and start to build our relationship with our horse. In a successful relationship the horse will first trust the rider and then respect him. From this respect and trust we can begin to educate the horse to react to our aids of leg, seat and rein.

In the modest early stages of schooling we are concerned with a basic control of speed and direction so that we can ride out or exercise our horses safely. If these early stages are accomplished correctly, then they will form the foundation of a language and influence that can take us to the dizzy heights of advanced dressage.

Dressage is a fascinating and unique sport. It requires an appreciation and understanding of the horse's structure, posture and locomotion. Training the horse in dressage is partly about schooling a reaction to the rider's aids, and partly about his gymnastic development, and to enhance his athletic development he should work through a well structured programme of routines and exercises. Every rider needs an extensive repertoire of these routines: they are the format of the horse's training.

They are:

❏ diagnostic – pinpointing weak areas of the horse's understanding or skills;
❏ educational – giving the rider the opportunity to teach the horse a new feel, step or response;
❏ gymnastic – to test and stimulate development in strength, suppleness, dexterity and co-ordination.

The exercises compiled in this book have been carefully selected to provide good value in each of these three areas, but great care should be taken over the manner in which the horse executes them. If the horse in his general way of going is incorrect, perhaps losing balance or running against the hand, then mindless repetition of any exercise will just serve to compound the problems.

For best effect the horse needs to be carrying himself in correct balance, to be on the seat, in front of the leg, and accepting the bridle. He needs to follow the rider's lateral position, and must know to stay within the corridor of aids.

Carrying himself
This is the expression used to distinguish between the horse that falls forward off the hind leg, and the horse that carries himself with support of the hind leg. It is a sophistication of balance and a prerequisite of collection.

Being 'in balance'
A horse is said to be 'in balance' when he is maintaining perfectly consistent rhythm with constant impulsion, neither falling left nor right from his rider's chosen line.

Being 'on the seat'

This describes the desirable state where a horse is not running away from a rider's bodyweight, and whose speed and rhythm can be regulated by the rider's bodyweight and seat. This is a pre-requisite of balance.

Being 'in front of the leg'

This is the state in which a horse understands to maintain his own efforts or impulsion, and not to be only active provided the rider is kicking. For a horse to be simultaneously in front of the leg, yet also on the seat, gives us access to his engagement.

Accepting the bridle

This expression describes a horse that has learned to adopt a rounded outline in accordance with the rider's hand position and rein length. When correct, the horse knows to not press or strain against a rider's hands, nor to tuck his chin in on his chest leaving the rider with loose reins, but to maintain a light contact in self-carriage. When the horse is:

❏ on the seat
❏ in front of the leg and
❏ within the bridle

we say he is correctly 'on the aids'.

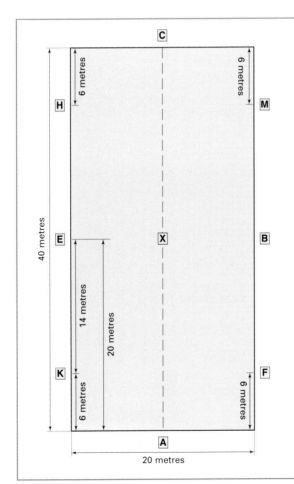

Setting Up an Arena

The best place to school your horse is in a purpose-built indoor school or outdoor arena with a fibresand or sand and rubber surface. However, where these facilities are not available, it is possible to school in a paddock or field. First select the flattest corner available that is free from any obstructions. It is helpful to have boundaries to your schooling area to keep you and your horse focused, to put you both in the right mental state for schooling, and to help contain your horse if necessary. The corner will provide two natural 'walls'. Use whatever is available to you to create the remaining boundaries. Some suggestions are: railway sleepers, jump poles, a white line marked on the earth or grass, a mown line – even bales of straw. At least one of your boundaries should be straight, as a guide when you need to practise riding a movement where it is important to stay straight.

Your arena should measure 20m x 40m (or 20m x 60m). Plastic cones or wooden boxes can be used as markers. The A, B, C and E markers are all exactly midway on the appropriate side, and the H, K, F and M markers are 6m in from the nearest corner.

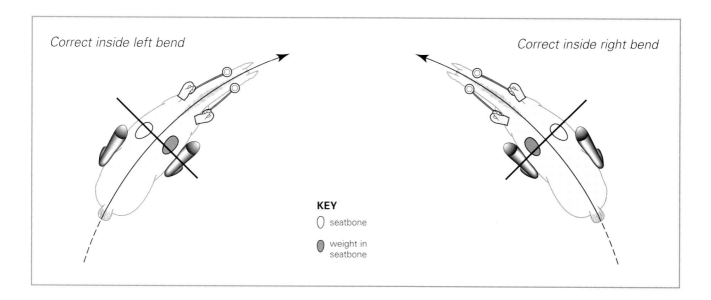

Correct inside left bend

Correct inside right bend

KEY

◯ seatbone

⬤ weight in
  seatbone

Lateral aiding

For a horse to work correctly, his spine should bend according to the line on which he steps. This is true in all cases except shoulder out, renvers, counter positioning and counter canter. To control the horse's spinal bend, the rider has to teach the horse to 'copy' his body position. Thus to ask the horse to bend, he should keep the inside leg to the girth and draw the outside leg back from the hip. This will retract the outside seat bone and transfer the weight to the inside seat bone. The rider's upper body should turn in the direction of movement, bringing the inside shoulder back and the outside shoulder forward, depending on the arc of the bend required.

The rider's hand position should change only as much as the shoulder position dictates, so the four influences of leg, seat, shoulders and hands should be related and fluid.

The aiding channel

Finally the horse needs to understand to stay within the corridor of the aids. This means that he should respect both the inside aids (he doesn't fall in) and the outside aids (he doesn't fall out), and should remain under the control of the rider's outside leg (the quarters don't slip out on turns).

These are all complex concepts, but to gain maximum value from this book it is important that they are understood so that we can work towards establishing them. With care over the above details, the exercises in this book will help you to develop a comprehensive and effective training programme.

Good luck!

RHYTHM, BALANCE AND IMPULSION

The fundamental requirements

THE EXERCISES

The first things you are taught in early riding lessons are how to stop and how to steer. These are basic requirements, but as you learn more about schooling a horse, your appreciation of the finer points of training, and establishing a harmonious relationship with him, will very quickly develop. For the horse, the fundamentals of flatwork are impulsion, balance, rhythm and suppleness, and the exercises in this section focus on improving these prerequisites. Moreover these are exercises that every rider needs to come back to at certain points in the training of a horse, however advanced that training might be.

EXERCISE

1

BEGINNERS ✪✪✪✪✪
PRELIMINARY ✪✪✪✪✪
NOVICE ✪✪✪✪✪
ELEMENTARY ✪✪✪✪✪
MEDIUM ✪✪✪✪✪

Walk-to-halt transitions

This may sound a bit basic, but it is essential in the early stages of schooling to ensure that your horse is fully attentive to your aids. Be sure that you are telling your horse when to halt and when to walk on.

BONUS

If you get this right now, you are establishing an excellent first building block in your training.

How do I ride this exercise?
- ❏ Establish walk. At a chosen marker, ask for halt.
- ❏ As soon as your horse has halted, reward and reassure him and then walk on.
- ❏ If your horse doesn't respond immediately, use your aids just a little more sharply.
- ❏ Once he has responded, relax the aids.

What should happen?
Your horse's weight should be distributed evenly over all four of his legs, and he should have 'a leg at each corner'. His poll should be his highest point. He should remain collected, with a supple jaw, and he should be attentive and ready to move off at your command.

How do I ride a perfect halt?
- ❏ It's important to differentiate between halting correctly, and merely pulling up: all downward transitions should be prepared with a period of increasing collection.
- ❏ To ask for halt, both legs should be closed, a little behind the girth.
- ❏ Stretch up with the chest and upper body, and close the hand.
- ❏ As the horse squares, relax the hand and leg.

Double check
Your horse should learn the habit of halting still, straight, and on the bit before you begin to teach him to square himself up.

Moving on
Once you've mastered walk to halt, try trot to halt. Watch out for too many walk steps. Let your horse find his balance in the downward transitions and don't push him on to his forehand.

What can go wrong?
1 Your horse pushes his weight on to the shoulder and may even yaw against the hand as he halts.
This is the result of not enough collection during the preparation for the halt.
2 Your horse stops abruptly.
Again due to unsuccessful collection, your horse has not stayed in front of your leg: use more leg in your preparation.

If it's not working...
If your horse is really not listening to you, seek professional help.

CELEBRITY
EXERCISE

2

BEGINNERS ✪✪✪✪✪
PRELIMINARY ✪✪✪✪✪
NOVICE ✪✪✪✪✪
ELEMENTARY ✪✪✪✪✪
MEDIUM ✪✪✪✪✪

Using the centre line to work on straightness
from Pippa Funnell

This may sound a bit basic, but it is essential in the early stages of schooling to ensure that your horse is fully attentive to your aids. Be sure that you are telling your horse when to halt and when to walk on.

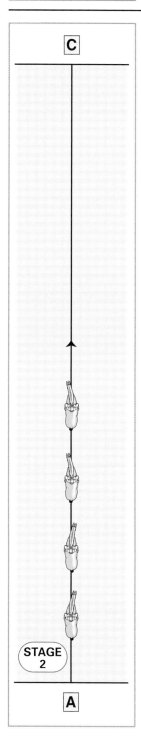

C

STAGE
2

A

How do I ride this exercise?

❏ Turn up the centre line and ride from A to C. Focus on keeping your horse straight using your legs rather than your hands. To check on your effectiveness, give one rein away for four strides and then take it back, then give the other rein away for four strides and take it back.

❏ Now repeat the exercise, but this time ask for a little neck bend for four strides, then straighten, then neck bend the other way for four strides and then straighten. Once again make sure that, as you change the bend and straighten before bending the other way, the horse's body stays absolutely straight while you are doing it.

What should happen?

Your horse should be able to maintain his straightness when you give and take the reins, and ask for the neck bend, then straighten: all the while he should stay absolutely true to that centre line.

Double check

Make sure that you are sitting in balance and correcting with your leg.

Moving on

Try riding this exercise in trot and canter.

What can go wrong?

1 When you ride the first part of this exercise the horse either deviates from the centre line or 'rubbernecks' (gives you too much bend one way or the other). *If your horse deviates from the centre line when you give the rein, you must be ready to intervene at the very onset of this problem. The moment your horse begins to deviate you have to catch him – not just in the act, but before it. If your horse is 'rubbernecking' you have to be very quick to take back the appropriate rein contact. Then ask again, by giving the rein, to see if your horse can understand to keep his neck straight while you give away the rein.*

2 Your horse falls in to the left or the right in the second part of the exercise. *If, when you ask for a little neck bend for four strides, the horse falls to the left, you have to use your legs to correct this, and once again make sure that you intervene before it becomes too big an issue.*

If it's not working...

If your horse is not well enough balanced to maintain his position on the circle, work on Exercises 4 and 9.

EXERCISE

3

BEGINNERS ✪✪✪✪
PRELIMINARY ✪✪✪✪✪
NOVICE ✪✪✪✪✪
ELEMENTARY ✪✪✪✪
MEDIUM ✪✪✪

Working on balance: the hourglass pattern

This exercise is appropriate for horses just starting their training. However, to ride it perfectly could take many hours of practice.

How do I ride this exercise?
- ❑ Starting at A on the right rein, ride a rounded corner (see diagram) in walk to K.
- ❑ From K, continue the curve to the quarter line, then ride straight over X to the opposite quarter line.
- ❑ Commence a gradual left curve to blend with the track at M.
- ❑ In the next corner ride a large rounded corner.
- ❑ Repeat the exercise from C.

What should happen?
Your horse will have to adjust his balance between a right-hand curve and a left-hand curve, thus improving his balance skills.

Double check
Be sure that you are not compensating for your horse's lack of balance with your shoulder position.

Moving on
Ride this exercise in trot; this is the pace that will bring most benefit.

What can go wrong?
Your horse suddenly falls off the track.`
Once you have recognized which shoulder your horse is inclined to drift through, prepare to support him before the bend with your outside leg and outside rein when the weaker shoulder is to the outside, and with your inside leg and inside rein when the weaker shoulder is to the inside.

If it's not working...
Go large around the school, riding rounded corners.

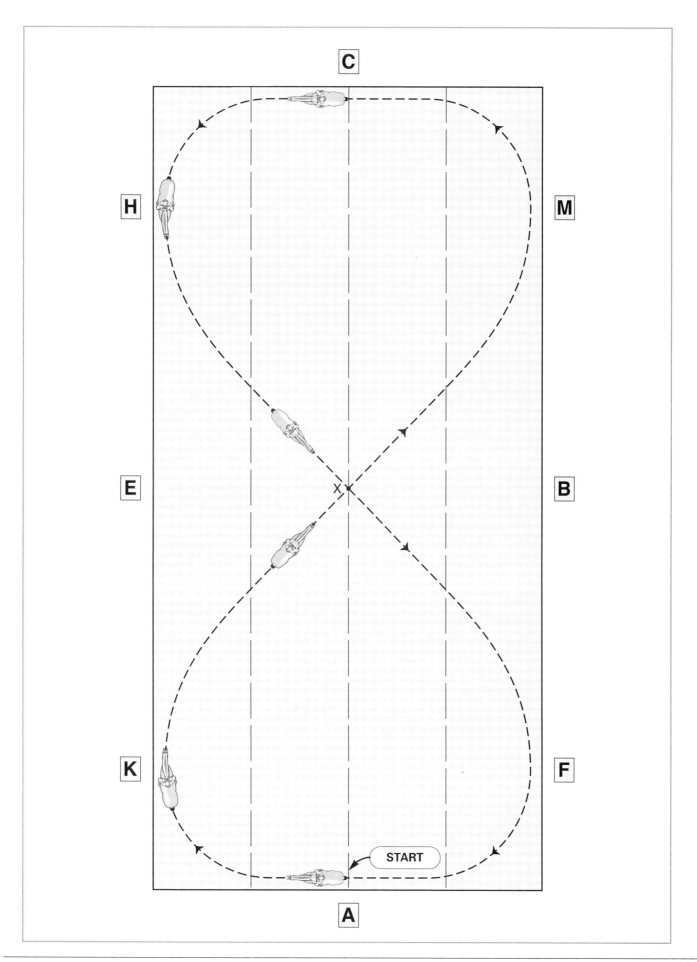

Working on balance: long sides and half circles

Before you even start to think about turning, you have to be sure that your horse is in balance; do this with half-halts. Work on your horse's reaction to your aids as you ride through the turn, as this will help to improve his balance.

BONUS

Although this appears to be a simple enough exercise, perfecting your horse's reaction to your aids through the turn will do much to improve his balance.

How do I ride this exercise?

❏ On the left rein, ride the long side straight from F to B in walk.

❏ Continue, and just before M, ride a 20m half circle to just past H.

❏ At H stay large on the track and repeat the exercise at K, until you feel you have got it right.

❏ Repeat the exercise on the opposite rein.

What should happen?

Your horse should be able to move up the long side in perfect balance, in a consistent rhythm, neither falling in nor falling out. Prior to the turn your horse should be asked for a little inside bend with the inside rein; at this point the inside leg should be used on the girth to remind him not to fall in. At the marker, the outside rein should be used in short guiding signals against the horse's neck. Your outside leg should be behind the girth, helping to keep the haunches from stepping out.

Double check

Be sure that you are not twisting your shoulder to counter balance your horse's tendency to fall in one way or the other.

Moving on

Ride this exercise in trot and in canter.

What can go wrong?

1 Your horse falls out through the inside shoulder.
  Use your inside leg.

2 Your horse falls in through the outside shoulder.
  He is ignoring your outside rein and leg, so you should be a little firmer and make sure that his rhythm is not too fast.

If it's not working...

This is a very basic exercise, so if your horse is not listening to you, you need to go back to establishing both his attention and his reaction to your aids: it may be that you need some professional help. Alternatively if you are working in trot or canter, go down a pace.

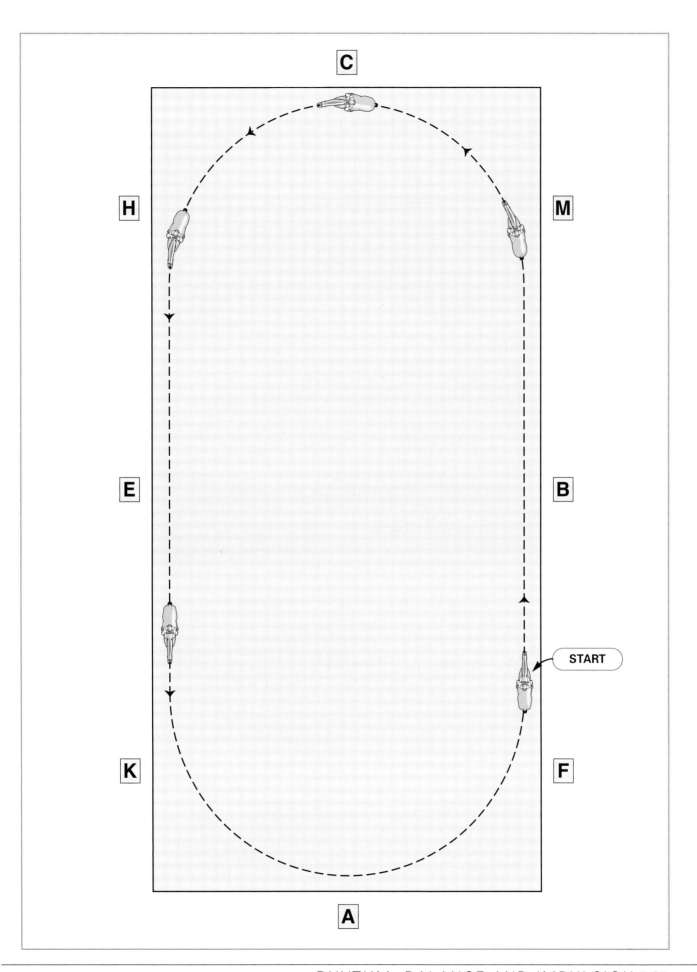

CELEBRITY EXERCISE

5

BEGINNERS	⊙
PRELIMINARY	⊙⊙
NOVICE	⊙⊙⊙
ELEMENTARY	⊙⊙⊙⊙
MEDIUM	⊙⊙⊙⊙⊙

An exercise to check that you are sitting straight
from Pippa Funnell

Any problems of straightness that occur in the horse's performance can usually be traced back to the rider's position and lack of straightness. This exercise will help you identify and correct any tendency to be crooked in your riding.

How do I ride this exercise?

❑ Ride a circle on both reins in trot.

❑ Take your knees and thighs completely away from the saddle to check whether you are sitting in balance.

'So often when I am watching dressage I see riders losing marks because their own crookedness is making the horse crooked.'

What should happen?

If you don't fall either way you will be sitting straight, and the horse will be able to keep straight and upright under you. If you are slipping one way or the other you will find yourself gripping particularly hard with one thigh. The combination of this and the inevitable pull on the rein to keep you in balance will result in the horse losing straightness: he will be receiving a mixed message – the inside rein is asking him to bend, but your position is making it difficult for him to do so. This is how horses become stiff and one-sided.

Double check

Be sure that your horse is in balance and upright before you begin this exercise.

Moving on

Once you are adept at riding this exercise in trot, with caution try riding it in canter.

What can go wrong?

1 You slip to one side!

If you feel yourself sliding one way or the other, you will know that you are not sitting in balance. For an exercise to help correct this crookedness in your riding – and as long as your horse is steady and reliable – ask a friend to lunge you whilst you hold your arms out to the side like a tightrope walker.

2 You bounce uncontrollably.

This is because you are missing your knee grip. You need to improve your sitting trot technique, working on getting your lower back into the right position.

If it's not working...

Begin by trying the exercise at halt, then at walk along the sides of the school. At the same time, consider taking regular lunge lessons to help improve your balance.

PIPPA'S PRIORITY POINTS

❑ The rider can maintain straightness by not letting their inside hip collapse but by remaining tall in the saddle, by keeping the inside leg long and pressed down, and by mentally dropping the outside shoulder.

❑ It can help to look behind you, over the outside shoulder, as an exercise; or if the horse is sensible enough, put both reins into the outside hand, and then put your inside hand behind your back and place it on your outside shoulder blade.

❑ If you aren't sure about your own straightness, ask someone to watch you from behind to check that your weight isn't falling more heavily on one side.

CELEBRITY
EXERCISE

6

BEGINNERS ✪✪✪✪✪
PRELIMINARY ✪✪✪✪✪
NOVICE ✪✪✪✪✪
ELEMENTARY ✪✪✪✪✪
MEDIUM ✪✪✪✪✪

Riding diamonds to improve your circles from Lizzie Murray

Lizzie Murray has 'a big thing' about straightness, and returns to this exercise, which she describes as four points of the circle, whenever it becomes an issue with even the most advanced of the horses she trains. 'I usually ride this exercise having first established corners and straight lines on squares and smaller squares.'

'Most horses are bent too much to the inside, and when you bend a horse's neck, the shoulders fall the other way.'

How do I ride this exercise?
❑ On the right rein and in trot, ride a diamond shape.
❑ On a 20m circle the points of the diamond should be one half way between the E and H markers, one at C, one half way between the M and B markers, and the fourth at X (see diagram).
❑ Concentrate on keeping the horse straight in between the turns: this will really make him engage himself, and in the canter it creates much better balance.

What should happen?
The horse should start to react more to the outside aids, and should become straighter, and in better balance.

Double check
Make sure you are bringing the horse's forehand around his haunches at the points of the diamond. When riding in trot, ride the points as 90-degree corners, keeping the outside leg back and pressing. This will help to keep the haunches working and prevent the horse swinging his back end out and leaning in on his inside shoulder.

Moving on
Try counter flexion on the straight lines. This exercise can be ridden in all three paces.

What can go wrong?
1 Your horse's quarters fall out to the outside.
   Be prepared to support him with your outside leg.
2 Your horse's shoulders fall in on the turn.
   Use more inside leg, and put a small circle in each corner to help establish bend around the inside leg, then straighten your horse on the straight sides.

If it's not working...
Try riding basic 20m squares at one end of the school (see diagram), reducing to 15m squares; then go back to trying this exercise. If you feel the need, there's no reason why you shouldn't try the exercise in walk initially.

BONUS

This is also a great exercise for helping a horse retain his balance and not fall through his inside shoulder, especially on circles. Once you can successfully ride the diamond, round it off into a circle of 20m: you should notice a marked improvement on previous performances.

> **CELEBRITY TIP**
>
> Says Lizzie: 'Most horses fall out through the shoulder. If you get your horse really balanced on the outside rein, you will hardly need the inside rein to turn a corner. You need the outside rein because that will bring the shoulders round.'

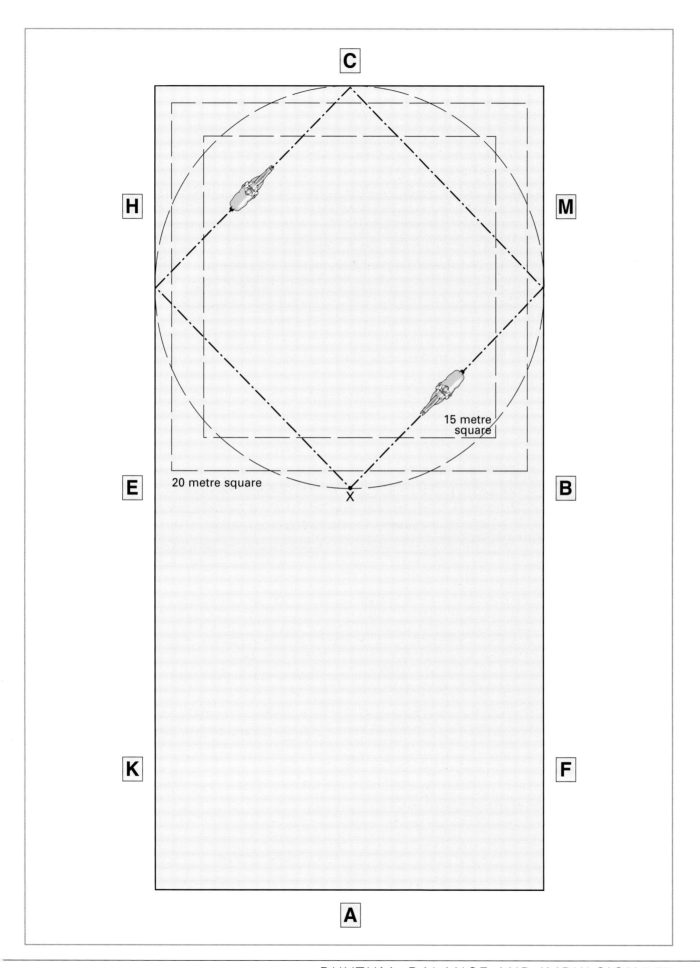

15 metre square

20 metre square

Riding a 'perfect' circle

Don't expect to find this easy. Obviously, because you need to mark the school with your foot or a stick or something, this exercise can only be performed on certain surfaces. But no amount of explanation can match up to actually seeing the line of a circle drawn in the 'sand', and this is a technique that could help with other exercises.

BONUS

This is a great exercise to revisit at any time in your training when the need arises, because it can be ridden in all the paces, including counter canter.

How do I ride this exercise?

❑ First you need to draw as accurate a circle as possible on your arena.
❑ Now ask your horse to step, foot perfect, along the line of the circle. This requires continual application of the aids to keep him on the curve of your line, and therefore a great deal of concentration on your, the rider's part.

What should happen?

The focus of this exercise is to help you become more spatially aware. As you and your horse work to maintain his steps exactly on the path of the circle, it helps you to appreciate and recognize his deviations!

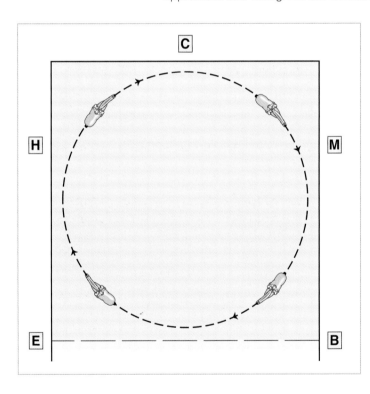

Double check

Be sure that your inside position and distribution of weight are correct.

Moving on

Try riding on a 15m and then a 10m circle, marked out as above. Also try riding the circle in trot, and then in canter.

What can go wrong?

Your horse starts to show resentment of what you are asking.
Make sure that your aids are clear.

If it's not working...

Mark the three-quarter line, and teach your horse to step correctly on a straight line.

CELEBRITY
EXERCISE

8

BEGINNERS ✪✪✪
PRELIMINARY ✪✪✪
NOVICE ✪✪✪✪✪
ELEMENTARY ✪✪✪✪✪
MEDIUM ✪✪✪

Five and fives
from Tim Stockdale

Tim says: 'Not only does this exercise aid collection, and help upward and downward transitions, but in a very short time it actually gets your horse to listen to you.'

How do I ride this exercise?
- ❏ Ride a 20m circle in a good, open, solid walk.
- ❏ Begin the exercise with five strides in walk in a soft manner, and a soft outline, and then strike directly into canter. This should be a proper canter, not a half canter nor a short collected canter, but a proper forward canter.
- ❏ Then come straight back down again into walk.
- ❏ And repeat, five strides of walk, five strides of canter, on the circle.
- ❏ Repeat this exercise on both reins.

What should happen?
Your horse will start to anticipate the five strides. As he comes down into walk, he'll already have his hocks beneath him, and he'll begin to hold his balance; and in the walk, he'll start to anticipate the canter, and collect himself ready to strike off. So what you're doing is using the anticipation to aid you. When he gets to this point, you can go into random strides (see Moving On).

Double check
Make sure the canter is a forward canter, and the walk is purposeful and regular.

Moving on
Once your horse is anticipating the 'five and fives', start to use random strides – for example, eight strides in canter and two in walk, or vice versa, or whatever suits you. Now your horse will really start to listen to you.

What can go wrong?
1 Your horse starts to anticipate your instruction and makes the transitions before you ask for them.
First, try being more positive with your aids: hold your horse until you are ready for the transition, counting the number of strides out loud if necessary. Alternatively you need to move on to random strides. Anticipation is good, but the horse must be saying 'I think we are going to go now', and not 'We're going to go now.'
2 Your horse 'throws his dollies out of the pram'.
He may be finding the 'five and five' repetition a bit stop-and-go. If that's the case, instead of going 'five and five', make the distance a bit bigger, 'ten and ten' for example.

If it's not working...
Go back to working through basic direct transitions (Exercises 15 and 21) before attempting walk-to-canter transitions.

EXERCISE

9

BEGINNERS ✪✪✪✪✪
PRELIMINARY ✪✪✪✪✪
NOVICE ✪✪✪✪✪
ELEMENTARY ✪✪✪✪
MEDIUM ✪✪✪

Introducing inside bend

This exercise works well with Exercise 4, Working on Balance: Long Sides and Half Circles, because it gives you the opportunity to correct the balance of your horse on a straight line without the support of the school wall or arena rails.

BONUS

Although one of the simplest balancing exercises, this is one of the most valuable available to a horse just starting his training.

How do I ride this exercise?

❑ Start on the left rein, in walk. Just before K, ride a half 15m circle to the three-quarter line.
❑ Ride up the three-quarter line.
❑ Once your horse is straight on the three-quarter line, ask for a left bend, and maintain the bend to the top end of the school.
❑ Once your horse has mastered the movement, repeat on the opposite rein.

What should happen?

Your horse should maintain a straight line with his forehand and haunches on the same path, and allow you to ask for a bend without distorting your position.

Double check

Be sure that you are not distorting your position in order to compensate for the horse's lack of balance.

Moving on

Ride in trot and canter.
Try bending to the outside.

What can go wrong?

1 Your horse falls in.
Use more inside leg.
2 Your horse falls out.
Use more outside leg and rein.
3 Your horse swings his haunches out.
Use more outside leg behind the girth, and take care that you are not asking for too much bend, or turning too suddenly from the track.

If it's not working...

Go back to riding a half circle to the three-quarter line without the inside bend.

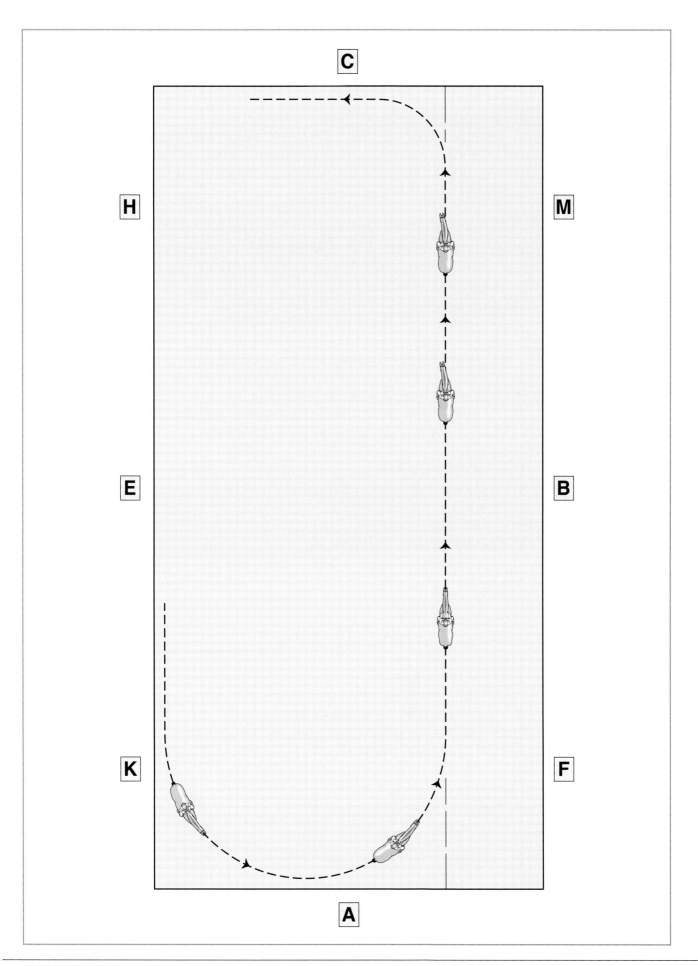

CELEBRITY EXERCISE

10

BEGINNERS ✪✪✪

PRELIMINARY ✪✪✪✪✪

NOVICE ✪✪✪✪✪

ELEMENTARY ✪✪✪✪

MEDIUM ✪✪✪

Using your inside leg to help with transitions
from Lee Pearson

Lee says: 'When your horse is a bit stiff or against your hand, rather than riding your transitions in a straight line with your horse straight, try bending him a bit more around your leg.'

CELEBRITY TIP

'Don't hold on to the inside rein, but keep it elastic.'

How do I ride this exercise?

❏ On the right rein in walk, at B ride a 10m circle.

❏ As you rejoin the track, keep the bend and ask for a transition to trot. If your horse maintains submission and doesn't hollow, gently straighten up and continue around the school.

❏ At E ride a 10m circle, making a transition back to walk, keeping the bend, as you come out of the circle. Keep your inside rein quite lively – I call it spongeing – to get and keep the submission.

❏ Straighten, and continue round the track to A.

❏ At A ride a 10m circle, and ask for the transition up to trot again, continue around the track. If you are satisfied with the transition, at B ask for a transition up to canter.

❏ Continue in this manner, using a 10m circle to help with your transitions whenever necessary, up and down through the paces.

❏ Repeat on the opposite rein.

What should happen?

The bend should encourage the horse to accept the bridle better and to stay supple; making consistent repetitive transitions should help to establish a good habit.

Double check

Your horse stays straight (on one track) and does not swing his quarters out when he makes the transitions.

Moving on

Ride the transitions without using the circles to assist.

What can go wrong?

1 Your horse puts his haunches to the outside.
Try using more outside leg.

2 Your horse becomes anxious with the frequency of the transitions.
Miss out a section to give him more thinking time.

If it's not working...

If you are not satisfied with the horse's submission, repeat the exercise at C or E until he understands what you are asking for. Then continue with the exercise.

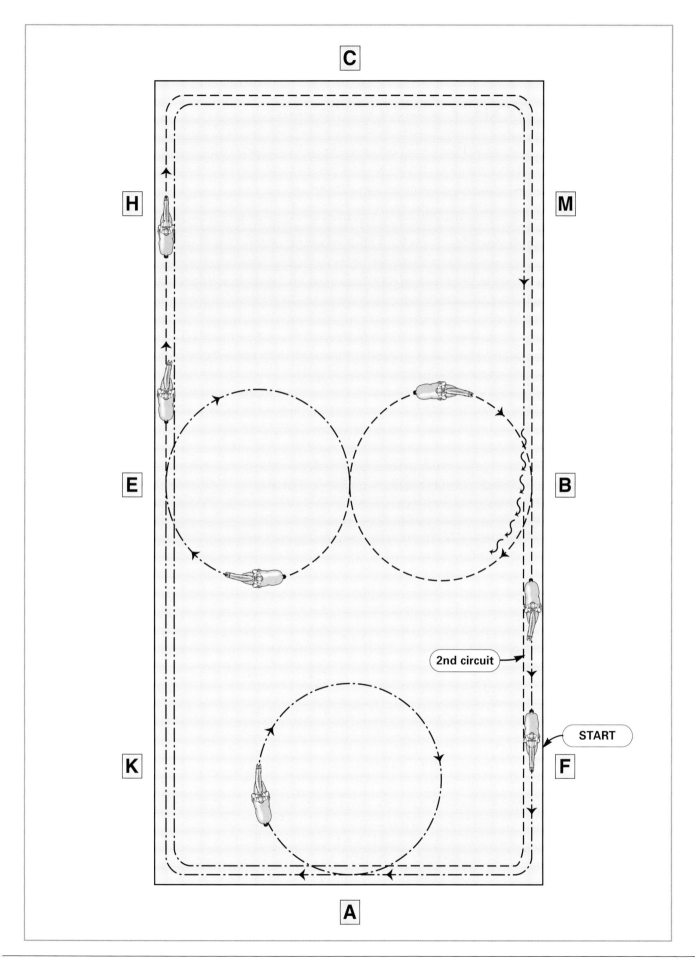

CELEBRITY
EXERCISE

11

BEGINNERS ✪✪✪✪✪
PRELIMINARY ✪✪✪✪✪
NOVICE ✪✪✪✪✪
ELEMENTARY ✪✪✪✪✪
MEDIUM ✪✪✪✪✪

Introducing the indirect aids from Sylvia Loch

Sylvia says: 'This exercise introduces your horse to the indirect aids – your outside rein and outside leg. Until your horse responds to the indirect aids he will never be truly straight, supple or "through".'

CELEBRITY TIP

'Your inside leg must be like a pillar leading the horse back: it must stay in alignment directly under your hip. Your leg should be at the girth to support the horse, because that feeling of the inside leg at the girth is what will return him to the track and keep him forward and straight. If your leg slips a little, or your hips slip, your horse will start to lose the quarters again: he'll fall in at the shoulder and his quarters will swing out.'

How do I ride this exercise?

❏ Ride down the long side of the school at walk (right rein).
❏ Halfway down, at E or B, make a right half circle to the centre line.
❏ Return to the track just before K, or just before F.

What should happen?

I tell the rider to ask the horse for a little bit of bend prior to the half 10m circle. Without bend, you won't have straightness – if a horse can't flex, he can't be straight. This exercise gets this idea across to the rider. Having completed the half circle I then ask the rider to bring the horse back to the track thinking of her outside rein and outside leg to control the quarters, as opposed to the inside rein and leg, which starts the movement off.

Double check

It is important not to change the bend until the rider arrives back at the track. This is the first step towards engagement.

Moving on

As the horse gets more experienced you can develop the exercise to returning to the track in half pass, first in walk and then in trot. It will also help your counter canter enormously.

What can go wrong?

Your horse brings his neck to the inside and throws his quarters out.
*If that happens, the point of the exercise will be lost. Going back to the track in the second phase will help to correct this, as you start to introduce the outside rein and the outside leg. I see a lot of riders who ride down the track and onto the half circle with too much neck bend hoping that they are getting suppleness. They tend to pull back on the inside rein, which allows the quarters to drift when they should come back to the track with the outside leg and the outside rein. The fact that the exercise is introducing the indirect aids – the outside leg and the outside rein – should hopefully stop the rider from feeling that he needs always to use the **inside rein** to guide the horse.*

If it's not working...

You are probably not keeping your inside hip forward, or supporting with the upper body. Even going down the long side you should be slightly advancing your inside hip preparatory to the half circle. When you return to the track, think of leading the horse back to the track slightly with your inside hip.

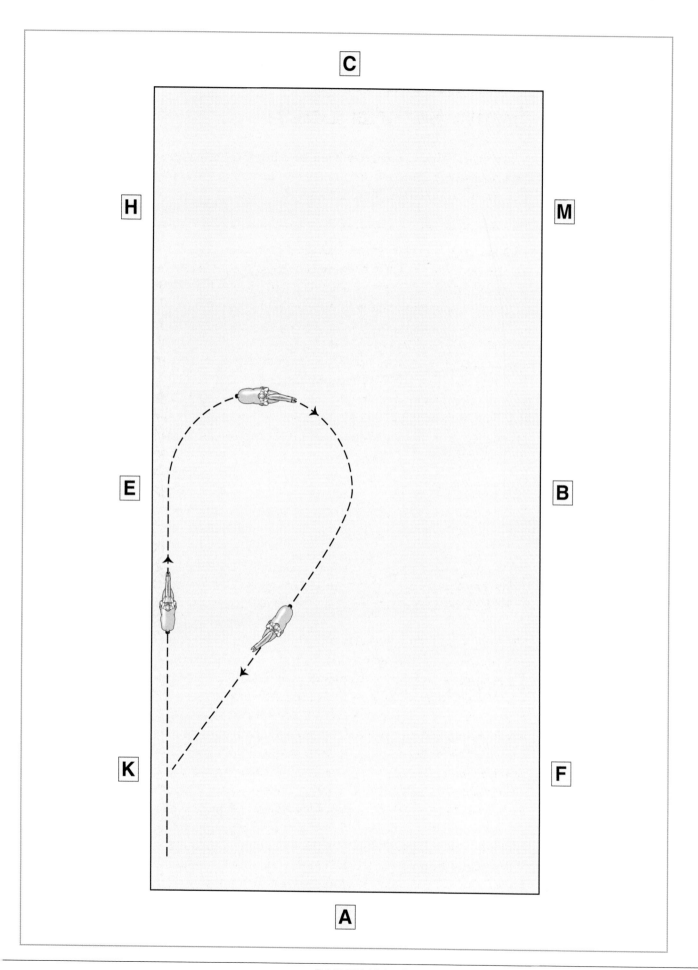

EXERCISE

12

BEGINNERS
PRELIMINARY ✪✪
NOVICE   ✪✪✪
ELEMENTARY ✪✪✪✪✪
MEDIUM   ✪✪✪✪✪

Using turn on the haunches for supling and collection from Sylvia Loch

'Once the rider can make the half circle and return to the track using their outside aids correctly, the turn on the haunches is my favourite balancing/collecting exercise.'

How do I prepare for this exercise?

❏ Ride down the long side of the school at walk on the right rein.
❏ Before E ride a 10m circle right, straighten up to E then ask for a two step 90 degree turn on the haunches. Then ride straight across to B on the other side. This should help encourage the horse on the bit, working more from the hind end.

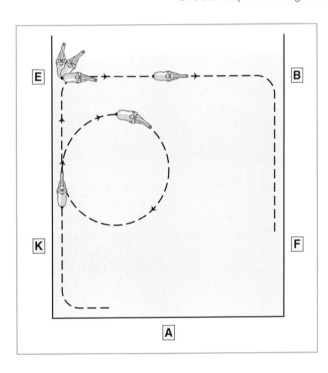

How do I ride turn on the haunches?

❏ On the right rein, straighten the horse on the track keeping a degree of inside poll flexion.
❏ Gently half halt with your upper body and outside rein, then apply lateral pressure with your outside leg behind the girth; the inside leg should remain 'neutral' and 'allowing' at the girth. There should be a little more downward weight into the inside stirrup.
❏ Apply pressure behind the girth with the outside leg at the same time as your outside rein guides the forehand to the right. Never cross the outside rein over the wither.
❏ Your inside rein must not pull back in the turn, but should gently give, to allow the horse to move into it.
❏ Having completed the turn, immediately apply a forward aid with the inside leg, and ride straight across the arena.

RIDER'S TIP

Be careful not to soften through the waist to the inside, as that's when your body-weight may slip to the outside.

How your riding can avoid problems

Rather than a nice slick turn, with your horse looking as though he's riding a square, it may look like a rather bad half circle. To improve this, sit very, very tall so that your seat doesn't slip to the outside. I often say to the rider: 'Imagine you've got an extra rib to the inside.' Keep the inside of your body very erect and supportive, and that keeps the inside seat bone in the correct position. You've almost got to think about the inside of your body being like a soldier on parade, so you keep a very long inside leg, everything hanging down with gravity, like a plumb line.

The outside of your body can be a bit softer, because that's what's allowing the turning. Remember, your horse has got to stretch to the outside, so the outside of your body can be a little more 'giving' as it accommodates your horse; then your horse will come round you. You act almost as a pivot for your horse: your horse comes around you – you don't push your horse away from under you in the turn.

What should happen?

Your horse's weight should move gently to the rear as he brings the inside leg more under his belly to make the turn. His poll should be his highest point. He should remain collected, with a supple jaw, and he should be attentive and ready to move off straight again, having completed the turn.

Double check

So many riders think they're asking with the outside rein, but they still bring the inside hand back. By doing this they're really turning the horse on the forehand, and when that happens, instead of the horse using and bringing the hind legs underneath him to push himself around, he pulls himself around with the forelegs.

Moving on

Quarter pirouettes are performed in walk or canter, although the latter is only for a very advanced horse. At a higher level the quarter pirouette in walk is ridden as a demi pirouette. Full canter pirouette is only ridden at Grand Prix standard. However, if you can't do a good turn on the haunches, it's unlikely you'll ever be able to ride good, accurate turns in walk, trot or canter, let alone canter pirouettes!

What can go wrong?

1 Your horse turns too much on the forehand or around the centre of his body.
You're probably using too much inside rein. You must appreciate that this exercise is mainly controlled by the rider's weight, the outside rein and the outside leg: it has nothing to do with the inside rein (other than gently flexing your horse to the inside, which is what you should already have done going down the long side).

2 Your horse manages his two steps to the right, and then goes crooked to B, rather than straight.
This is because you have asked correctly with the outside leg back behind the girth, you've given the horse a little nudge or a little pat, but your inside leg forgets to say to the horse that having completed these two steps he must now go forward. If the inside leg is not quick to say 'forwards', the horse will tend to fall right instead of coming out of a nice turn straight across to B. Without guidance he will drift on to the right shoulder.

3 Your horse goes into a shoulder-in, or jack knives.
This is a common occurrence, and is because you have turned before your horse. When you do this, your inside hip falls back and doesn't support your horse through the turn, so the horse moves away. Your bodyweight slips to the outside, and instead of supporting and leading your horse into the turn, it collapses and pushes him sideways. The horse will obviously move away when your bodyweight slips to the outside. Instead, always feel you have a little more weight on the inside seat bone and the inside stirrup, so your horse moves into your weight, not away from it.

If it's not working...

Work on letting go with the inside leg, and realize that the inside leg, whatever you are doing, has always got to be the 'pillar' around which the horse wants to bend. If it's not there, he's got nothing to bend around. Work on lengthening your inside leg, and make sure that it isn't in the wrong place: if it's too far forward, so that your heel is at the girth instead of the toe, you may find your weight no longer plumb from hip to stirrup. If it's too far back and pushing against the horse, it will merely prevent him from moving into the exercise.

EXERCISE

13

BEGINNERS
PRELIMINARY ✪✪
NOVICE ✪✪✪
ELEMENTARY ✪✪✪✪✪
MEDIUM ✪✪✪✪✪

Teaching half-halt to you and your horse

This technique is recommended in Jennie Loriston-Clarke's book *The Complete Guide to Dressage*. It makes use of repetition and association of location to help rider and horse understand the half-halt.

BONUS

The half-halt has all the collecting benefits of a downward transition.

How do I ride this exercise?

❑ Start in walk. Ride a 20m circle in the centre of the school, and each time you cross the centre line, ask for halt.

❑ Repeat this until your horse begins to anticipate the request. As soon as you feel he has reached this point, squeeze him on again.

❑ Now repeat the exercise in trot, asking for walk, using your voice, legs, seat and hands, as you cross the centre line. Once again, as soon as your horse begins to anticipate the downward transition, ride him forwards.

THE AIDS FOR HALF-HALT

❑ Sit in the correct upright position.
❑ Close the lower legs on the girth, gently squeezing the horse into a restraining but allowing hand.
❑ Lighten your seat.
❑ Close your legs on the girth again, and as your horse responds, allow him to go forwards.
❑ Apply the aids for the next movement.

What should happen?

Your horse should gather himself together, remain properly on the bit, but still feel as if he has sufficient impulsion to go forwards.

Double check

Once you are certain your horse understands your aids for the half-halt across the centre line, try the exercise in different parts of the school.

Moving on

Try riding this exercise in canter.

What can go wrong?

1 Your horse dies on you.

Work on teaching your horse to be more obedient to your leg aids before you start.

2 Your horse comes above the bit.

This is most likely because you are being a little heavy in your requests. Try to be rather more cautious, and use a gentler and more progressive approach when you ask for the half-halt.

These two problems are usually linked.

If it's not working...

Soften your aids, soften your demand, and revisit the exercises on teaching your horse to listen to your legs. Try Exercises 2 and 10.

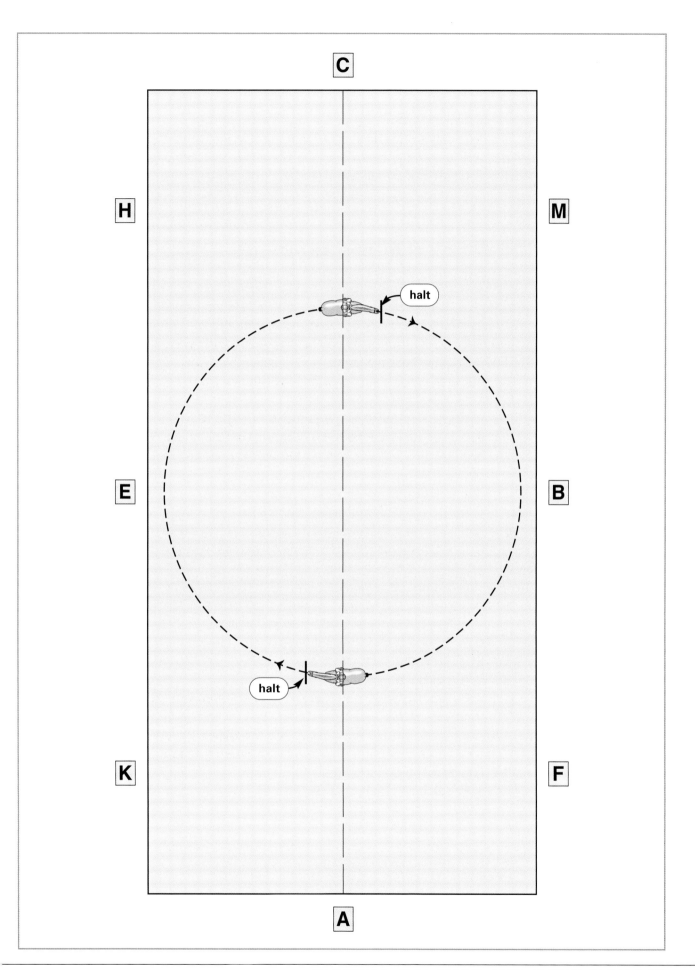

RHYTHM, BALANCE AND IMPULSION ▌37

CELEBRITY
EXERCISE
14

BEGINNERS

PRELIMINARY

NOVICE   ✪✪

ELEMENTARY ✪✪✪

MEDIUM   ✪✪✪✪

The square exercise to teach or refine the half-halt
from Richard Davison

The first part of this exercise prepares your horse for half-halt. Once you've mastered that, move on to the second part to complete his training! Richard says: 'I use this exercise about a thousand times a day!'

RIDER'S TIP

Use only your wrist to encourage flexion – not your arm. The wrist action is similar to signing your name with a pen, or turning a door key.

How do I ride this exercise?

- ❑ At the A or C end of the school, in trot, ride a 20m square.
- ❑ As you ride into your first corner, make a transition into as collected a walk as possible.
- ❑ Make a very deep corner with lots of little walk steps through the corner.
- ❑ Just as you come out of the corner, go into trot again and then repeat in the next corner.
- ❑ Repeat on the opposite rein.

The second stage:

- ❑ Ride the exercise without really quite walking. Your horse should almost anticipate your request as he comes to the corner, he should give you a slight bend, and reach his hind legs underneath his body. Like this you will go round the corner in collection, and then be ready to go forward again. This combination is the preparation for half-halt.

CELEBRITY TIP

I make my upper body slightly taller, and as I come out of the corner I allow it to go slightly forward: this way the horse associates upper body tall as a directive to 'come back' (so I don't have to use much rein) and upper body forward as a directive to 'go forwards' (so I don't have to use much leg). This makes him more sensitive.

What should happen?

This exercise uses transitions to supple and activate your horse. The downward transitions will improve his suppleness and engagement, the upward transitions will make him more responsive and active.

Double check

Be sure that you are applying your aids clearly just before every downward transition.

Moving on

1 Ride the exercise in canter/walk/canter.
2 Ride a 15m square, and then a 10m square.
3 This is a good preparation for Exercise 38, quarter pirouettes on a box to collect and engage the hocks.

What can go wrong?

You can't keep your lines straight.

Use poles on the open sides of the square; once your horse is riding the exercise correctly, you can remove them.

If it's not working...

'It always does,' says Richard. 'However, you should analyse whether the horse is better at the downward or the upward transitions, and concentrate on refining whichever are the weakest.'

RICHARD'S PRIORITY POINTS

❏ As you make the downward transition, keep your back supple in order that the horse's hind legs can step underneath him. You also ask the horse to flex a little to the inside before riding a very controlled and acute corner with very small walk steps.

❏ When you go from walk to trot, you should use just one single aid: your horse must be very responsive.

❏ Always encourage your horse to be round over his topline, so he brings his hind legs well under his body in the transitions.

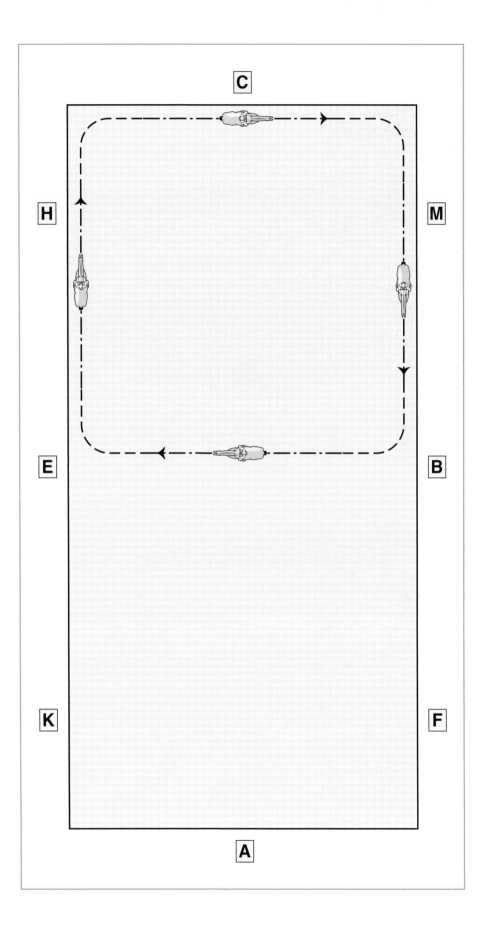

EXERCISE

15

BEGINNERS

PRELIMINARY ✪

NOVICE ✪✪

ELEMENTARY ✪✪✪

MEDIUM ✪✪✪✪

Quality transitions on a circle

Any transition is only as good as the preparation you put into it. And the way in which your horse makes his transitions is only as good as your training, because it must become a habit.

How do I ride this exercise?

❏ On a 20m circle in the centre of the school, establish a correct, consistent trot.

❏ With good preparation, ride a correct walk transition.

❏ Maintain the walk until it is correct in rhythm, energy, outline and straightness.

❏ Then prepare and ride a correct upward transition to trot.

❏ Stay in trot until this is correct in the same characteristics.

❏ Prepare and repeat the walk transition.

WHAT IS A CORRECT WALK AND WHAT IS A TROT?

❏ **The walk:** must be four equal hoofbeats, meaning that the time that elapses between the footfalls of the left hind and the left front hooves should be the same as between the left front and the right hind ones. The horse should have a generous overstep, and he should accept the bridle and use his neck in a stretching arc, as this encourages suppleness through the back.

❏ **The trot:** in a correct trot, the horse's legs move in diagonal pairs, working in perfect synchronization with a period of suspension between. The hind legs should step well under the body, lifting the horse sufficiently clear of the ground so as to emphasize the period of suspension. As in the walk, he should be accepting the bridle and using his neck in a stretching arc, so as to encourage suppleness through the back.

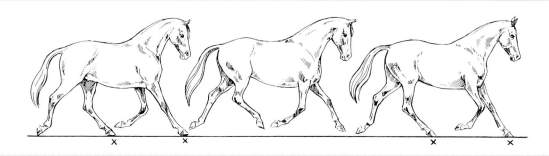

What should happen?

In the downward transition your horse should catch and support his bodyweight on his haunches. In the upward transition, whilst remaining in balance and accepting the bridle, he uses his hind legs to lift himself up into the next pace.

Double check

Be sure that your horse remains straight on the circle, and that his quarters do not swing in or out.

Moving on

Try this exercise in trot to canter.

What can go wrong?

1 Your horse uses his head and neck to pull himself up into the next pace.
   Ask him to be a little rounder and deeper first.
2 Your horse stops abruptly.
   Be prepared to use more leg to push him into the bridle.

If it's not working...

Go back to Exercise 13, teaching the half-halt.

EXERCISE

16

BEGINNERS

PRELIMINARY ✪

NOVICE ✪✪

ELEMENTARY ✪✪✪✪

MEDIUM ✪✪✪✪✪

Working on lengthening and shortening the strides

This is an exercise that will really teach your horse to listen to you, and will make him much quicker off your leg aids.

RIDER'S TIP

The best way that you can understand engagement, which is different from collection, is to compare it to its opposite, which is 'limp'.

How do I ride this exercise?

❏ Commence on the right rein, in working trot. Along the next long side, ask for lengthened strides.

❏ Return to working trot across the short side.

❏ Change the diagonal from either M or K.

❏ Repeat along the next long side, asking for lengthened strides, changing the rein across the diagonal and rejoining the track at F or H.

❏ Once you feel your horse has understood what is being asked of him, along the next long side, ask for lengthened strides from the first marker, shortening for two or three strides just before the centre marker, and then lengthening again.

❏ Repeat on the other rein.

What should happen?

By alternately lengthening and shortening your horse's strides you will help to increase his engagement.

Double check

Ensure that you are creating sufficient excitement and energy, rather than just chasing your horse into the lengthened strides.

Moving on

Try riding a number of shortened strides at the B and E markers on the long side. Ride this exercise in canter, returning to trot across the diagonal.

What can go wrong?

Your horse runs away from you.

In order to make a good lengthened stride your horse needs a sufficient level of engagement. If you have not achieved this, he will 'paddle' with his front legs and try to run forwards.

If it's not working...

Practise simple lengthened strides on an oval shape, Exercise 18.

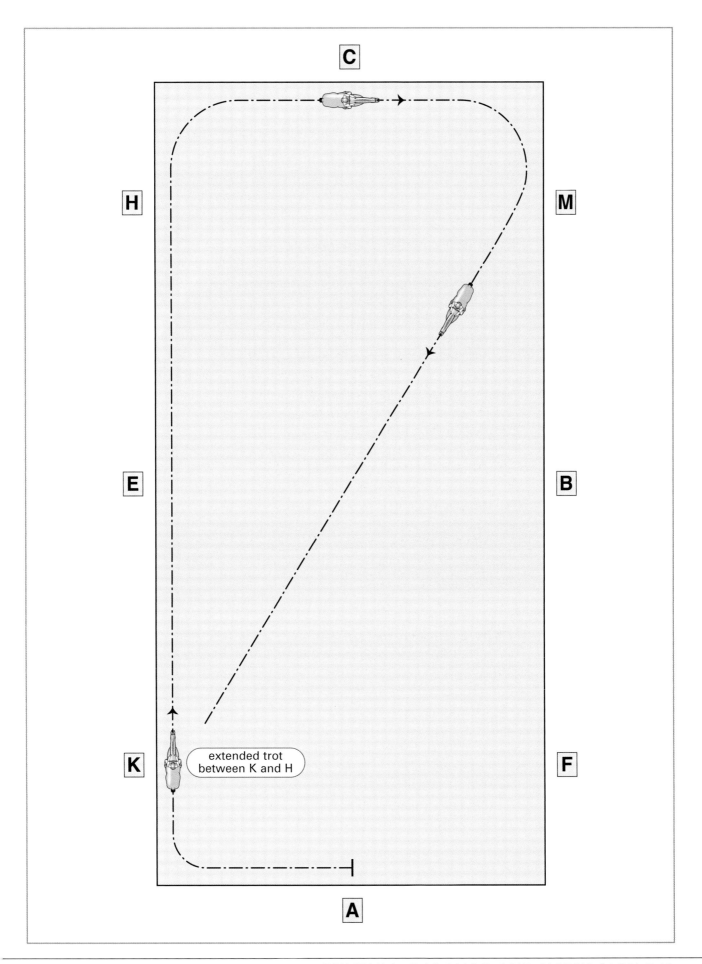

extended trot
between K and H

Lengthened strides into halt

BEGINNERS

PRELIMINARY ❂❂

NOVICE ❂❂❂

ELEMENTARY ❂❂❂❂❂

MEDIUM ❂❂❂❂❂

Ridden by an experienced rider, this exercise teaches a horse to make transitions from a faster pace in a very effective and relaxed way.

How do I ride this exercise?
❏ On the right rein establish a good working trot on a 20m circle at A.
❏ From K, build the medium trot on the diagonal.
❏ Just before M, collect.
❏ After M ask for halt, using the corner of the school to help reinforce the aid.
❏ Reassure your horse with a little pat.
❏ Repeat on the other rein.

What should happen?
This exercise will bring the horse's hind legs underneath him. It is particularly good for a big horse, and will help with the balance of the medium trot and the transition back to collected trot. The horse should gather himself together to collect for the transition, and should not be pulled up together by the rider.

Double check
Make sure that your horse is not intimidated by this procedure. If he is not yet in good balance he may find being ridden into the corner threatening.

Moving on
This exercise can be ridden in canter as a training exercise for tests.

What can go wrong?
Your horse loses balance and canters.
Make the upward transition to medium trot more progressive.

If it's not working...
Go back to the basic walk-to-halt exercise, Exercise 1.

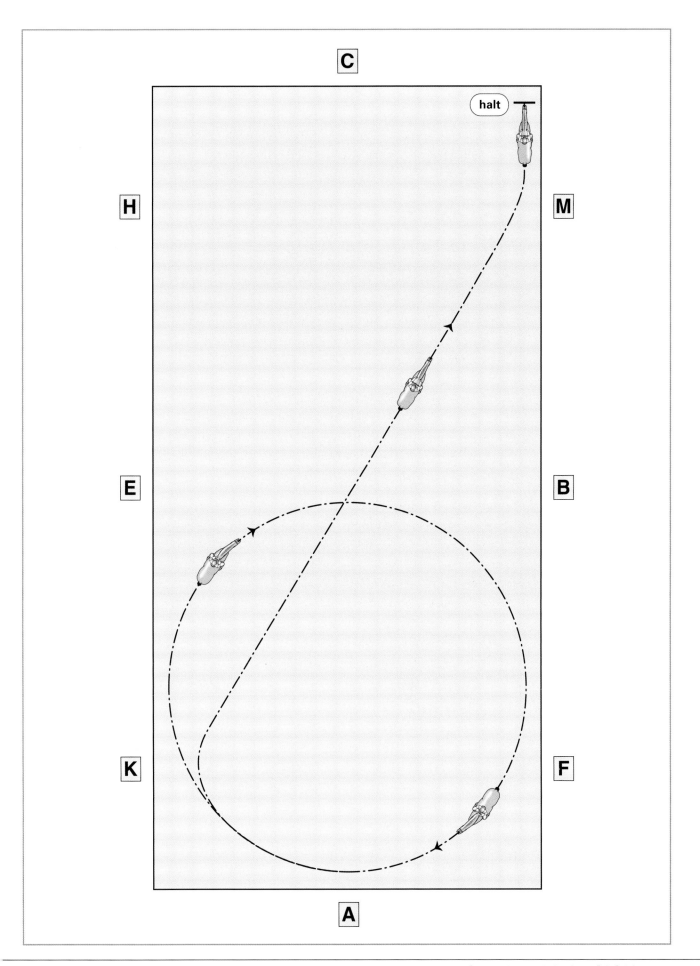

EXERCISE

18

BEGINNERS ✪✪✪✪
PRELIMINARY ✪✪✪✪✪
NOVICE ✪✪✪✪✪
ELEMENTARY ✪✪✪✪
MEDIUM ✪✪✪

Building up your trot on a big oval

Although this appears an innocent enough exercise, the half 20m circle, if ridden exactly, sets your horse up correctly for the medium trot on the straight line.

How do I ride this exercise?

❏ On the right rein starting at K, ride up the long side in trot until 10m before the corner.
❏ At this point commence a 20m half circle, finishing a little after M.
❏ Ride straight to 10m before the F corner, and once again repeat the 20m half circle to the right.
❏ Using this oval pattern, work on improving your horse's lengthened strides towards medium trot.
❏ Before he becomes tired, rest and then repeat on the opposite rein.

Why are we riding this on an oval?

Not only do the gentle half circles at the end provide a general rebalancing opportunity, they also permit the medium trot to be sustained around the entire school; the rider can build up the trot as and when they feel the horse is ready.

How do I ask for lengthened strides?

The important issue with lengthened strides is that you 'rally up your horse' and excite him; thus he will pick himself up and move forwards with the necessary enthusiasm and impulsion. Only you will know if it is the use of your seat, your legs, or both that will achieve this. Remember, however, that 'less' is always 'more'!

What should happen?

The gentle arc of the half 20m circles permits your horse to rebalance and collect himself together, and thus to sustain his medium trot; this in itself builds up his confidence, and will help increase the reach of his medium strides.

Double check

Maintain equal rhythm and power all the way around this figure.

Moving on

Try sustaining the medium trot around the whole school.

What can go wrong?

The horse falls on to his forehand and paddles.
This is usually because you have asked too suddenly for the medium trot.

If it's not working...

Rebalance your horse using the exercise on a 20m circle to re-establish his trot before trying this exercise again.

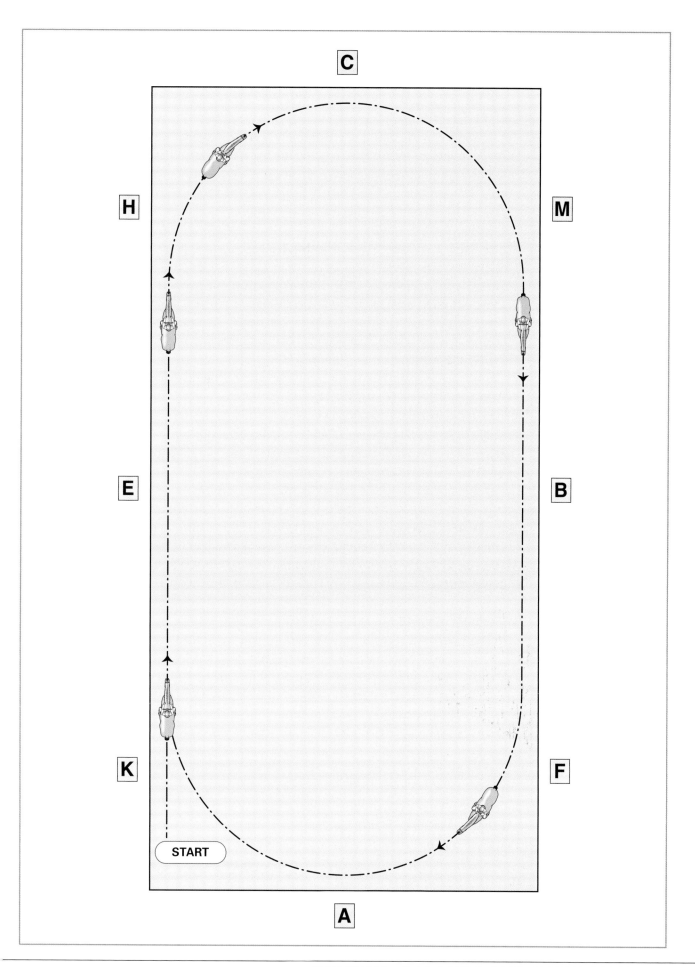

C

H

M

E

B

K

F

START

A

CELEBRITY
EXERCISE

19

BEGINNERS

PRELIMINARY ✪

NOVICE ✪✪✪

ELEMENTARY ✪✪✪✪✪

MEDIUM ✪✪✪✪✪

Working on collection and extension on a circle from Mary King

'This exercise works for two different sorts of horse: those that need to learn to flex a little more; and those that need to be more forward and in front of your leg. I would use this exercise once my horse is warmed up and has done some suppling exercises, but before beginning on lateral work.'

How do I ride this exercise?

❏ At E, ride a 20m circle in trot and ask your horse to make various transitions on the circle within the pace. First, establish a good, forward working trot for, let's say, half a circle (this could be a shorter or longer distance depending on your horse's abilities).

❏ Then ask your horse to come back to a collected trot that's really active.

❏ When you've completed a quarter of a circle, move him forwards into an extended trot.

❏ Repeat this exercise on the opposite rein.

What should happen?

This is an exercise that a young horse can do as well as an older horse, but you have to judge how strong the youngster is, and avoid being tempted to ask him to do too much. To begin with, a young horse will find it difficult to open up his stride, but in this exercise the fact of being slightly on a turn teaches him to engage his inside hind leg – and until he can achieve this fairly well, he will not be able to maintain a regular open stride on a turn.

Double check

It is important that your horse keeps very engaged so that he's ready with his hind leg underneath him when you ask him to go forward into extended trot. If his hind leg is well underneath his body, then you can get a big, open stride.

Moving on

Ask for even more collection!

What can go wrong?

1 Your horse is reluctant to come back to collected trot.

With the forward-going horse that's happy to 'power on', you may experience a little more resistance in the rein when you ask him to come back to the collected trot, because he's being asked to step under more with the hind leg into the collected gait. It's important that you bring your upper body back on the downward transition, and keep your leg on to keep the hind leg active so you can ride him forwards into your hand.

2 Your horse goes flat in the collected trot.

This is quite common. Be sure to maintain the rhythm within the collection, keeping the trot active enough and your horse engaged in preparation for the extended trot.

If it's not working...

Continue on a circle and do walk-to-trot transitions, making sure that your horse is being attentive to your aids. If he is really struggling, try working the exercise on a straight line initially until he understands what you are wanting him to do.

EXERCISE

20

BEGINNERS

PRELIMINARY

NOVICE ✪✪

ELEMENTARY ✪✪✪

MEDIUM ✪✪✪✪✪

Establishing lengthened canter strides on a circle

Establishing a lengthened canter is the first step towards performing medium canter. Medium trot and medium canter on a circle are being used more in competitions, and have now been introduced at Novice level.

BONUS

Not only is this a good exercise for lengthening the canter, it also greatly improves the strength of your horse's back and haunches.

TURNING TIP

Remember that it is the inside aids that bend a horse, and the outside aids that turn him. Often circles fail because a rider is trying to turn the horse from the inside rein instead of guiding him with the outside rein and outside leg combined: like this the rider will assert the correct influences, so preventing the horse from falling in or out on the circle, and therefore being able to maintain better control over the shape of the circle.

How do I ride this exercise?

❏ On a 20m circle, establish working canter and count the number of strides your horse takes to complete half the circle.

❏ On the second half of the circle, with a stronger seat but in the same rhythm, push him out a little and use a bigger stride. Try to take at least one or two steps off your original stride count.

❏ Repeat the exercise until you can see a clear difference between the two half circles every time.

How do I ride a 'bigger stride'?

To ride a bigger stride you are asking for more 'electricity' and power from your horse.

❏ Rally him up with your inside leg, and ask for a bigger step by asking for a bigger swing with your hips…

❏ … though be careful not to make a bigger swing with the shoulders.

What should happen?

As your horse improves through this exercise he will become better engaged and so come up off his forehand.

Double check

Be aware of the accuracy of your circle, and whether or not your horse is falling through his outside shoulder.

Moving on

Try medium canter on a circle with more accurate transitions up and down within the canter pace, at, say, X and C.

What can go wrong?

1 Your horse may fall through his outside shoulder.
  Ensure you are turning the circle from the outside aids (see Turning Tip above).

2 Your horse comes above the bit.
  Make sure you re-collect him by holding with your back, seat and legs – not just by pulling with the hands.

If it's not working...

Go back to working on transitions, as in Exercises 15, 16 and 19.

Trot-to-canter transitions on a straight line

The aids for a canter strike-off are inside leg on the girth, and outside leg behind the girth; however, the horse is often either ignorant of, or oblivious to this directive from his rider, and only goes on the left lead, for example, because he happens to be going through a left corner. This exercise teaches your horse to acknowledge and react to your aids for the canter strike-off.

BONUS

This is one of the most important and helpful exercises that can be used when teaching the horse flying change.

How do I ride this exercise?

❑ Ride round the school on the left rein in trot, and ride a canter transition at B; continue around the arena.

❑ Make a diagonal change of rein from H to F.

❑ At F make a canter-to-trot transition; remain on the track to E.

❑ Make a canter transition at E, followed by…

❑ …a diagonal change of rein from M to K.

❑ Make a canter-to-trot transition at K.

What should happen?

When your horse learns to canter on a particular leg, he usually understands which leg you want him to strike off on because it relates to the direction in which he is travelling: for example, left-hand curve, left lead. However, as an introduction to flying changes, your horse should understand to canter on the left lead because of your position in the saddle, regardless of the curve on which he is travelling.

In this exercise, before asking for the trot-to-canter transition the horse should feel and react correctly to your inside position: thus he should take notice of the rider's outside leg, which should be held a little back, telling him how he should hold his haunches prior to and during the canter transition – that is, not slipping them to the outside. Consequently he will make a balanced and obedient inside lead canter transition.

Double check

The clarity and emphasis of your leg position, with the inside leg a little forward and the outside leg back, is the most important factor in this exercise.

Moving on

Try this exercise on the centre line with the trot-to-canter transition at X.

What can go wrong?

Your horse runs forwards a little in trot, and in so doing, turns his quarters to the outside and then picks up an outside lead canter.

Bring him back to trot, and wait for the next long side to ask for canter once again. Be sure your aids are consistent and clear, and give him time to understand what you are asking.

If it's not working...

Try riding a walk-to-canter transition on the straight line so he understands not to go bowling off ahead of your aids.

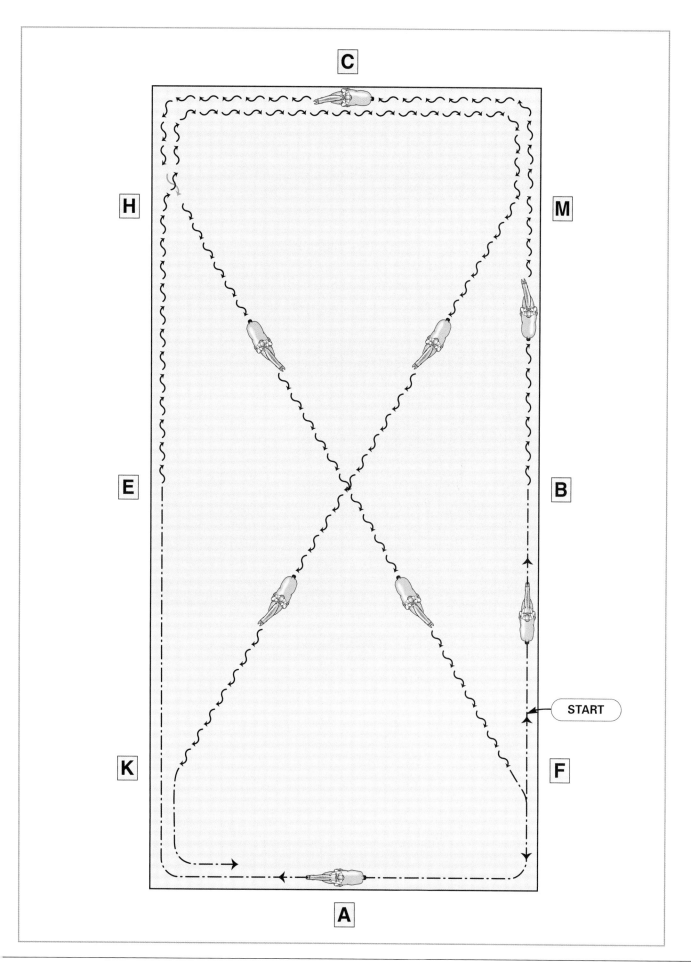

CELEBRITY
EXERCISE

22

BEGINNERS

PRELIMINARY

NOVICE ✪✪✪

ELEMENTARY ✪✪✪

MEDIUM ✪✪✪✪✪

Freeing up your horse's back
from Tim Stockdale

Tim says: 'A number of years ago I realized that the best engaged horses are racehorses. Watch Frankie Dettori canter to the start of a race: he's very relaxed, up in his stirrups, his reins bridged over the horse's neck, and the horse is totally engaged – you can see the back opening and the horse coming through from behind: and as the horse's back is free, he's able to use it so much better. So I put this exercise into my training, and it works. I use it probably twice a week within a training programme for a horse. Control is the ultimate key to this exercise – galloping flat out around the school is only dangerous.'

How do I ride this exercise?

❑ Shorten your stirrups two to three holes and ride around the arena, off your seat, on your hands with your reins bridged almost racing style.

❑ Once you are in balance, canter the full circuit of the school in a normal half canter: if trot is zero and gallop is ten, I'm talking about a five to a five-and-a-half.

❑ You are controlling the horse via the bridge in your hands, and what you do is keep rolling your wrist gently just to get the horse nice and soft in his forehand, and to keep him like that.

What should happen?

It's amazing the number of horses that will now use their back because it is free; this is especially good if your horse is not great from behind or through his back. Eventually when you go into a half seat the horse will automatically start to open up from behind and maintain his engagement.

Double check

If you are doing this on a young horse, or one that is rather stiff, take care, because, believe it or not, this exercise will make them quite sore as they are using muscles in their backs that they have probably not used before.

Moving on

Try to maintain this canter over a slightly greater distance: thus if the horse can hold this canter over
a circuit and a half, see if he can do it over two – though be very aware of not doing too much at a stretch: this exercise is more tiring for the horse than you might imagine.

What can go wrong?

Your canter goes out of control.

Firstly, you've probably gone too forward. This exercise must be done at a half canter (see preceding page) and your horse must learn to hold this canter. He must not go too much on his forehand, which is why you roll the wrists to lighten the front end.

If it's not working...

This exercise must be done in a confined area such as an arena or school. It is all about balance and control, and if you are at all unsure, try riding it in a half seat (or light seat) without shortening your stirrups. Once you and your horse have gained in confidence, then shorten the stirrups up. If the horse goes a little too forward and you are on the verge of losing control, use the corners of the school or diminishing circles to restore control.

CELEBRITY TIPS

Get someone to watch you doing this exercise from the ground. It's amazing that when you first start this you think, after a couple of circuits, 'This isn't doing anything!' But somebody on the floor, watching, can see the horse's back become more springy and more concertina-like as he starts to use himself.

This exercise should not be ridden in deep going.

23

Deeper and taller

Before you attempt this exercise your horse must be working 'on the bridle' as a matter of course, and also working through a supple and correctly swinging back.

BONUS

Even if your horse can't work in a correct 'uphill' position, he will still be able to perform to his optimum ability and achieve his full potential.

How do I ride this exercise?

❏ This is best ridden on a circle, and in trot.

❏ Ask your horse to work deep and low for one circuit…(below left)

❏ …then gradually bring him to a shorter, taller, 'uphill' position (below right), with the poll as the highest point.

How do I ride this?

❏ Invite your horse to work deep and low by gradually lengthening your reins, taking care to correct him if he tries to evade your request by coming above the bit.

❏ Continue to allow the longer rein, provided he maintains his supple roundness.

❏ Gradually shorten the reins supported by half-halts and maintaining the lively impulsion with your legs until your horse's poll is his highest point.

❏ In this position, reward him with a subtle giving of the reins.

❏ It is crucial that he is comfortable at this point, and not held in position.

What should happen?

Your horse should learn to step under more with his hind leg, and to use his haunches to lift his shoulders up off the ground and move in a genuine uphill position. As your horse works deeper and lower he should maintain his balance and improve the subtle swinging use of his back.

Double check

As the horse goes from the deepest position to the tallest, 'uphill position' he should show increasing impulsion.

Moving on

Alternate between trot and canter.

What can go wrong?

1 Your horse falls on to his forehand in the deeper position.
Settle your horse on a circle and keep riding him deep and low until he has established his balance.

2 Your horse becomes confused and resistant when ridden in the shorter frame.
Check that your aids are not too demanding, even by a little, and question whether his ability is compromised by his confirmation.

If it's not working...

Alternate between deep and low and a halfway point, and question whether your horse is comfortable in the uphill position.

SUPPLE AND STRAIGHT

Circles and Turns

THE EXERCISES

It is said that no horse can be truly straight until he can bend equally well in both directions. Working on circles and turns helps improve your horse's bending and suppleness, but you will almost undoubtedly find that he is stiffer on one rein than the other. Wherever possible start each exercise on the more supple rein. If your horse is in the early stages of training, ride mostly 20m and 15m circles in walk, trot and canter. Introduce 10m circles in walk and trot gradually, and only tackle the smaller 8m and 6m circles (knows as a volte) when your horse can cope with a higher degree of collection and bend. Remember that every corner is a part of a circle, the size of this circle depending on your horse's abilities. When riding a circle or turn your horse's hind legs should follow on the same track as the forelegs (confusingly known as 'being straight'), and he will need to take extra weight on the inside hind leg. This is achieved by riding from the inside leg to the outside hand. Throughout the circle your horse should remain on a constant bend (see diagram) and should not be bending just through his neck, in which case his quarters would 'drag' to the outside.

THE AIDS TO A TURN OR CIRCLE

❏ Check your position.
❏ Use your inside rein intermittently to ask for an elastic contact and a slight flexion to the inside; this will also let your horse know in which direction you are turning.
❏ Allow your horse to bend through his neck and body with your outside rein, whilst maintaining a constant contact – unless you need to use the rein to control impulsion or degree of bend.
❏ Look to where you are going: then you will automatically turn your shoulders subtly to the inside.
❏ Allow a little more weight on your inside seatbone and into your inside stirrup.
❏ Your inside leg used on the girth will encourage your horse's inside hind leg to step forward.
❏ Your outside leg, just behind the girth, is used as necessary to prevent the quarters swinging out.
❏ Use both legs and a supple seat to encourage and maintain impulsion.

Correct   *Incorrect*

EXERCISE
24

Half circles and straightening to the track

If your horse's strides are quick and uneven, use this exercise to help establish a more regular rhythm, and later a more powerful lengthened or extended stride.

RIDER'S TIP

Encourage the horse to look upwards by looking up and ahead yourself.

How do I ride this exercise?

❏ Establish trot on the right rein passing E.

❏ Just before H, ride a 10m rounded turn, straightening in the direction of B. but maintaining the bend.

❏ Rejoin the track and repeat the exercise, turning just before F and straightening in the direction of E.

❏ Repeat on the opposite rein.

What should happen?

The balanced turns before C and A should help the horse come up off his outside shoulder, and to engage his inside hind leg. If he is looking up, his shoulders become looser and freer, so the hind leg can come through and carry his weight better.

Double check

Be sure that your horse stays on the correct inside bend throughout (see diagram).

Moving on

Try lengthening your strides as you ride out to the track. This is also good in canter.

What can go wrong?

Your horse swings his quarters out through the turn.

Guard against this with the outside leg, or make your turn earlier or more gradually.

If it's not working...

Go back to working on the three-quarter line with inside bend (Exercise 9).

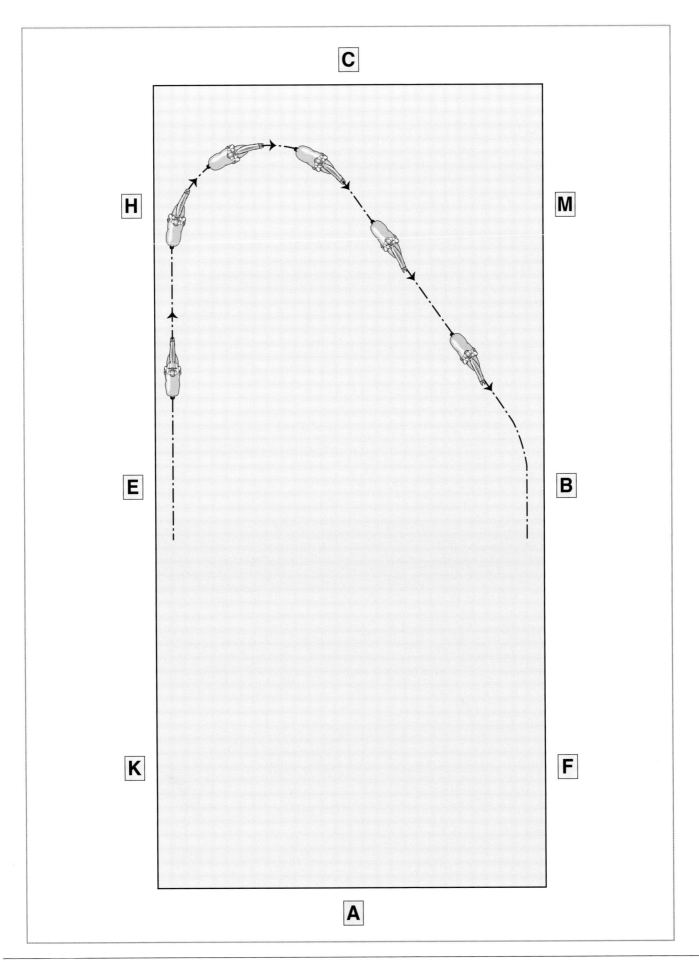

Simple spirals in and out

This is a kind way to introduce your horse to 10m circles. If your horse always comes above the bit in downward transitions, this is a great exercise to help him take his weight on to his haunches, to find his balance, and come up off his forehand.

How do I ride this exercise?

❏ Ride a 20m circle in the centre of the school in walk.
❏ From this, gradually spiral in to a 10m circle, with the same centre point.
❏ Sustain the 10m circle until you feel your horse is in balance and bending correctly.
❏ Then spiral out again.

What aids do I use?

❏ Maintain the appropriate bend with the inside rein.
❏ The size of the circle is reduced by applying pressure from the outside leg and outside rein.

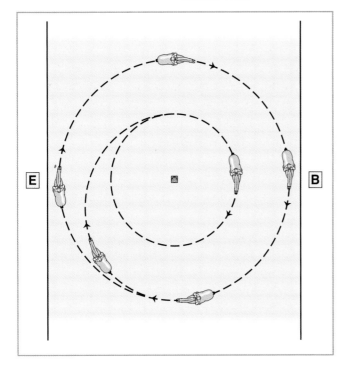

❏ It is increased with pressure from the inside leg, taking care to support the outside shoulder with the outside hand.

What should happen?

The horse should be able to reduce the size of the circle in a balanced way, neither anticipating, nor being reluctant to move into the smaller arc. In the 10m circle he should maintain a uniform bend through his spine, without any twisting or tilting of the head. His hind feet should step into the imprint of the front feet, and not to the inside or the outside of their track.

Double check

Be sure that your shoulders are not twisting to compensate for any loss of balance by your horse.

Moving on

This exercise can also be ridden in trot and canter.

What can go wrong?

Your spiral arc is not uniform.
This is because your horse is either falling in, or falling out through his shoulders. Support him with your outside rein and outside leg if he is falling to the outside, or your inside leg if he is falling to the inside.

If it's not working...

Go back to riding separate 20m, 15m and 10m circles until your horse is more balanced.

EXERCISE

26

BBEGINNERS ✪
PRELIMINARY ✪✪
NOVICE ✪✪✪✪
ELEMENTARY ✪✪✪✪✪
MEDIUM ✪✪✪✪

Perfecting 20m, 15m and 10m circles

Make no mistake, a circle is one of the most difficult shapes to ride accurately. This exercise will help you to focus on getting the size of your circles right – though don't forget to concentrate on the shape, too.

How do I ride this exercise?
❏ Starting at B, ride a 20m circle in trot.
❏ When you rejoin the track at B, ride a 15m circle.
❏ Follow this with a 10m circle.
❏ Change the rein and repeat.

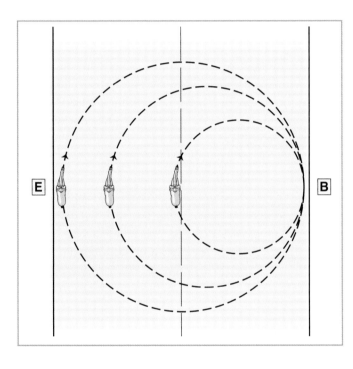

What should happen?
The constant bend will encourage your horse to use a balanced and rhythmic stride. The smaller circles will encourage him to bring his hind legs underneath his body.

How do I ride this?
❏ Help your horse to achieve the correct bend through his body by keeping your own shoulders in line with the desired bend, using plenty of inside leg, and giving him support through your inside seatbone and upper body.

Double check
Don't forget to check your inside position.

Moving on
Move up a pace.

RIDER'S TIP

Remember that it is the inside aids that bend a horse, and the outside aids that turn him. Often circles end up being an odd shape because the rider is trying to turn the horse with the inside rein instead of guiding him with the outside rein and outside leg. This is the correct way to ride a turn or circle, and it is the only way that the rider will assert the correct influences.

What can go wrong?
You will ride inaccurate circles, where the first quarter is always too big.
This is usually because your horse is not set up properly for the circle, and expects to continue along the track. Make sure that you are using the correct aids, and be prepared with your outside leg and outside rein.

If it's not working...
Go back to a simpler 20m circle exercise to perfect your circle (Exercise 7).

EXERCISE

27

BEGINNERS

PRELIMINARY ✪

NOVICE ✪✪✪

ELEMENTARY ✪✪✪✪

MEDIUM ✪✪✪✪✪

Shallow changes of rein

The key to this exercise is fitting three circles of approximately 15m into your school! This reads like a really complicated exercise, but it is actually very simple, and it's worth the effort as the changes of rein asked of your horse are shallower than those in a figure-of-eight, and give you more time to maintain control of your horse's shoulders.

BONUS

Circles and serpentine changes are wonderful exercises for suppling your horse. If they are used progressively to develop each side of your horse, he will develop evenly and eventually be able to ride a true straight line.

How do I ride this exercise?

❏ See diagram to establish circles 1, 2, and 3 in your mind.

❏ In walk, take the left rein at K, and follow circle 1.

❏ At the point when you are facing E, change the bend and join circle 2.

❏ Continue around circle 2, until you are facing M.

❏ Then change the bend and join circle 3.

❏ Follow circle 3 until you are facing B, halfway between H and B.

❏ Then change the bend and rejoin circle 2.

❏ Follow circle 2 until you face E.

❏ Change the bend, rejoin circle 1 and the track at K, which completes the exercise.

❏ Repeat on the opposite rein.

What should happen?

Frequent changes of bend encourage alternate relaxation and contraction of the main muscle groups used for lateral work.

Double check

Be sure that your weight is on the inside stirrup and your inside seatbone.

Moving on

Try the French serpentine (Exercise 42).

What can go wrong?

Your horse's neck bends suddenly or bends too much.

He is most likely falling out through his outside shoulder. Focus on your outside bend aids, and try again.

If it's not working...

Work on a three-loop serpentine (Exercise 41).

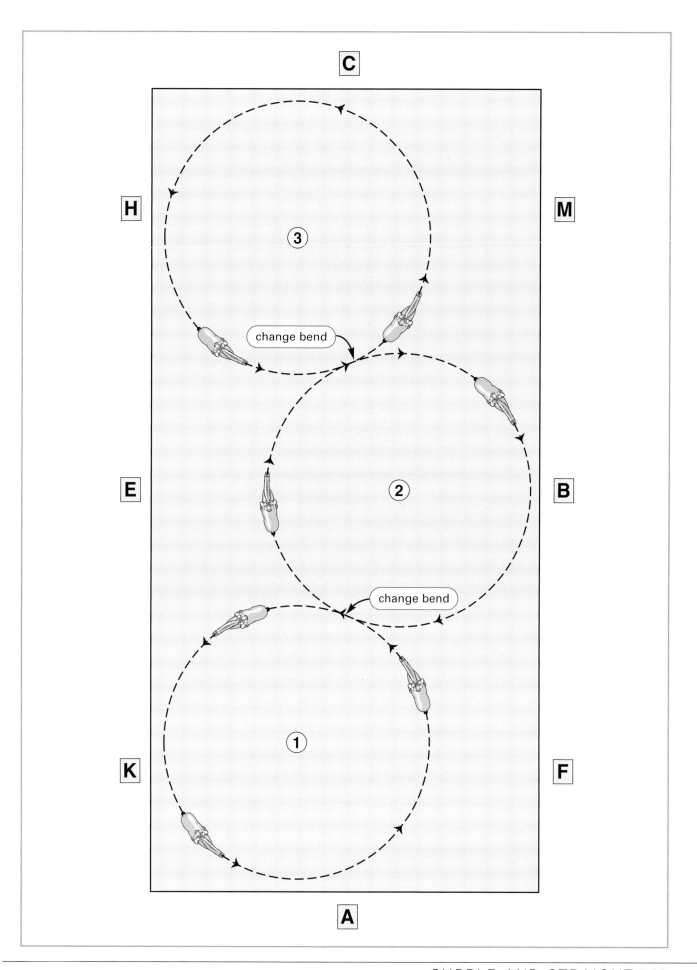

EXERCISE

28

BEGINNERS ✪

PRELIMINARY ✪✪

NOVICE ✪✪✪

ELEMENTARY ✪✪✪✪

MEDIUM ✪✪✪✪

Four small collected circles in a 20m circle

Whether you are attempting this exercise in walk, trot or even canter, it works for all three paces. For the more advanced horse this exercise is a good preparation for canter pirouettes.

How do I ride this exercise?

❏ Ride a 20m circle.

❏ Within this circle, ride four smaller 10m circles.

❏ On the small circles, collect the horse to generate more impulsion.

❏ Make sure the circles are accurate, and that the horse bends correctly.

❏ Once you have completed four small circles in this way, go on to the 20m circle again, and go up a gear in pace.

❏ Remember to ride this exercise on both reins so your horse doesn't become one-sided.

What should happen?

If your horse's hind legs are in correct alignment with his forehand, he will bend his hocks more and lower his haunches.

Double check

Be sure that the horse has the correct bend, and is turning from the outside rein.

Moving on

The faster the pace, the harder this exercise becomes: according to your horse's stage of training, if he is quite comfortable in the pace you have been trying, you could move up a gear.

What can go wrong?

Your horse may try to avoid bending by tilting his head.

Use a little more outside rein for a moment, and less inside rein.

If it's not working...

Try riding two 15m circles at E and B.

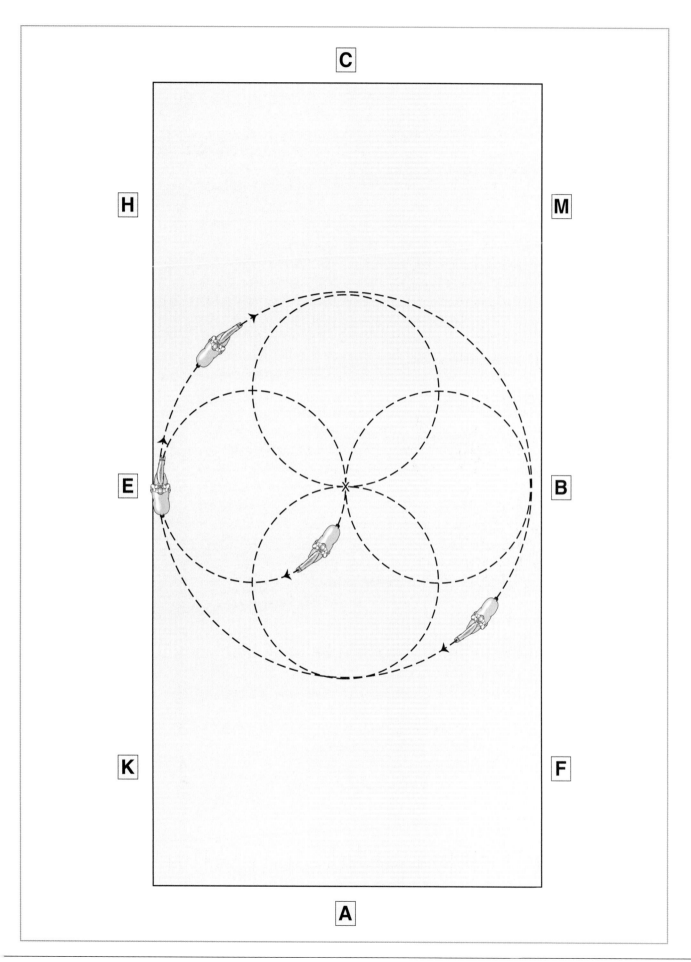

BEGINNERS ⬤⬤⬤⬤⬤
PRELIMINARY ⬤⬤⬤⬤⬤
NOVICE ⬤⬤⬤⬤
ELEMENTARY ⬤⬤
MEDIUM

Testing control and flexibility on half loops

This is a good exercise to practise using the quarter and three-quarter lines of the school, and to ensure that your horse is listening to you. Once you've mastered the basic exercise you can either move up a pace, or you could add the half 10m loops (see Moving On, below).

BONUS

This is a good exercise for helping your horse to establish his balance.

How do I ride this exercise?

❑ Ride round the school on the right rein, in walk.
❑ Between K and E, ride a half circle right to the quarter line.
❑ Change the bend, and ride a half 15m circle left.
❑ Change the rein diagonally across the school from just past F to mid-way between E and H.
❑ Then ride a half 15m circle right to the three-quarter line.
❑ Change the bend, and ride a half 5m circle left, rejoining the track just past M.
❑ Repeat on the other rein.
❑ Once you feel your horse is really balanced throughout the exercise in walk, try this exercise in trot – but make the circles 8m and 12m.

RIDER'S TIP

Half-halt and ride a few steps straight each time you plan to change bend to help your horse's balance and to prepare yourselves for the change of rein.

What should happen?

This exercise is a test of your control and your horse's flexibility, as he has to manoeuvre between left and right bends and be straight.

Double check

Be sure to keep your horse well between hand and leg to help him keep his balance and negotiate the turns successfully.

Moving on

Having rejoined the track just past M, at B ride a half 10m circle right to the centre line, change the bend and ride a half 10m circle left to rejoin the opposite track.

What can go wrong?

Your horse can fall through the inside shoulder.
Support him with the outside rein and outside leg and ride him forwards.

If it's not working...

Work on a simple three-loop serpentine (see Exercise 41).

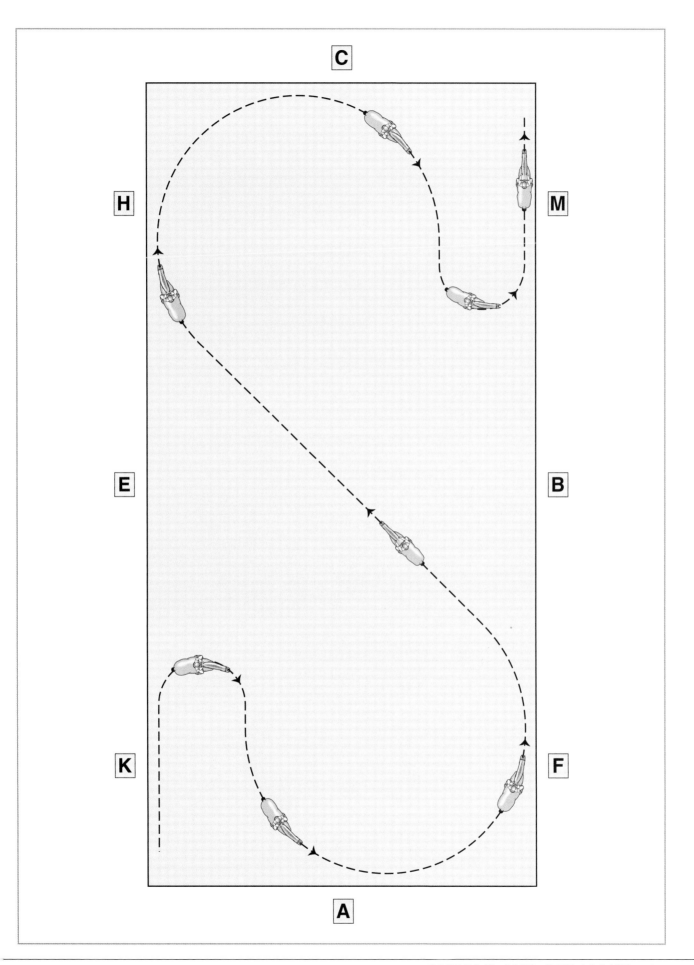

Using the outside aids to ride a long figure-of-eight

BEGINNERS	✪
PRELIMINARY	✪✪
NOVICE	✪✪✪✪
ELEMENTARY	✪✪✪✪✪
MEDIUM	✪✪✪✪

This long and thin figure-of-eight uses the sides of the arena to limit the size of each half circle and prevent your horse drifting to the outside on the turns. It helps you to understand how your outside aids control turns, and will get your horse listening to your outside rein and leg.

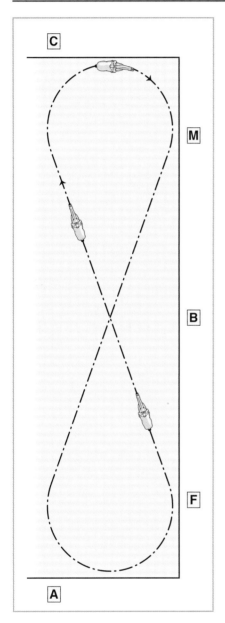

How do I ride this exercise?
❏ Ride round the school on the left rein in trot.
❏ Come off the track at F, and ride a straight line diagonally towards C.
❏ Ride a half 10m circle right to the corner.
❏ Come off at M and head towards A.
❏ Ride another half 10m circle left, to bring you to your starting point

What should happen?
By using the corners of the school, the horse learns to make controlled turns without being pulled by the reins.

Double check
Be sure to prepare the horse for the turns by asking for the correct bend, and at the same time make sure you sit in the 'future' inside position.

Moving on
Collect the trot at the ends and ask for lengthened strides or medium trot along the diagonal. Or, trot the ends and canter along the diagonals, using the corner to set up the transition to canter. This is also a good exercise to do in canter, with flying changes across the diagonal.

What can go wrong?
Your horse could be falling on the 'future' inside shoulder.
Try leg-yielding away from the track instead of a simple diagonal.

If it's not working...
Make your half circles 12m or 15m.

31

The wonderfully versatile figure-of-eight

BEGINNERS ⊙

PRELIMINARY ⊙⊙

NOVICE ⊙⊙⊙

ELEMENTARY ⊙⊙⊙⊙

MEDIUM ⊙⊙⊙

Once you've mastered the basic figure-of-eight, it can be put to many uses. For example, riding one circle in one pace and the second in another, or each circle in two paces, changing the pace across the centre point and/or the A and C markers. Combine a 20m circle figure-of-eight with a 10m circle figure-of-eight, and you could be in the arena all day!

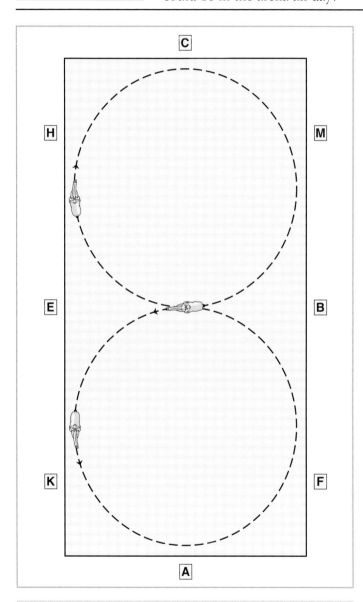

How do I ride this exercise?

❏ Ride round the school on the right rein, in walk.

❏ Begin a 20m circle at either A or C.

❏ Just before you cross X, straighten for one or two strides then change the rein.

❏ Ride a 20m circle at the opposite end of the school.

❏ Just before you reach X, once again straighten for one or two strides, and change the rein.

❏ Complete the original 20m circle.

What should happen?

The particular challenge of this exercise is to show that your horse can change his bend without losing balance. Use straight strides over X to give him time to change bend gradually and, as his balance improves, reduce the number of strides.

Double check

Be sure that your contact is even on both sides, and that you are not riding with more rein contact in either the left or the right hand.

Moving on

Ride the figure-of-eight in different paces. Repeat the exercise, riding a 10m circle, commencing at E or B.

What can go wrong?

Your horse has problems maintaining the arc of the circle through the left to right change on the right rein.

Spend longer on the straight strides over X.

If it's not working...

Go back to working on your basic circles (Exercises 23 and 25).

BONUS

Use the figure-of-eight to compare your performance on each rein. Our aim in training is for the horse to be evenly balanced and supple on both reins, so as you ride this exercise, compare each 'half' to see if you are achieving that. Check that your riding is the same in position left and in position right, that the two are a mirror image, and that there is not a bias in the shoulders or legs.

BEGINNERS	✪✪✪✪
PRELIMINARY	✪✪✪✪✪
NOVICE	✪✪✪✪✪
ELEMENTARY	✪✪✪✪
MEDIUM	✪✪✪✪

10m circles on to short diagonals

This exercise is to help the horse's straightness and bend. 'A horse with a correct bend is a straight horse.' 'Straight' means correct alignment of head, forehand and haunches, whether on a straight line or curve. Therefore the hind feet should step into the print of the front feet.

How do I ride this exercise?

❏ Ride a short side in walk, and then a 10m circle at the corner.

❏ Coming out of the circle, head across a short diagonal line to E or B.

❏ Just before the marker, ride another 10m circle, this time in the opposite direction to the first.

❏ Ride from this marker across another short diagonal to the far corner.

❏ There ride another 10m circle in the same direction as the first.

❏ You should therefore have ridden three 10m circles and two straight lines on the short diagonals: after each circle, straighten the horse on the diagonal line.

❏ End this exercise by riding a straight line up the centre line, with good turns before and after.

How do I ride this exercise?

As you approach each circle, prepare your horse by half-halting and bending him in the new direction. Ride the circles, straighten your horse, then prepare him for the new bend. Each time you cross the school, you and your horse should be straight for about 10m before preparing the new bend.

Double check

Make sure of the accuracy of your circles.

Moving on

For the more advanced horse this exercise is good in canter with flying changes over the centre line.

What can go wrong?

Your horse falls in on his inside shoulder.
Support him with the inside leg and inside rein.

If it's not working...

Try 15m circles.

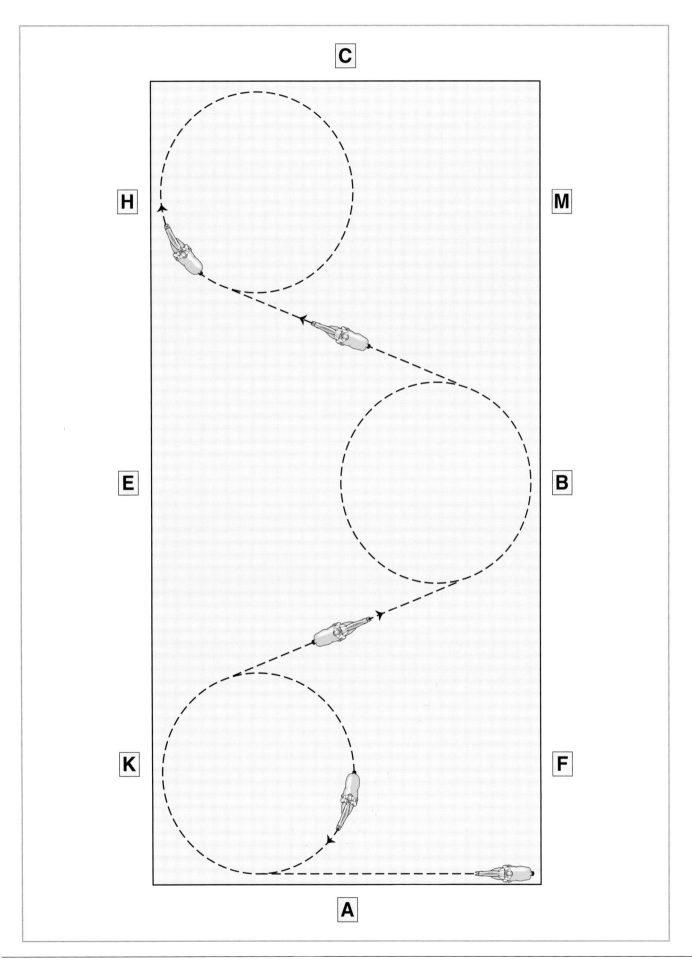

Using corner circles in canter to improve your horse's response to your aids
from Mary King

'This is a good exercise for teaching your horse obedience and getting him in front of your leg. The smaller circle will help with engagement.'

RIDER'S TIP

To do this exercise correctly, your horse has got to be quick to move off your leg. If he is a little bit sluggish, give him a quick, sharp nudge – but be careful not to restrict him with your reins: it's very tempting to hold on to your reins while you give him a nudge because you know he's going to run forwards, but that's what you want him to do, even though it may be a bit fast – you want him to react immediately. So, give him a sharp nudge with your leg, and keep your reins soft. Let him go forwards for a number of strides before steadying him, giving him a pat and getting him back. This way he will learn to respond with a forward movement when he is asked.

How do I ride this exercise?

❑ On the right rein and in canter, turn right up the centre line from A; keep your horse moving forwards.

❑ As he approaches the short side, between H and M, ask him to collect a little bit more, and ride a three-quarter 10m circle to the right in right canter.

❑ As you cross the three-quarter line of the school, ride forwards three or four strides parallel to the short side of the school.

❑ Upon reaching the opposite quarter line, collect your horse again and ask him to do another partial 10m circle right in that corner.

❑ As you rejoin the centre line, ride down the school to A.

❑ Just before A, between K and F, repeat the two circles in the same manner at this end of the school, finally rejoining the centre line.

❑ Come back to trot, and strike off in left canter to repeat the exercise on the left rein.

What should happen?

Your horse will have to collect at the end of the long sides to be able to maintain his balance around the circle.

Double check

Be sure to turn him on the circles with your outside rein and leg; and don't restrict him with the rein.

Moving on

As you finish the final circle, at K ask for a transition to trot and ride a full diagonal in a medium or extended trot across the arena. In a dressage test you are often asked to ride a full diagonal at medium or extended trot out of a corner. This exercise prepares you for that, and you know that when you come to the end of the diagonal your horse is going to be very responsive and come back to you because he's been doing it in this exercise at home.

Another exercise is to move your 'centre lines' to either side of the school centre line and, remaining in canter, ride smaller, 8m circles in the corners.

What can go wrong?

1 Your horse is running on to his forehand as you go down the long side.
Bringing him back to collection for the corner will help, as he's got to come back on to his hind legs to maintain his balance on the circle.

2 Your horse resists collection.
Turning him on to the small circle will help him come back to you without you having to be strong with your hands.

If it's not working...

If your horse cannot maintain the canter and breaks into trot, try riding a 20m circle at A and C, gradually reducing to a 15m and then a 10m circle at A and C before attempting the exercise again.

CELEBRITY TIP

'Always reward the horse with a pat or with your voice. Always correct mistakes straightaway.

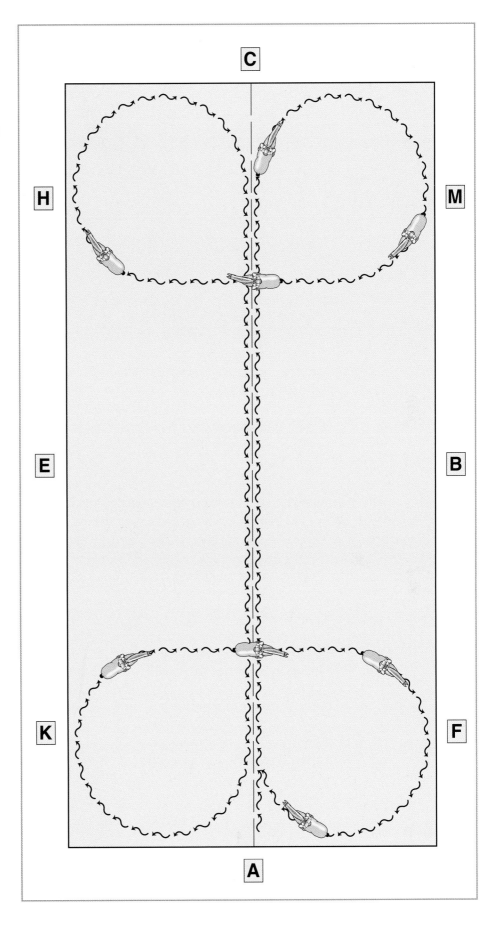

EXERCISE

34

BEGINNERS ⊙⊙⊙⊙⊙
PRELIMINARY ⊙⊙⊙⊙⊙
NOVICE ⊙⊙⊙⊙
ELEMENTARY ⊙⊙⊙
MEDIUM ⊙⊙

10m circles off the centre line to test your aids

This exercise looks deceptively simple! It has two very different objectives, depending on whether it is ridden in walk or trot. In walk, it teaches the horse a better understanding of the rider's aids; in trot it is a great strengthening exercise.

How do I ride this exercise?

❑ Ride down the centre line in walk, and ask for a bend to the right.
❑ Once your horse is doing this correctly (not falling in through the shoulder or turning right), ride a 10m circle on the right rein.
❑ Rejoin the centre line, and ask for a slight left bend.
❑ When it is being performed correctly, ride a second 10m circle on the left rein.
❑ Rejoin the centre line, and if space permits, repeat the exercise on the right rein.
❑ The aim of this exercise is to fit on the centre line as many correctly balanced circles as possible.

Why are we doing this exercise?

We do this in walk to teach the horse not to fall in through the inside shoulder, and to listen to the rider's aids: when the initial bend to the right is requested, the horse will often either fall in through the inside shoulder or turn right, rather than bend right. It is important to have this bend correct before riding the circle!. In trot it is a great exercise to build stamina and strength and to maintain a working outline, and is of use to riders up to advanced medium level.

What should happen?

Your horse should allow you to bend him without his quarters swinging out. Ridden correctly, this exercise should result in improved balance and bend on the 10m circle.

Double check

Be sure your outside leg is back and controlling the haunches throughout.

Moving on

Ride the exercise in trot.

What can go wrong?

1 Your horse may fall in through his inside shoulder or out through the outside shoulder.
   In this case go back to working on half-circle and circle exercises (see Exercises 18, 20 and 23).
2 Your horse could run away from your outside leg control.
   You need a bit more work on response to outside leg aids (see Exercises 3 and 31).
3 He may hollow through his back.
   See below.

If it's not working...

If you find your horse hollowing his back he is probably either trying to avoid your contact, or to avoid stepping under properly with his inside hind leg, or both! Whichever is the case, go back to working on a 20m circle and use Exercises 23, 25 and 28 to help generate his better acceptance of the bit and improved engagement of the hindquarters.

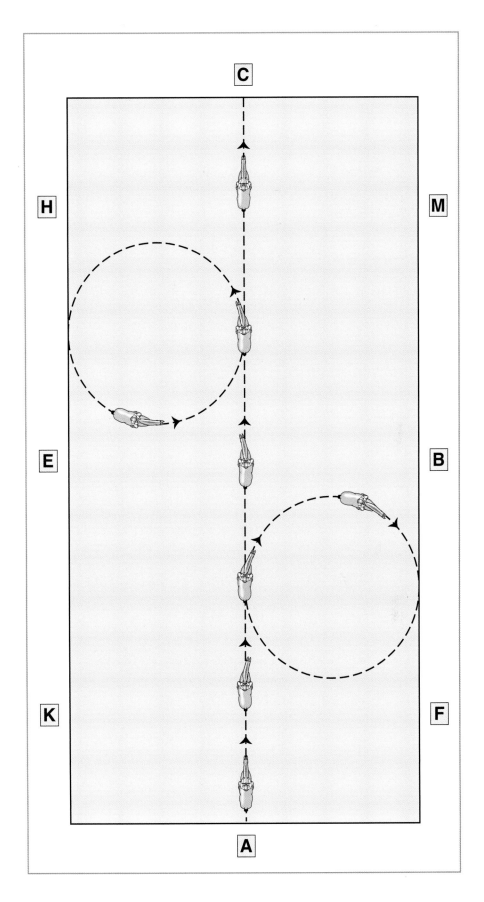

Collecting and engaging the hocks

This exercise requires a great deal of concentration! We're assuming these exercises are being ridden in a 20m x 40m school, but if yours is large enough, progress to riding this exercise in trot, enlarging the circles to 10m.

How do I ride this exercise?

❏ On the left rein and in walk, ride a 6m circle around X.

❏ Continue on this circle, but each time you cross the centre line ride a 6m circle on the right rein.

❏ Return to the original circle and ride a new 6m circle, on the right rein, towards B or E.

❏ Rejoin your original circle and ride another new 6m circle on the opposite side to this.

❏ Repeat, commencing with the right rein.

What should happen?

The frequent changes of bend and the small size of the circles in this exercise will really encourage your horse to collect and engage his hocks. The rein contact should become softer after a few attempts.

RIDER'S TIP

It's easy to become disorientated in this exercise. Place a marker at the centre of your original circle – it will help.

Double check

Accuracy is important in this exercise, so be sure that each circle is bisected either by the centre line or the half-school line (see diagram).

Moving on

If your school is large enough, increase the size of your circles to 10m, and ride this exercise in trot.

What can go wrong?

Your horse loses his balance through the sharp changes in direction.

Be careful that you are not asking for too much bend on the inside.

If it's not working...

Go back to working on 10m, 15m and 20m circles (see Exercise 26).

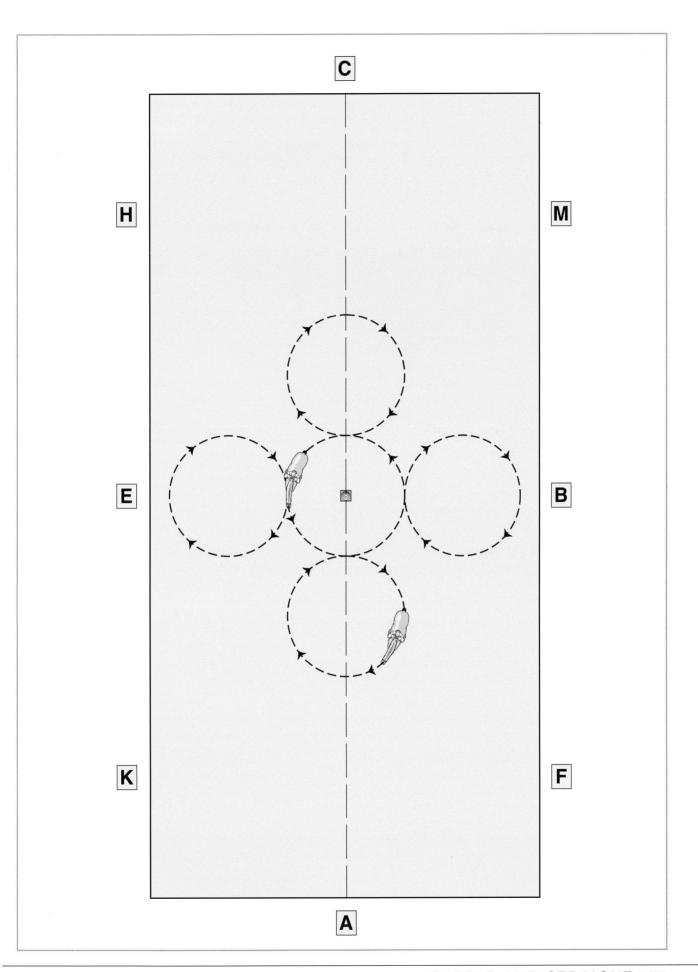

EXERCISE

36

BEGINNERS

PRELIMINARY ○

NOVICE ○○○

ELEMENTARY ○○○

MEDIUM ○○○○○

How to ride a correct corner

A short turn is the correct way to ride a corner on a well trained horse. This exercise is the best format for teaching the horse to work into his corners, as it makes the same demands without the intervention and support of the fence.

How do I ride this exercise?

❏ Ride on the left rein from F in walk up the long side, with a slight bend to the inside.

❏ 2 to 3m before B, commence a short turn (see below) left, to bring you exactly to the half-school (B to E) line.

❏ Ride straight to X, and then ask for a little left bend again.

❏ 2 to 3m before E, short turn left to join the track.

❏ 4m before K, ride a 20m half circle to the track just past F.

❏ Repeat.

❏ Ride on the opposite rein.

What is a short turn?

A short turn is a 90-degree turn in six equal steps.

What should happen?

The act of turning a horse is all about repositioning his forehand. A horse that is heavy on the forehand is difficult to turn. Frequent, correctly aided turns encourage your horse to lighten his forehand.

Double check

Be sure that your turn is coming from the influence of your outside hand, and not from your inside rein.

Moving on

Ride this exercise in canter.

What can go wrong?

Your horse's haunches swing out over the E-to-B line.

You are probably asking your horse to turn too suddenly and with insufficient use of your outside leg.

If it's not working...

Go back to a simpler turning exercise, such as riding the three-quarter line with inside bend (Exercise 9).

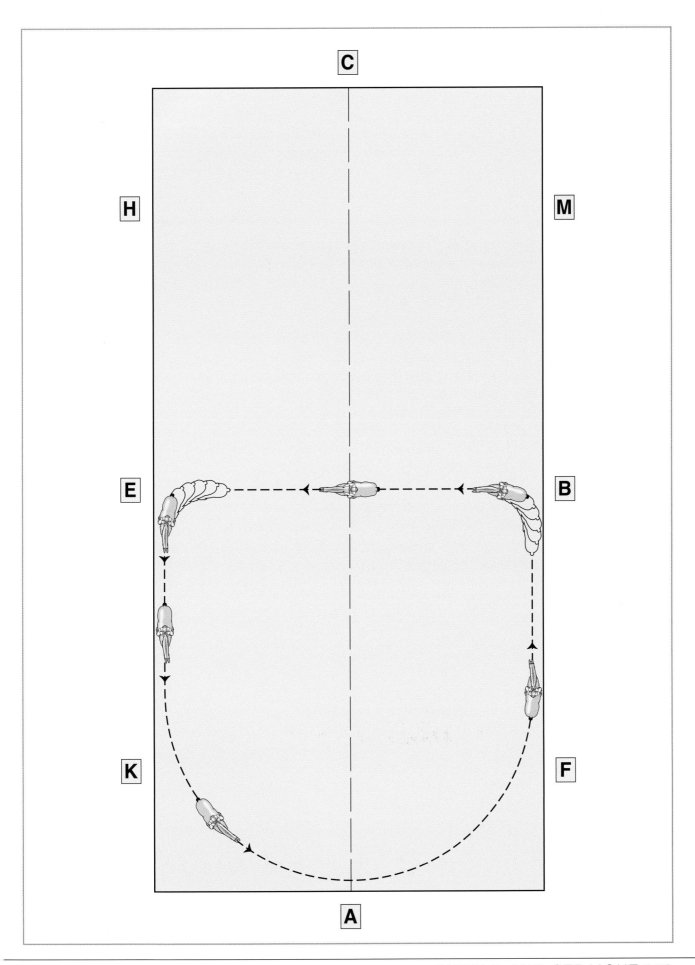

EXERCISE

37

BEGINNERS

PRELIMINARY ✪

NOVICE ✪✪

ELEMENTARY ✪✪✪

MEDIUM ✪✪✪✪✪

Perfecting accurate corners

This exercise is a good test of your horse's attention to your aids and, as corners feature strongly in all levels of test, they are great mark earners – and a well-turned corner looks very smart!

How do I ride this exercise?

❑ On the left rein from F, ride a straight line in walk.

❑ From B onwards ask for a little left bend, and ride into the corner from M, with a neat, short turn.

❑ Proceed straight along the short side.

❑ From C onwards, again ask for a left bend, and ride a neat, short turn in the corner before H.

❑ Proceed along the long side.

❑ At E, ride a half 20m circle to B.

❑ Go large, and repeat the exercise for the two corners.

❑ Once satisfied, do this exercise on the opposite rein.

What should happen?

You should be in control of your horse's forehand as he approaches the corners, to prevent his natural inclination to fall in on to the inside shoulder. Make use of the straight track to prepare him for what comes next.

Double check

Be sure that your outside leg is back to prevent his quarters slipping out as he makes the turn.

Moving on

Try this exercise in trot and canter.

What can go wrong?

Your horse falls in on the corners.

Use your inside leg and rein together to support the inside shoulder.

If it's not working...

Work on the three-quarter line with inside bend and short turns on to the half-school line (Exercises 26 and 34).

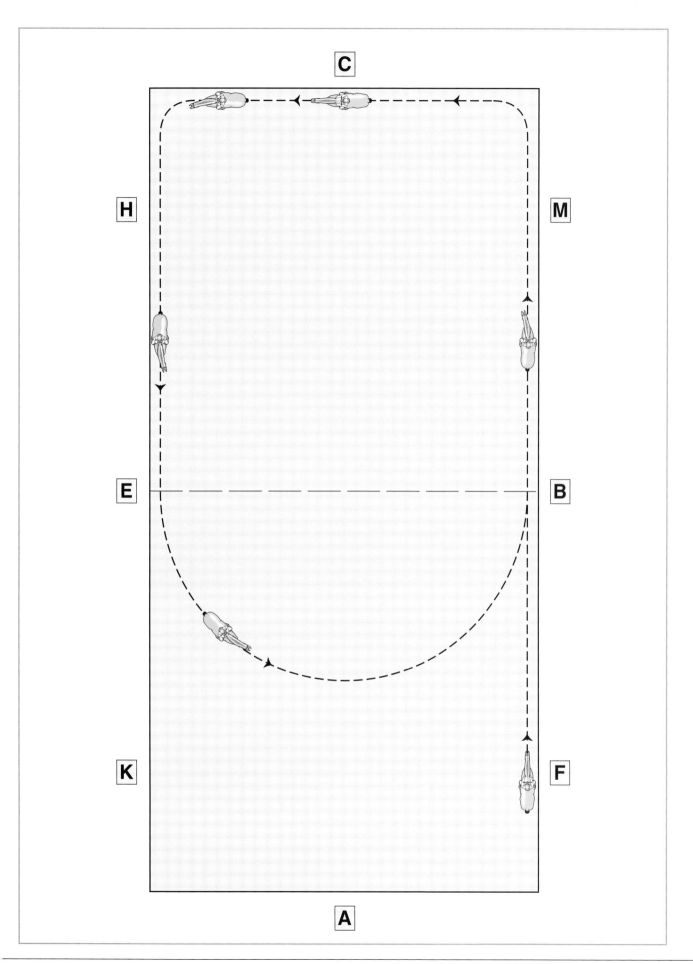

38

Lightening the forehand using quarter pirouettes

BEGINNERS

PRELIMINARY ✪✪

NOVICE ✪✪✪✪

ELEMENTARY ✪✪✪

MEDIUM ✪✪

The aim of this exercise is to increase suppleness and to lighten the horse's forehand by using walk pirouettes at diagonally opposite corners of a box. The exercise is ridden between the three-quarter lines of the school.

BONUS

This exercise also tests your leg aids, and whether your horse is generally in front of the leg.

How do I ride this exercise?

❏ On the three-quarter line, establish a collected walk and ask for a slight inside bend.

❏ At corner (A) of your 'box' (see diagram), ride a quarter pirouette.

❏ Continue in walk to corner B, making a simple turn at this corner.

❏ Halfway between corner B and corner C, check that you are still in collection, and then ride a quarter pirouette at corner C.

❏ Make a simple turn at corner D.

❏ Check your collection once again before corner A. Repeat the exercise on the opposite rein.

WHAT ARE THE AIDS TO PIROUETTE?

❏ Be sure to sit in the correct inside bend position.

❏ Inside hand asks for the bend.

❏ Outside hand uses gentle half-halts as required.

❏ Inside leg employs small, rhythmic nudges on the girth for impulsion and tempo.

❏ Outside leg remains behind the girth to guard the haunches, and uses small rhythmic nudges for tempo.

What should happen?

As the horse has to lift his forehand in order to turn through the pirouette, he takes his weight on to his hocks. With his weight on his hocks, he is now able to bring his front legs across in big wide steps, making good use of his shoulders. As he has to maintain flexion to the inside of the pirouette, he learns to be supple through his back and neck, to work into the outside rein, and to soften into the inside rein.

Double check

Your horse should maintain the rhythm of the footsteps in the collected walk throughout the pirouette.

Moving on

Try riding half pirouettes on the centre line.

What can go wrong?

1 Your horse's rhythm slows down.

In this case it is most likely that your horse is not sufficiently well trained to stay in front of your leg, and additional work needs to be done on sharpening up his response to your leg aids.

2 Your horse twists on his inside hind hoof instead of marking time.

Try using a sharper rhythm with your inside leg to be quicker with the tempo, or to make the pirouette bigger.

If it's not working...

Work on travers (Exercise 71).

❏ It is more difficult for
the horse without
the school walls for
support.

❏ If your horse has his
nose 'against the
wall' as he makes
the pirouette it is
inclined to stop him
'moving forwards'.

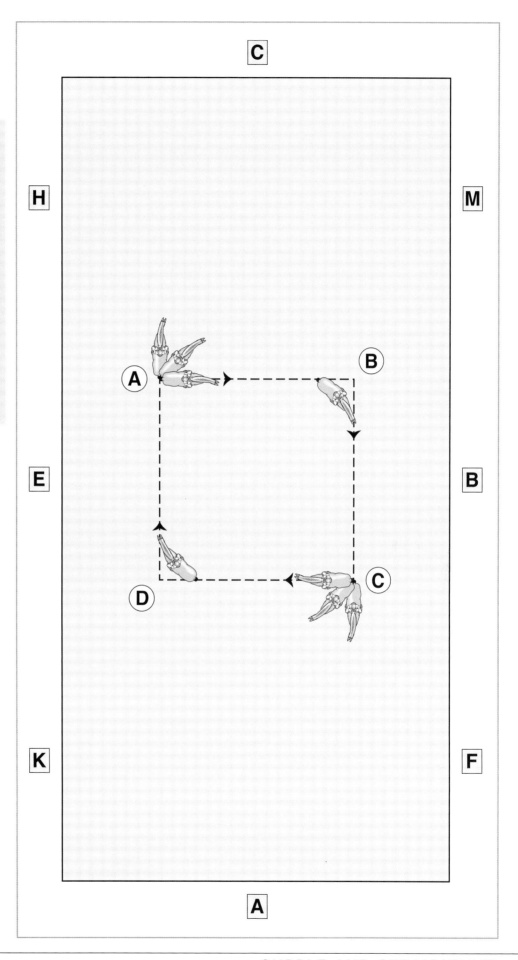

EVEN ON BOTH SIDES

Serpentine Exercises

THE EXERCISES

Serpentines are great for novice riders and horses. However, their role in any training programme, from novice to advanced, as an exercise to aid suppling and prepare for collection, should never be underestimated. Their value is in developing the dexterity of the horse by changing the bend from one rein to another and back again (any exercise that includes this formula is known as a serpentine), and because there are so many permutations of serpentine exercise, to suit the training level of rider and horse. For example, if you are having problems with a change of rein in one of the exercises featured here, try putting in an extra straight stride or two, where possible, before asking for the change. And as your horse's collection develops you can increase the number of loops (again, where possible) to suit his abilities.

YOUR AIMS

❏ The loops should be of a similar size and shape.
❏ The horse's rhythm and stride should be maintained throughout.
❏ The correct bend should be maintained throughout.

EXERCISE

39

BEGINNERS ⬢⬢⬢⬢⬢
PRELIMINARY ⬢⬢⬢⬢⬢
NOVICE ⬢⬢⬢⬢
ELEMENTARY ⬢⬢⬢
MEDIUM

The simplest of serpentines

This exercise is intended to help your horse improve his straightness and balance, and to command his attention. Ride it in trot initially, and once you feel you have mastered this pace, move up to canter. Get a friend to stand in the apex of the loop for you, and watch to ensure that you and your horse are in balance.

How do I ride this exercise?
❏ Establish the trot along one long side of the school.
❏ Ride across the short side, and into the next corner.
❏ Make a 3–5m loop in from the track on the long side.
❏ Straighten, and ride round the short side.
❏ Head straight up the opposite long side, and across the short side again.
❏ Repeat the loop down the long side.
❏ You could then ride the loop up the opposite long side of the school…
❏ …and then on the other rein.

What should happen?
The essence of the loop lies in its perfect geometry: it should be exactly symmetrical, the second half being a mirror image of the first half, and the mid-point exactly on the E–B line. The angle at which the horse leaves the track should be exactly the same as the angle at which he rejoins it. He should be balanced and guidable, neither falling in nor falling out.

Double check
Are you sitting up and looking straight ahead to where you are heading? Is your horse being guided by your leg as well as your hand?

Moving on
Try this in canter, remembering to keep the bend in accordance with the canter lead – that is, over the leading leg.

What can go wrong?
Your horse may be unbalanced at first, possibly because he is not listening to you, and may fall in at the corner.
Make sure you have not turned him too suddenly: his departure from the track must be very gradual.

If it's not working...
If you are riding this exercise in trot, mark out the track you should be following before attempting to ride it again. If you are trying a 5m loop, go back to a shallower loop.

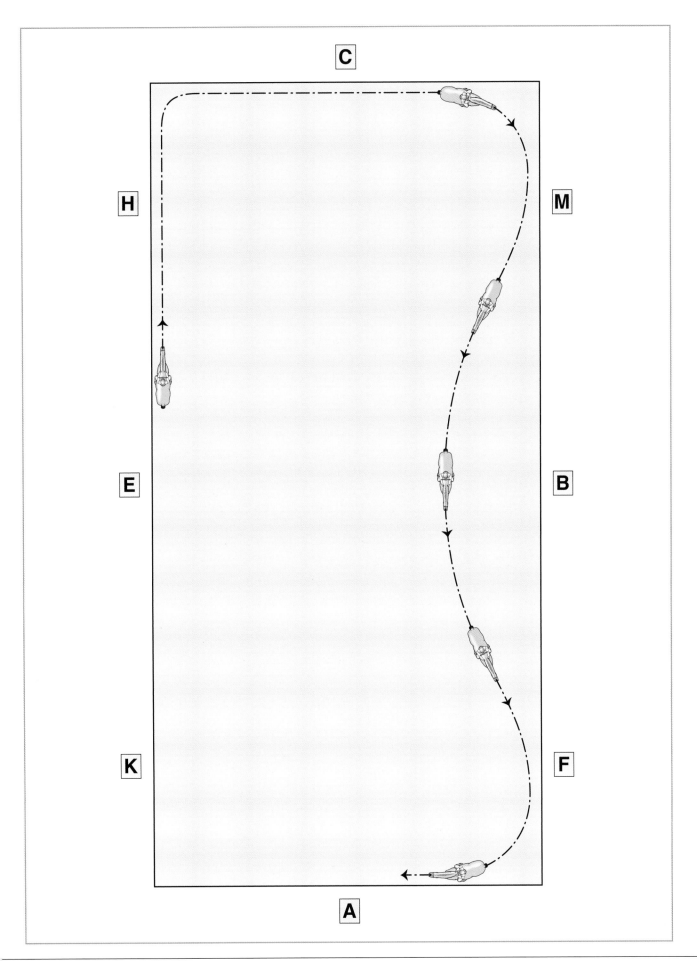

Shallow loops

This is an excellent exercise for teaching a horse to listen and follow your lateral aids. This is a good movement to practise for your preliminary tests. It is also a great exercise for helping you to develop your skills controlling your horse's balance.

How do I ride this exercise?
❏ On the right rein, turn down the centre line from C in walk.
❏ Ride four shallow loops, 1–2m either side of the centre line.
❏ Go large and repeat.

What should happen?
Your horse should step exactly over the line you planned, allowing you to bend him left and right with relaxed submission, and staying in good balance as you change your body position from left to right.

Double check
As you change bend you should also change your leg, seat and hand position.

Moving on
This exercise can be ridden in trot. You could also ride it maintaining the same bend throughout.

What can go wrong?
He could fall in or out through the shoulder on the curves.
Support him with the leg and rein on whichever side he is falling.

If it's not working...
Go back to an easier format of shallow loops (Exercises 27 and 39).

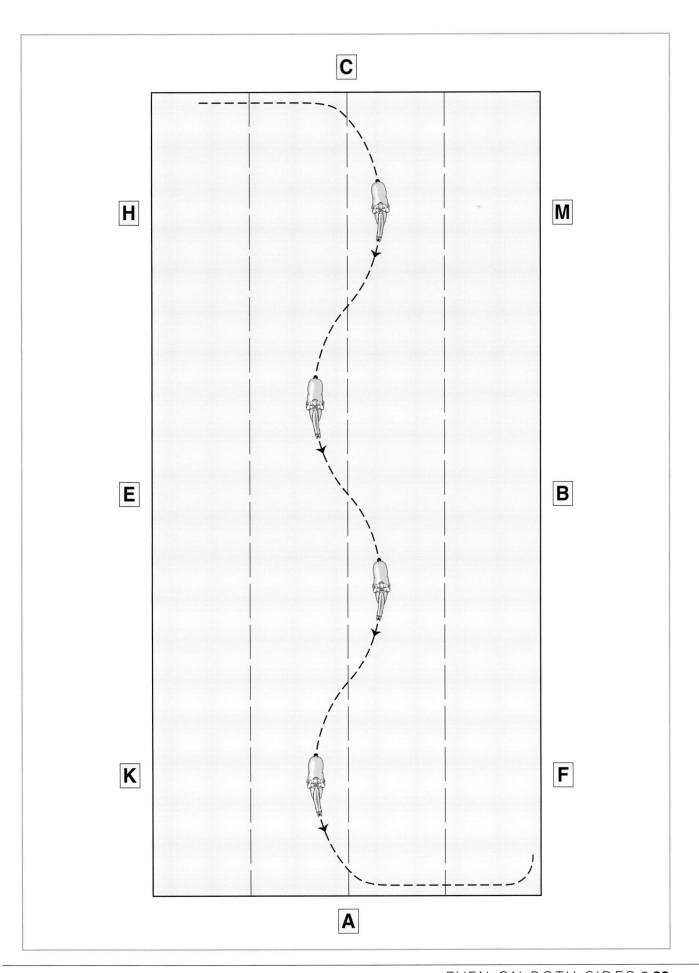

Classic three-loop serpentine

This exercise is not as easy as it looks, as you need to make two changes of bend within a short space, and your horse must show that he can do this without losing balance. Your horse is also going to find it easier to bend and turn one way than the other, so your challenge is to ensure that the loops on each rein are absolutely equal.

BONUS

Making regular changes of inside position prepares both rider and horse for the sequence of actions required in flying changes.

How do I ride this exercise?

- ❏ This exercise can be ridden from either end of the school.
- ❏ In trot, three strides past A or C, ride a half 13.3m circle. (In theory! As near as you can, its diameter would be a third of the length of a 40 x 20m school).
- ❏ Straighten for six strides or so (depending on the length of your horse's stride) crossing the centre line.
- ❏ As you cross the centre line, change the bend. After the six strides, ride a second half 13.3m circle.
- ❏ Once again cross the centre line in six or so straight strides…
- ❏ …then change the bend to ride a half 13.3m circle, rejoining the track at A or C.

What should happen?

Your horse should remain upright in the shoulders, and allow you to finish one curve and prepare him for the next so that he can negotiate it in balance.

Double check

Make sure you are changing your entire position – leg, seat and rein – to make the change of bend, and are not just using your hands.

Moving on

For the more advanced horse, this exercise can be ridden in canter, initially with simple changes (coming back to trot and asking for a change), and eventually with flying changes.

What can go wrong?

Your horse falls in as you ask for the change of bend, and leaves the line.
On a serpentine there will be either one or two loops that will be on your horse's stiffer side, when to avoid making the correct bend he falls in, rather than bends.
  To help him make the bend, see that he is softly accepting the inside rein contact and reacting correctly to the inside leg. The outside leg is responsible for controlling his haunches.

If it's not working...

Go back to working on simpler loops and circles (Exercises 27 and 39).

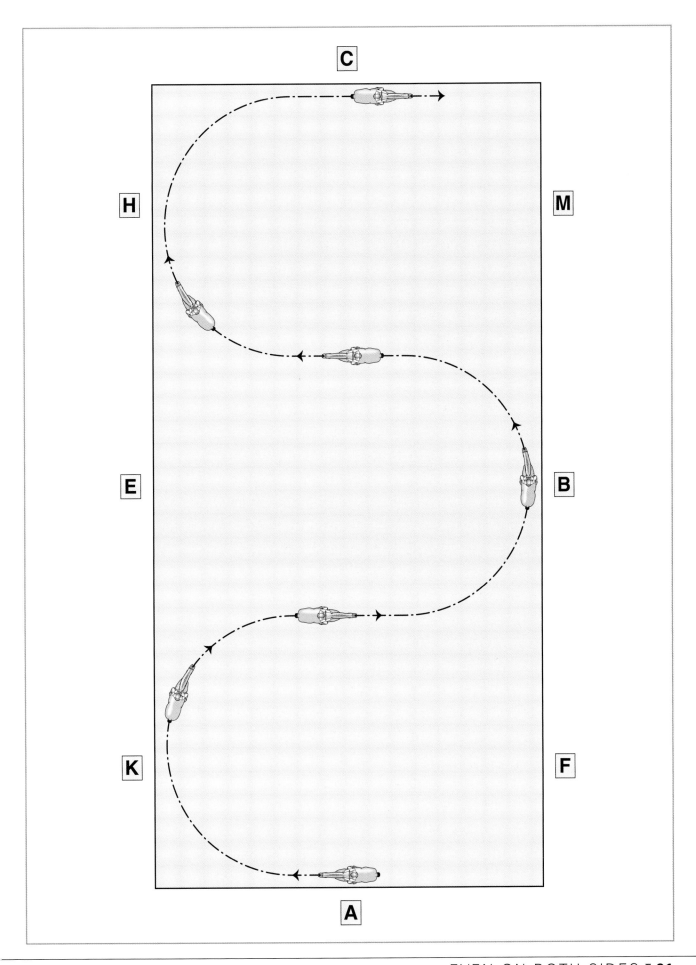

EVEN ON BOTH SIDES ▌91

EXERCISE

42

BEGINNERS

PRELIMINARY ○

NOVICE ○○○

ELEMENTARY ○○○○

MEDIUM ○○○○○

The curvy French serpentine

Serpentines have many applications in schooling – for example, in between loops, if you ride straight from one side of the school to another, this straight section can be used for a change of pace. Another favourite is to ride a halt each time you cross the centre line. However, this exercise is about improving rhythm and bend, and uses a rounded serpentine to help the horse's movement flow.

BONUS

Believe it or not, riding serpentines is one of the best ways to teach you and your horse to be straight.

How do I ride this exercise?

❏ Between each loop of your serpentine, exaggerate its curves so that, as you make each loop from the long side, you almost come back on yourself across the centre line.

❏ Use a half-halt to help set up the change in bend, and try to achieve it in one stride.

❏ Aim for a three-loop serpentine.

❏ Repeat on the other rein.

What should happen?

Your horse should make equal and even loops left and right, bending comfortably and keeping a smooth, regular rhythm, allowing the rider to adopt the correct inside position on both curves.

Double check

Make sure you maintain rhythm and movement flow in this exercise, by keeping the horse forward from the leg, and turning him with the outside aids.

Moving on

Once you are happy with three loops, decrease their size and try to fit in five (see Exercise 43).

What can go wrong?

Your horse comes above the bit and resists the hand during the change.

Spend longer on the straighter strides between the curves, and make a less exaggerated bend. Make sure you are not pulling on the horse's mouth.

If it's not working...

Go back to the classic three-loop serpentine (Exercise 41).

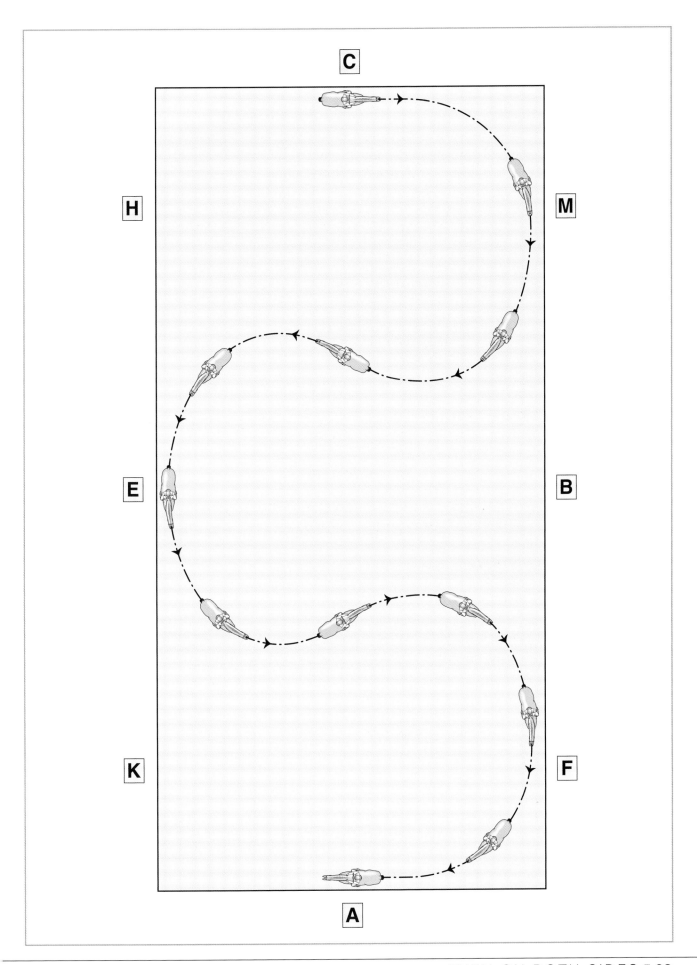

EXERCISE

43

BEGINNERS

PRELIMINARY ✪

NOVICE ✪✪✪

ELEMENTARY ✪✪✪✪

MEDIUM ✪✪✪✪✪

Five-loop French serpentine

Not only is this exercise most effective as a way to improve your horse's suppleness, it also helps in controlling his speed.

BONUS

Making regular changes of inside position prepares the rider and the horse for the movements required in flying changes.

How do I ride this exercise?

- ❑ On the right rein, just past A, ride a three-quarter 10m circle.
- ❑ Make a change of rein across the centre line and ride another three-quarter 10m circle on the left rein.
- ❑ Continue in this serpentine up the school, making five loops in the length of the arena (see illustration).

What should happen?

Your horse should remain correctly between hand and leg, and should be able to make the changes of rein without loss of balance and submitting softly to your aids.

Double check

Make sure you are changing your entire position – leg, seat and rein – to make the change of bend, and that you are not just using your hands.

Moving on

You could try the serpentine in canter, initially with simple changes, and eventually with flying changes.

What can go wrong?

Your horse runs off, or the change of bend is too slow.

Complete the 10m circle before proceeding.

If it's not working...

Go back to working on the three-loop French serpentine (Exercise 42).

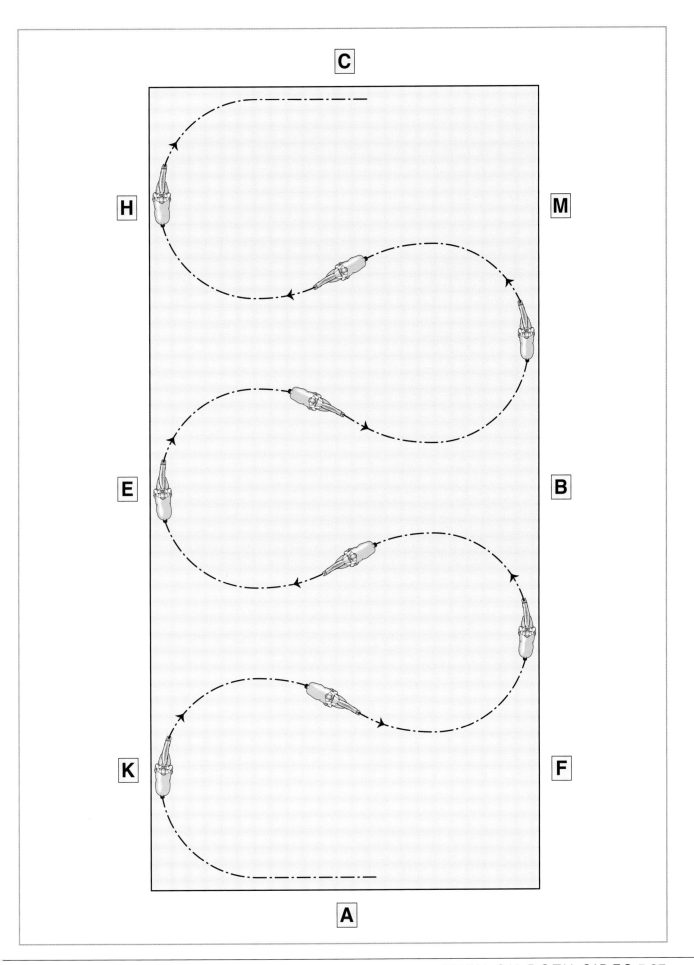

EXERCISE

44

BEGINNERS ✪
PRELIMINARY ✪✪
NOVICE ✪✪✪✪✪
ELEMENTARY ✪✪✪✪✪
MEDIUM ✪✪✪✪

Changes of pace across the serpentine

This exercise gives the rider more opportunity to direct and control his horse's balance: all downward transitions are wonderful collecting exercises.

How do I ride this exercise?

❏ On the right rein, in trot, and commencing at A: ride a three-loop serpentine.
❏ Having completed the first loop, as you cross the quarter line, ride a walk transition for two to three steps across the centre line.
❏ Return to trot again for the second loop …
❏ …repeating the transition to walk as you change for the third loop.
❏ Repeat on the opposite rein.

What should happen?

If the horse is performing his transitions correctly, it will cause him to take his weight more on his hind leg, and so he will become a little more collected.

Double check

Be sure that you make a correct shift of weight from position left to position right during the walk period of this exercise.

Moving on

This exercise can also be ridden in canter, with trot steps either side of the centre line.

What can go wrong?

Your horse stops abruptly in the downward transition.
Make sure you are riding your horse forward, and that he is in front of your leg.

If it's not working...

Go back to working exclusively on serpentines (Exercises 39, 40 and 41) and figures-of-eight in the walk (Exercise 31).

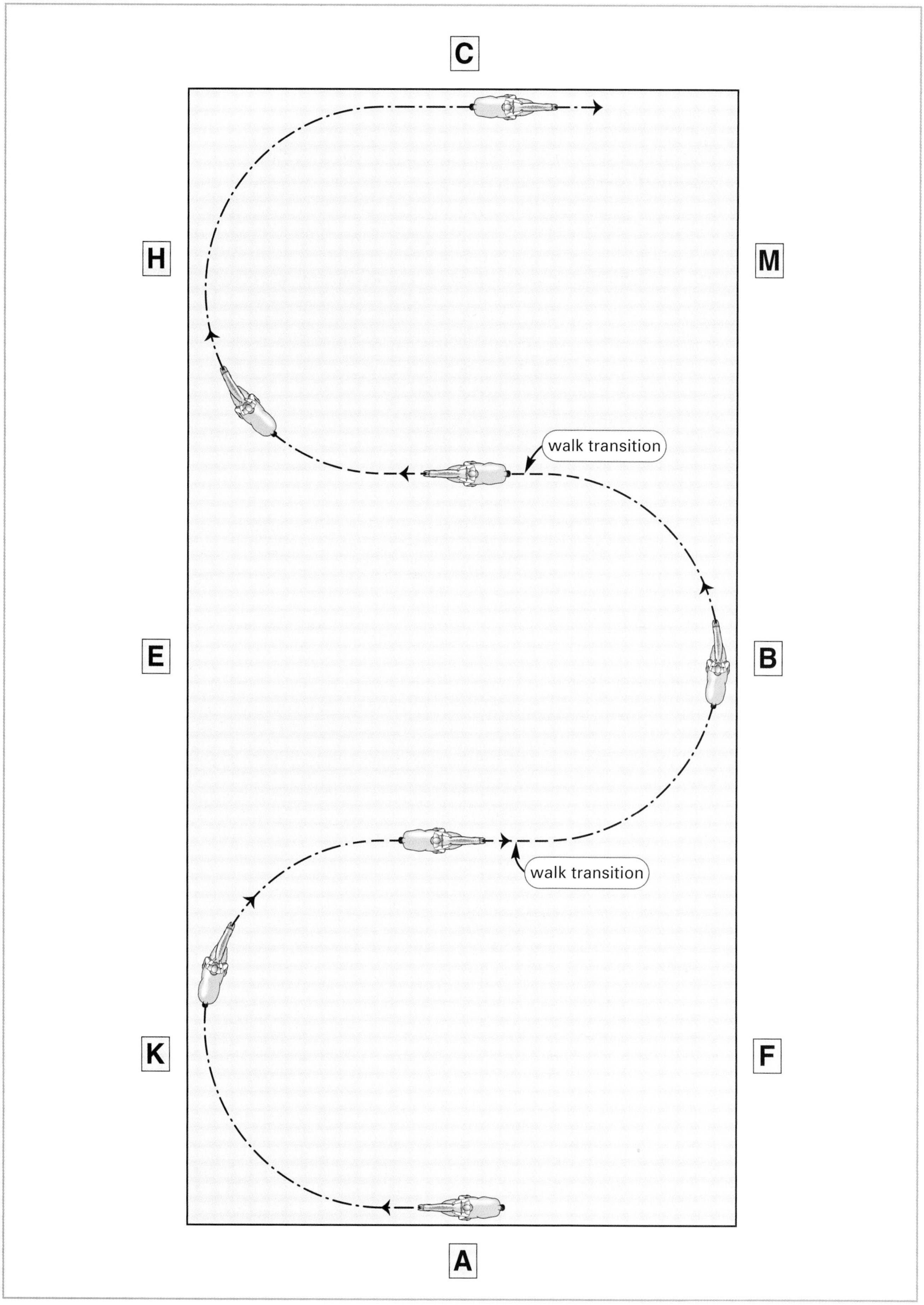
C
H
M
walk transition
E
B
walk transition
K
F
A

EXERCISE

45

BEGINNERS ✪
PRELIMINARY ✪✪
NOVICE ✪✪✪✪
ELEMENTARY ✪✪✪✪✪
MEDIUM ✪✪✪✪✪

10m half-circle serpentine

This is a great exercise for gaining your horse's attention, and a good suppling exercise – perfect for loosening up on a cold morning once you've warmed up.

RIDER'S TIP

After every two or three half circles, go large around the school, keeping your horse straight in order to regenerate his impulsion.

How do I ride this exercise?

- ❏ From A, on the left rein and in walk, ride a half 10m circle to the left.
- ❏ As you cross the centre line, straighten for one or two steps...
- ❏ ...then ride a half 10m circle to the right.
- ❏ Continue along the centre line, repeating the circles left and right.
- ❏ At C repeat the exercise.

What should happen?

The constant changes of bend and repositioning of your horse's forehand ensures that he has to pay attention to your aids in order to accomplish this exercise correctly.

Double check

Be sure that your half circles are comparable in size and shape.

Moving on

Once your horse is fully loosened up and feels balanced and on your aids, come back to riding this exercise in trot.

What can go wrong?

Your horse comes above the bit and resists your hands in the turns.

Make sure your contact is gentle, and don't underestimate the intimidating effect of metal on the mouth.

If it's not working...

Increase the number of straight steps between each half circle.

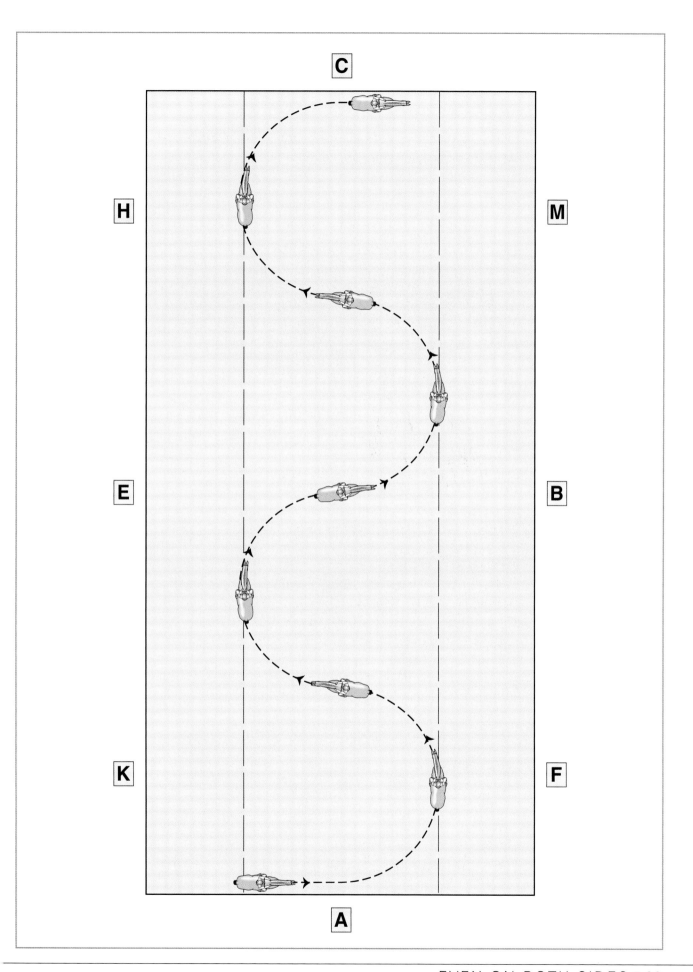

EXERCISE

46

BEGINNERS
PRELIMINARY ✪
NOVICE   ✪✪✪
ELEMENTARY ✪✪✪✪
MEDIUM   ✪✪✪

Serpentine ridden longways

Riding an accurate small half circle on to a long, straight line down the school is excellent practice for riding straight, and requires a good level of balance and engagement on the part of your horse.

How do I ride this exercise?

❏ On the right rein and in walk from F, leave the track and make a small half circle right to the quarter line.
❏ On reaching the quarter line, proceed in trot along the quarter line to the other end of the school.
❏ Go back to walk, and ride another small half circle left…
❏ …and proceed down the centre line in trot.
❏ Return once again to walk, and ride a small half circle right to the three-quarter line.
❏ Trot along the three-quarter line.
❏ Go back to walk at the other end, and make a final small half circle left to the track.
❏ Ride down the long side.
❏ Repeat on the other rein.

What should happen?

This is a good exercise to improve balance and straightness, training the horse to stay straight without the support of the fence or track.

Double check

❏ Be sure that the horse is being channelled straight by your legs, and is not just being pulled by your hands.
❏ Make sure you get a good change of bend. Half-halting at each end of the school will collect your horse and rebalance him so he is ready to set off straight down the length of the school.
❏ Make sure that you collect your horse for a correct transition to walk.

Moving on

Try riding your turns in trot, and the straight lines in canter.

What can go wrong?

Your horse swings his quarters out on the turns.
Check that you are riding with more influence from your outside aids.

If it's not working…

Ride two 10m half circles at each end of the school instead of four small half circles.

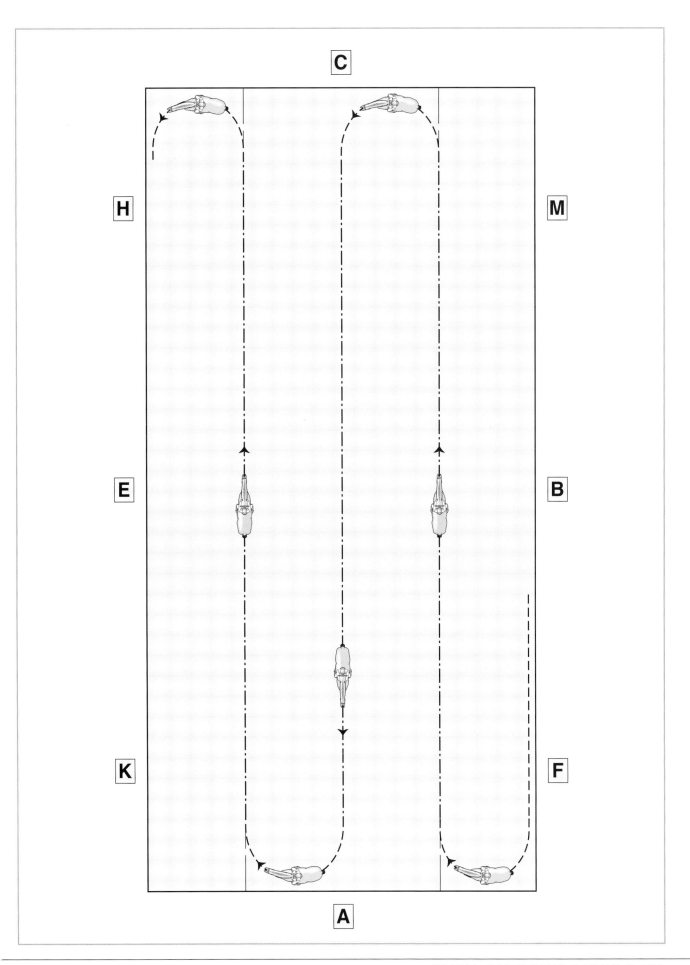

EXERCISE

BEGINNERS
PRELIMINARY
NOVICE   ✪✪
ELEMENTARY ✪✪✪✪
MEDIUM   ✪✪✪✪✪

Looping into a half serpentine

In a 20m x 40m arena, opportunities to ride counter canter of progressive difficulty are limited. This exercise in canter allows you a gentle alternative or two if your horse is finding it difficult.

How do I ride this exercise?

❏ On the right rein in canter with inside lead, just before H, ride a 10m half circle to the centre line.
❏ Incline back to the track arriving a little before E.
❏ From E adopt the path of a three-loop serpentine, riding counter canter until you cross the centre line.
❏ Resume true canter for the final loop.
❏ Work on the same rein until you are satisfied…
❏ …then change direction, starting at B…
❏ …and riding the initial 10m half circle (left lead) between M and C.

What should happen?

As your horse comes out of the initial 10m half circle he should remain balanced, upright and straight, maintaining the same bend with his nose over the leading leg.

Double check

Be sure that your weight is in your inside stirrup and on your inside seatbone, that your outside leg is back, and your inside shoulder is back. Don't forget that in this exercise, the term 'inside' refers to the horse's bend, and not the direction of his movement.

Moving on

Try making the initial half circle 15m: this will increase the difficulty of the counter-canter loop.

What can go wrong?

Your horse loses his balance and changes legs, either in front or behind (he becomes 'disunited').
Try riding a less severe middle arc.

If it's not working...

Go back to shallow loops (Exercises 27 and 40).

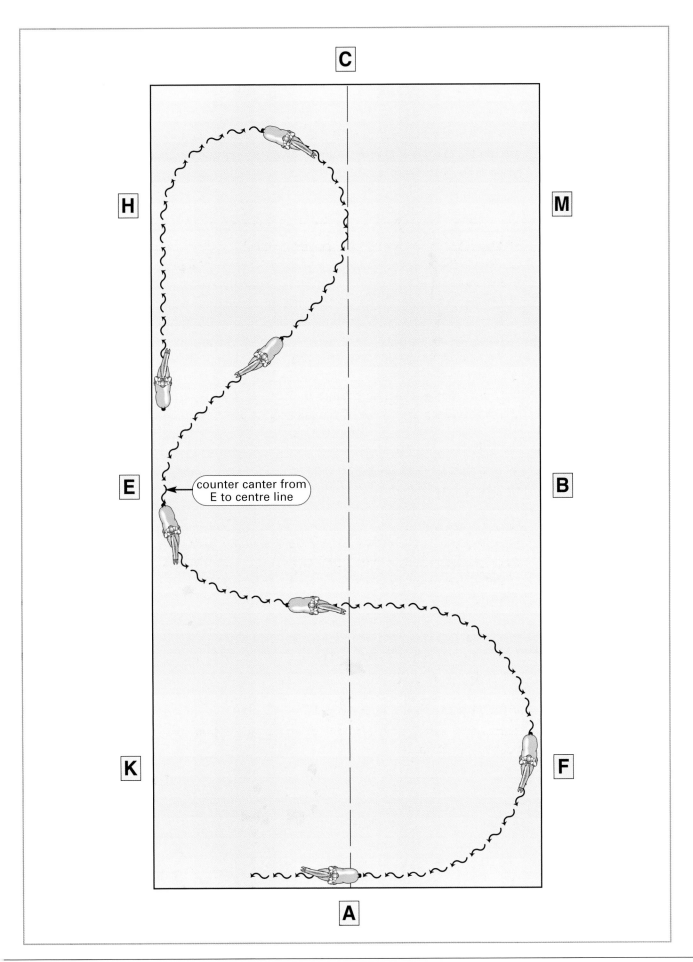

counter canter from E to centre line

EXERCISE

48

BEGINNERS

PRELIMINARY

NOVICE ✪

ELEMENTARY ✪✪

MEDIUM ✪✪✪✪✪

Serpentine of unequal loops

This is a counter-canter exercise that uses a version of the three-loop serpentine to add to our counter-canter repertoire, which is limited in a 20 x 40m arena. Two loops of the serpentine are in true canter, and the middle loop is in counter canter.

BONUS

Faults that crop up in this exercise are an indication of troubles that may appear in the flying-change exercises.

How do I ride this exercise?

❏ Start on the left rein, in canter.

❏ Half way between C and the corner, commence a half 10m circle.

❏ As you approach the centre line, ride a few straight steps.

❏ From the centre line ride a half 20m circle right in counter canter.

❏ At the centre line ride one or two straight steps...

❏ ...and then ride a half 10m circle left in true canter, bringing you back to A.

What should happen?

Your horse needs to maintain the same balance and rhythm through the counter-canter arc as he shows through the true canter arcs.

Double check

Be sure that your horse crosses the centre line at exactly 90 degrees.

Moving on

Once your horse is confident and comfortable in this exercise, try making the size of the loops equal.

What can go wrong?

Your horse falls out through his outside shoulder (right shoulder on the left rein) as he crosses the centre line and assumes counter canter.

This is because the initial half circle is quite tight. Make sure you make the turn for this circle with enough support from your outside leg and outside rein.

If it's not working...

Try an easier format, such as the half serpentine (Exercise 47).

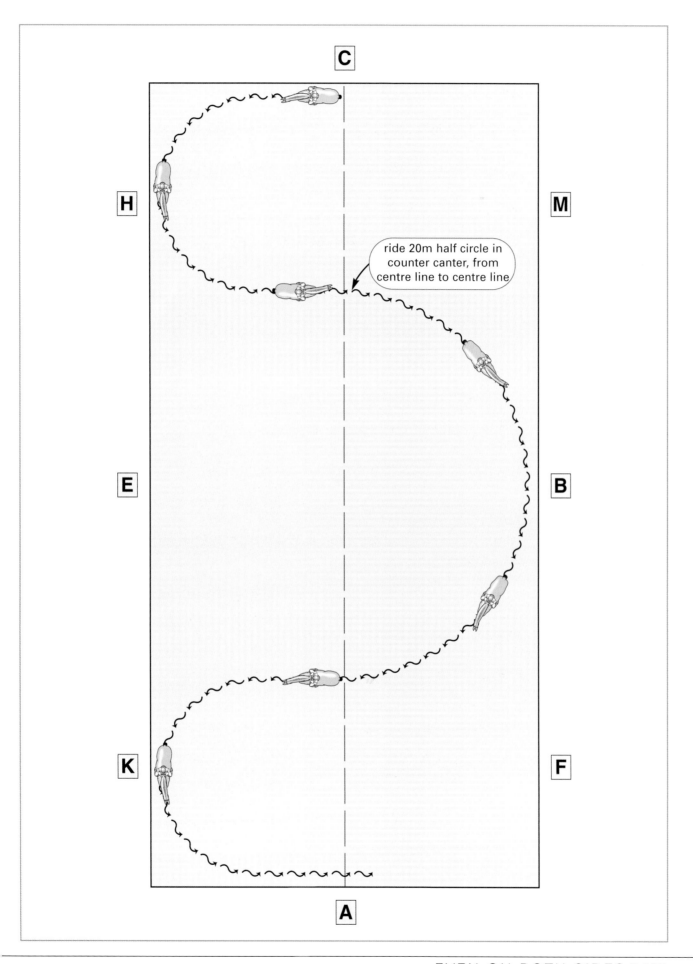

ride 20m half circle in counter canter, from centre line to centre line

LOOSE AND AGILE
Leg-yielding

THE EXERCISES

Leg-yielding is the first step in lateral work. Lateral work is aimed at loosening up your horse and making him more agile or supple, because it involves exercises in which the front legs and the hind legs move on different tracks, and the horse is required to move sideways and forwards in the same movement.

Whilst it is a logical introduction to lateral work for novice horses and riders, it is also an excellent training tool for re-schooling horses, and can be used as a warming-up exercise before your horse is ready to work on the bit.

THE AIDS TO LEG-YIELD

- ❏ Place more weight on your inside seatbone.
- ❏ Position your inside leg just behind the girth, and use it to encourage your horse forwards and sideways.
- ❏ Your outside leg should be behind the girth in case your horse moves his hindquarters too far sideways. It should also help to maintain the forward movement.
- ❏ Your inside rein should ask for just a slight bend.
- ❏ Your outside rein should give sufficiently to allow the bend, but should maintain contact to prevent your horse bending too much, or falling out through the outside shoulder.

EXERCISE

49

BEGINNERS ✪✪✪✪✪
PRELIMINARY ✪✪✪✪✪
NOVICE ✪✪✪
ELEMENTARY ✪
MEDIUM

Using quarter turns on the forehand to prepare for leg-yielding

A turn on the forehand teaches the horse to respond to your sideways aids. It can be done a step at a time, which gives both rider and horse the opportunity to master each aid, and to improve their overall co-ordination.

How do I ride this exercise?

❏ On the right rein in walk, turn down the long side before K and ride up the inner track 2m from the wall.
❏ Half way between E and H halt, and perform a quarter turn on the forehand to the right.
❏ Proceed straight across the school.
❏ 2m before the next long side, halt and repeat the quarter turn on the forehand.
❏ Proceed on the inner track 2m from the wall.
❏ Midway between B and F halt, and perform another quarter turn on the forehand.
❏ Walk across the school for one final halt and turn on the forehand.
❏ Repeat on the other rein.

How do I ride a turn on the forehand?

One of the advantages of this exercise is that it can be ridden step by step, giving you the opportunity to understand and co-ordinate your aids, and time to reward the horse as he completes each step. The exercise is ridden with a little inside bend.

❏ Take up a correct inside position: inside leg on the girth, outside leg a little further back, inside shoulder back, outside shoulder a little forward, and your weight on your inside seatbone.
❏ Because you want your horse to move his quarters over, your inside leg should come back just a little more, and therefore your outside leg needs to go back just a little further to maintain its guarding position.
❏ Ask your horse to step sideways away from your inside leg, and as he makes each step, relax and reward him, before asking for the next step.
❏ Once he fully understands, the steps can be performed in a more fluid manner.

What should happen?

Turn on the forehand is an exercise in which the horse moves his quarters sideways away from the rider's inside leg. He has a slight inside bend, and the centre of rotation should be the inside front foot, which is picked up and put down in the same place. He should make his side steps by crossing his inside hind leg in front of his outside hind leg, rather than moving the outside hind leg out as the inside hind leg comes up to it.

The horse should remain relaxed and calm whilst he performs this simple and absorbing exercise. The aim is to make correct turns on the forehand, in balance and on the aids.

Double check

Be sure that your horse is learning the good habit of accepting the bit calmly and with submission during this exercise.

Moving on

Try omitting the halt and riding the whole exercise in the same rhythm as the walk.

What can go wrong?

Your horse becomes anxious and swings his quarters before being asked to move away from the leg.

Go back to the walk – halt – walk routine (Exercise 1).

If it's not working...

Try reinforcing your leg aids with a light tap from the stick to help him understand what you want.

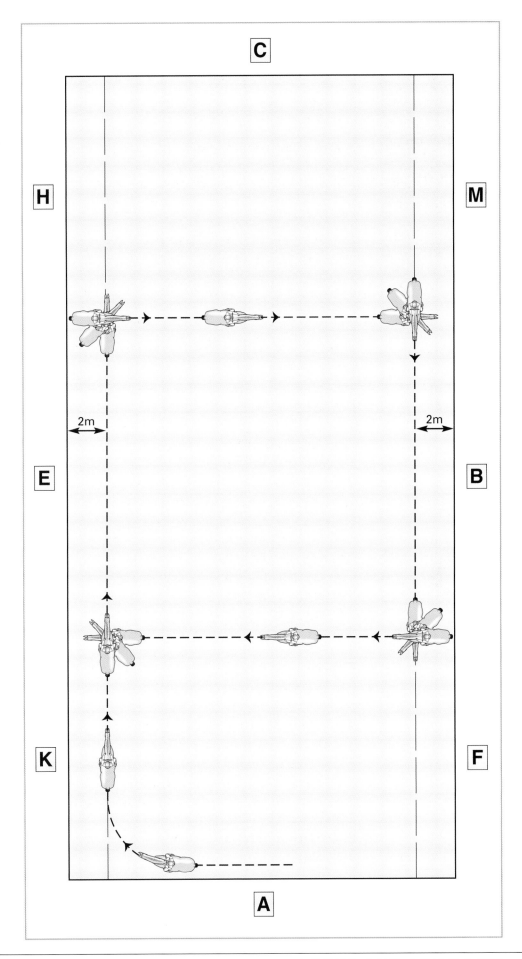

2m

2m

EXERCISE

50

BEGINNERS ✪

PRELIMINARY ✪✪✪

NOVICE ✪✪✪✪✪

ELEMENTARY ✪✪✪

MEDIUM ✪

Easy leg-yield from the three-quarter line to the track

Leg-yielding teaches the horse to move away from your leg, and has a suppling and strengthening effect on the muscles of the back and the hindquarters because they have to stretch more than in any work on a single track.

How do I ride this exercise?
❑ In walk, turn up the three-quarter line.
❑ Ride a few straight steps, then leg-yield to the outside track.
❑ This exercise is relatively easy, as most horses gravitate towards the track; but be careful not to let the horse fall sideways.

What should happen?
Having made the turn down the three-quarter line, be sure that your horse makes a few straight steps: then leg-yield sideways towards the track, keeping his forehand and haunches united. He should keep his body quite straight and just have a slight bend to the inside.

Double check
❑ Check your position, and make sure you are sitting up and that your body is straight.
❑ Check your reins are a suitable length, and that you have a good contact.
❑ Check that you are straight before asking for any sideways movement.

Moving on
Turn up the three-quarter line and leg-yield to the centre line.

What can go wrong?
1 Your horse loses impulsion and rhythm.
It is easy during lateral work to get bogged down with what you are working on, and it is always best to start again: so if your horse loses impulsion, send him forward and straight in a strong and positive fashion. If necessary, make a few transitions before having another go.

2 Your horse has too much bend in the neck and/or body, which leads to him falling out through the outside shoulder.
You will need to use the outside aids more strongly, and make sure you are not being too strong with the inside hand. Remember, you only want to be able to glimpse the horse's eyebrow, and not his whole eye!

3 Your horse's hindquarters either lead or trail.
It is important that the horse remains straight. If the quarters are ahead of the shoulder, your inside leg may be too far back, or your outside leg is being rather ineffective. If the quarters are trailing, the inside leg needs to be used a little further back and the outside leg should take greater control of the outside shoulder.

4 Your horse does not cross his inside legs in front of his outside ones, but shuffles instead.

This is a sign that he has lost energy and may be confused. Try again, asking for deliberate steps. Carry a long schooling whip in the outside hand, to reinforce your leg aid.

5 Your horse panics, his head goes up and a battle ensues.

Go back to basics, but ask an expert to check your position and application of aids.

If it's not working...

Go back to working on your horse's response to your aids (Exercises 6, 7, 21 and 23).

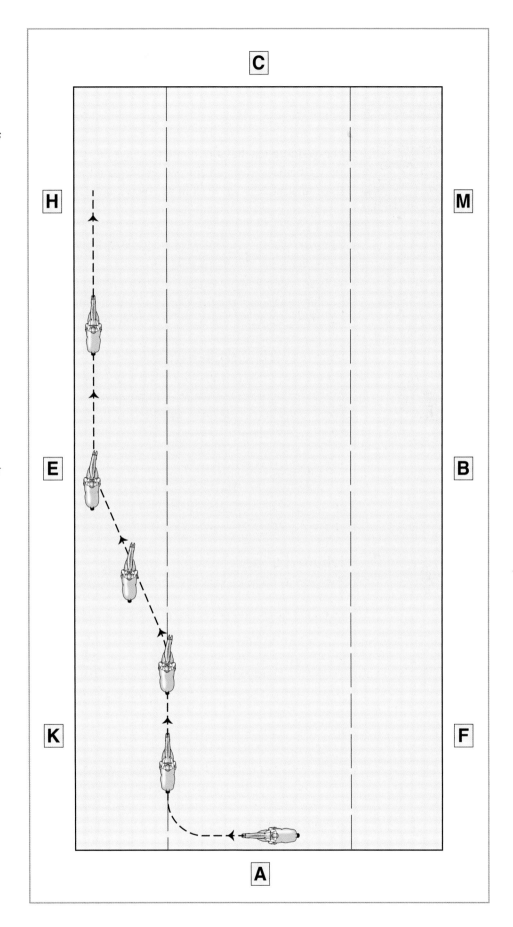

EXERCISE

51
BEGINNERS ○
PRELIMINARY ○○○○
NOVICE ○○○
ELEMENTARY ○○○
MEDIUM ○

Leg-yielding across the corner

This exercise is a good one for warming up an older or stiffer horse. It also ensures that you are in charge – not him!

How do I ride this exercise?
❏ Ride on the left rein in walk.
❏ Just before A turn, and ride in the direction of M.
❏ When your horse is facing M, leg-yield towards B.
❏ If you find that your horse has taken charge and is leg-yielding when he chooses, try riding him straight for two steps, then leg-yield for two steps, then ride straight for another two steps, and so on.

What should happen?
Your horse should stay balanced and purposeful, and shouldn't drift towards the track, falling out through his shoulder. He should move forwards and across without swinging his quarters, and without reluctance.

Double check
Be sure that you are not leaning over to the left.

Moving on
This exercise can be ridden in trot.

What can go wrong?
When you turn your horse at A he swings his quarters out.
You have probably turned too suddenly. Take time to prepare your turn.

If it's not working...
Check that your inside leg isn't creeping too far back and dislodging your horse's quarters, leaving his forehand unsupported.

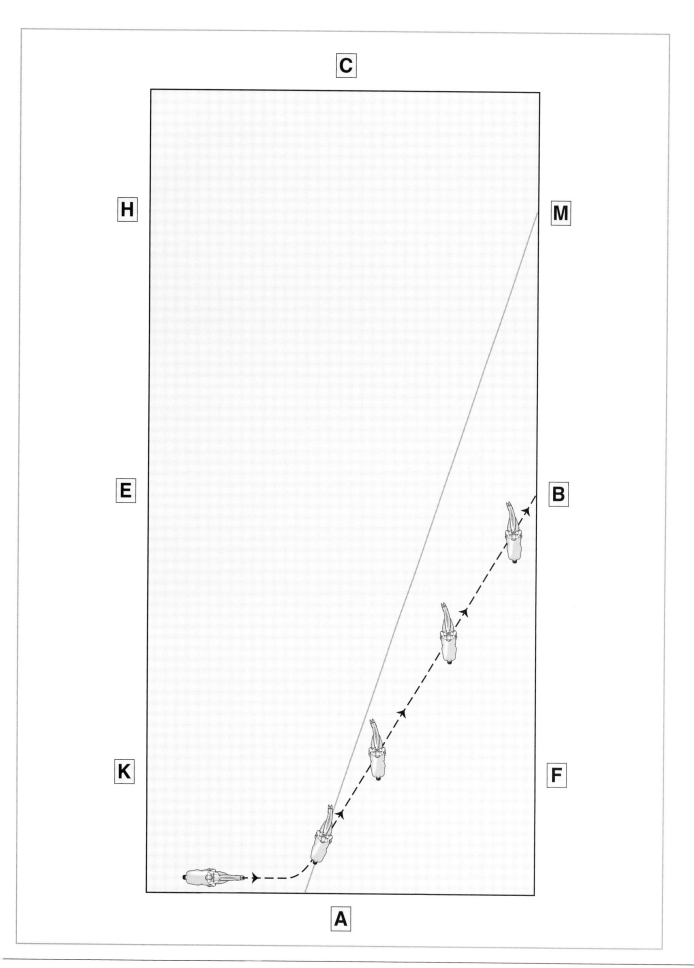

Leg-yielding across the diagonal

BEGINNERS ✪

PRELIMINARY ✪✪✪

NOVICE ✪✪✪✪

ELEMENTARY ✪✪

MEDIUM ✪

This is one of the most popular exercises for getting a horse correctly on the aids. It is an excellent training tool for re-schooling a horse, and can be used as a warming-up exercise before your horse is ready to work on the bit.

RIDER'S TIP

Remember to use your outside rein to prevent the horse from falling sideways. Be careful not to bring the inside leg too far back.

How do I ride this exercise?

❏ Begin on the left rein in walk.

❏ Ride a half 10m circle right from K to the centre line.

❏ Leg-yield diagonally across the arena in the direction of M.

❏ At M, make a 10m half circle left, and leg-yield diagonally across the arena back to K.

❏ Repeat on the opposite rein.

What should happen?

In complying with the rider's aids your horse is going to have to amend his balance to pick his weight up, and off his inside shoulder: he is going to have to carry himself at an angle forwards and sideways, and this will help with the engagement of his haunches and so free his shoulder. It will also improve his obedience and understanding of the rider's aids.

Double check

Be sure that you aren't trying to pull your horse over by sitting to the outside.

Moving on

This exercise can also be done in trot.

What can go wrong?

1 Your horse's quarters tend to lead in the leg-yield.

   Keep your inside leg further forward and your outside leg further back. You need to commence the leg-yield earlier from the half circle.

2 Your horse falls through the outside shoulder.

   Be careful to use more control through the outside rein.

If it's not working...

Make the circles a little bigger to give you more time, and so you are less demanding on your horse; or ride one-and-a-half circles before beginning the leg-yield.

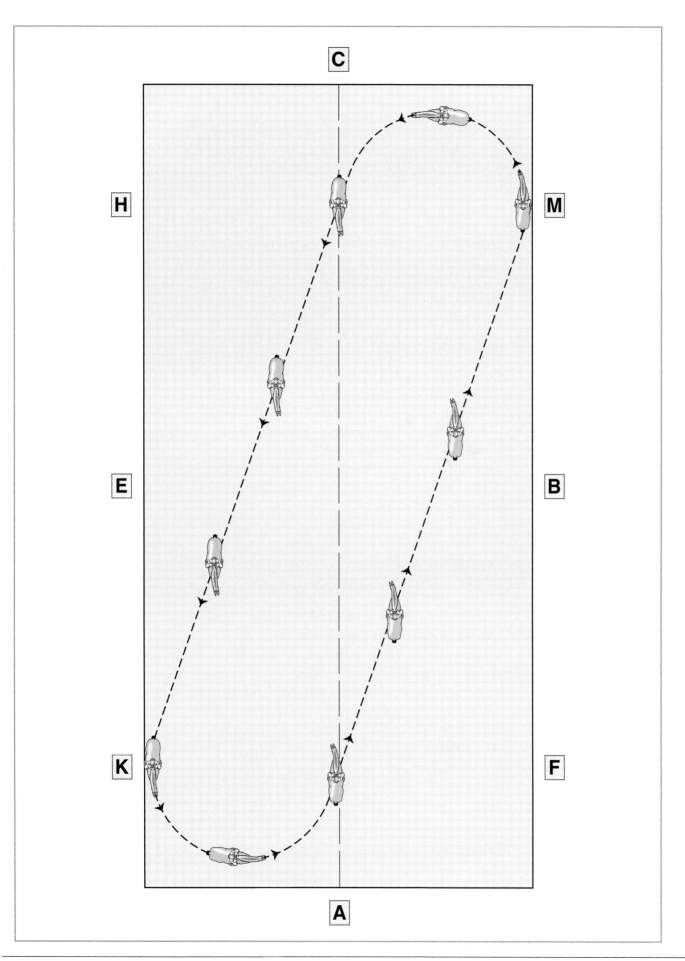

Leg-yield into the corners

This exercise will teach the horse to 'come off the leg' so that you can press him right into the angles of the school without losing impulsion; this will help you to perform really good turns and corners in a test.

How do I ride this exercise?

❏ Go large in the school, on the left rein and in rising or sitting trot.
❏ As you pass A, turn and ride up the three-quarter line, keeping your horse straight, until the middle marker.
❏ Now leg-yield out to the track at M, and…
❏ …continue the leg-yield aids so that you can ride deep into the corner between M and C.
❏ If your horse feels balanced and confident, repeat again from the C end of the school.
❏ Otherwise make a circle to restore his way of going.

What should happen?

The horse should arrive back at the track well engaged so that he is 'up' in front and off his inside shoulder, mindful and obedient to your inside leg, and readily obedient to your aids for the next corner.

Double check

Check the following: are you sitting crooked? Is your inside leg too far back?

Moving on

Turn down the length of the school at A and/or C, and leg-yield from X to M, or X to F – a bit further, and therefore more of a challenge.

What can go wrong?

1 Your horse leads with the haunches.
  Make sure your inside leg is forward, and your outside leg is guiding the haunches.
2 Your horse trails with his quarters, allowing his forehand to sweep sideways.
  Use little half halts on the outside rein to try to gain control of the forehand.

If it's not working...

Make a circle after the corner to give your horse time to recover. Try the exercise in walk.

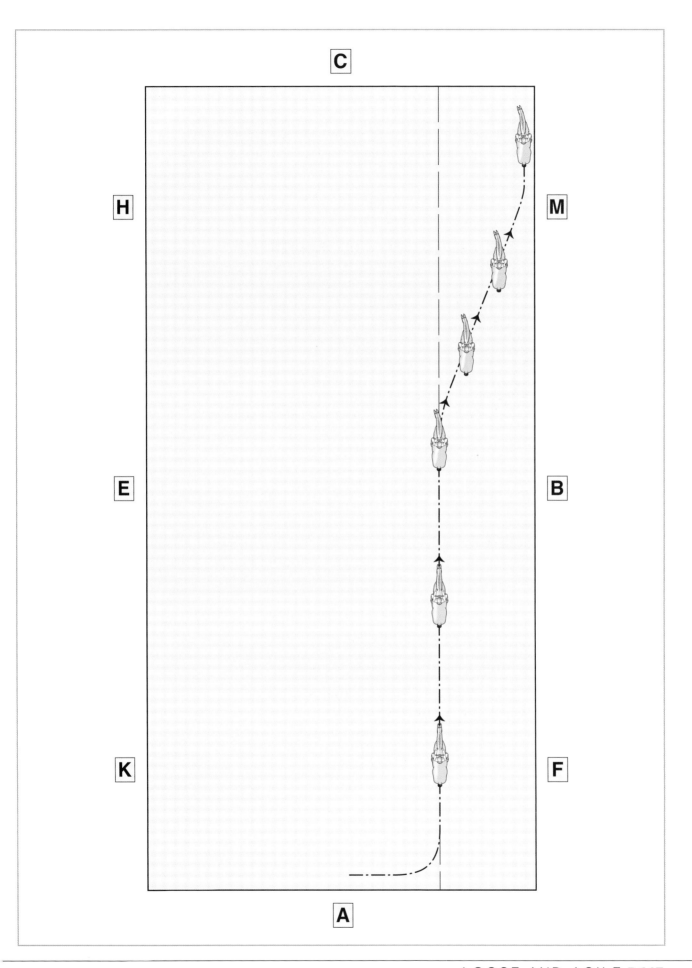

EXERCISE

54

BEGINNERS

PRELIMINARY ✪

NOVICE ✪✪✪✪

ELEMENTARY ✪✪✪

MEDIUM ✪✪

Leg-yield in shoulder-in position

This exercise prepares your horse for the challenges of shoulder-in. It is particularly good for loosening up your horse, and making him more agile and supple.

How do I ride this exercise?

❏ On the right rein in walk, collect through the corner after C.

❏ Bring your horse's forehand to the inside, and ride a 30-degree leg-yield along the long side of the school.

❏ Shortly after B straighten, and march forwards.

❏ Repeat from K.

❏ Repeat on the opposite rein.

What should happen?

Your horse should remain in position with his hind feet on the track, fairly straight in his body, with just a slight bend in his neck to the inside. He should maintain a consistent rhythm and good activity.

Double check

Be careful that your horse doesn't bend too much in leg-yield.

Moving on

Ride this exercise in trot, then try combining it with leg-yield in haunches-in position (Exercise 58), and give your horse a thorough muscular workout in one exercise!

What can go wrong?

Your horse tends to fall too much forwards off the track.

Use more half-halts with the outside rein, and more inside leg.

If it's not working...

Go back to working on leg-yield from the three-quarter line to the track (Exercise 50).

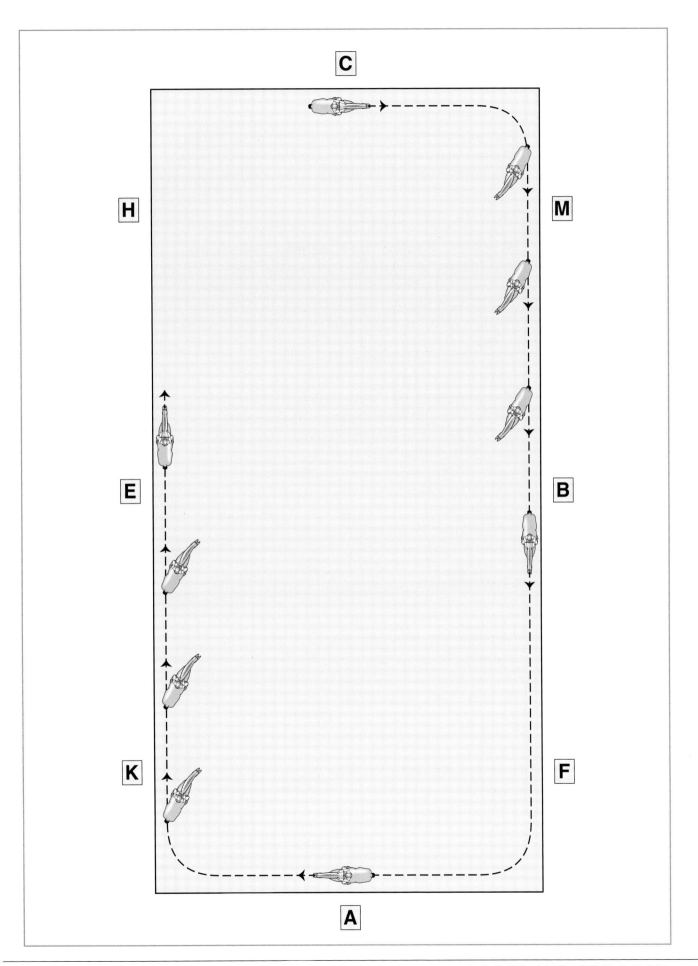

55

Leg-yielding away from the track

BEGINNERS

PRELIMINARY ◗◗

NOVICE ◗◗◗◗◗

ELEMENTARY ◗◗◗◗

MEDIUM ◗◗

Once your horse has mastered the simpler leg-yield from the three-quarter line to the track, try this exercise. If your horse is inclined to hug the wall he may find this a little harder, but it will teach him to become more independent.

> **REMEMBER**
>
> When leg-yielding, your horse's head is turned away from the direction in which he is travelling.

How do I ride this exercise?

❏ On the right rein, establish a good medium walk along the short side of the school.

❏ Make a turn just before the corner up the inner track.

❏ Ask your horse to leg-yield from this point to the centre line.

❏ At the centre line, straighten up and proceed to the opposite end of the school.

❏ Repeat on the other rein.

What should happen?

Upon receiving the aids, the horse should lift his weight up off the left shoulder and obediently leg-yield inwards towards the centre line.

Double check

❏ Are you riding crooked or leaning sideways?

❏ Try to maintain your own straightness, or you will cause your horse to move crookedly, too.

❏ Are you leaning forwards?

❏ This will push your horse on to his forehand and make subtle leg-aiding difficult.

Moving on

Try the exercise in trot.

What can go wrong?

Your horse increases his speed rather than leg-yielding.

This could be because he has misunderstood your leg aids, or it could be evasion (usually by falling out through the shoulder). Firstly, check that you are not using leg aids that are too strong: if that is not the case, use half-halts to help decrease the horse's speed and rebalance him. Think forwards, half-halt, and then sideways.

If it's not working...

If the horse is really having difficulty it might be easier to try this exercise from the three-quarter line to the centre line.

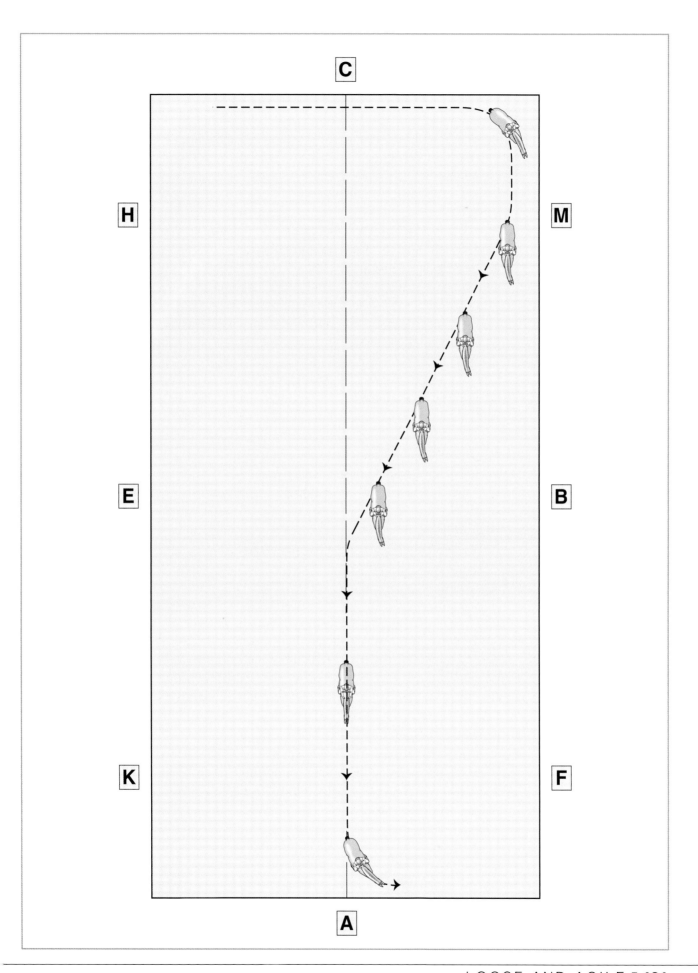

EXERCISE

56

BEGINNERS

PRELIMINARY ✪✪✪

NOVICE ✪✪✪✪✪

ELEMENTARY ✪✪✪✪✪

MEDIUM ✪✪✪✪

Leg-yielding on a circle with inner flexion

This exercise will teach the horse to engage his haunches to a greater degree, thereby becoming more collected; it will also make him much more responsive to the rider's aids.

How do I ride this exercise?
- ❏ Ride a 20m circle in walk.
- ❏ Ask for leg-yield, positioning your horse's forehand slightly to the inside of the circle.
- ❏ The hind legs should step sideways, describing the original circle's circumference.
- ❏ Repeat on the opposite rein.

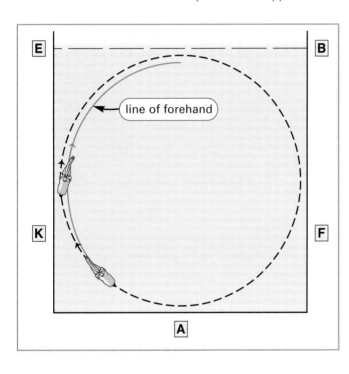

line of forehand

What should happen?
When asked to collect himself in the way in which this exercise requires, your horse should engage his haunches, accept the bridle and, being in balance, be ready and receptive to your aids.

Double check
Be sure that you are sitting in the correct position in the saddle: centrally, with a little more weight on the inside seatbone.

Moving on
This exercise can also be ridden as a counter leg-yield where the horse is on a left-hand circle bending right, and moving in a leg-yield away from the right leg. In these circumstances the front feet are travelling on the line of the circle, and the haunches are to the inside of the circle.

What can go wrong?
1 Your horse shows too much sideways and not enough forward movement.
Check that you are not applying too forceful an inside leg aid.

2 Your horse swings his quarters out and shows too much angle.
Check your outside leg. Are you using it too strongly? Is it in the correct position? Likewise, check that you are not applying too forceful an inside leg aid, or that your inside leg is not too far back. Ride the horse on more with the outside leg to maintain his forward reach of stride.

If it's not working...
Go back to leg-yielding on a straight line, or from the three-quarter line to the track (Exercise 50).

EXERCISE

57

BEGINNERS

PRELIMINARY ✪✪

NOVICE ✪✪✪✪✪

ELEMENTARY ✪✪✪

MEDIUM ✪

Spiralling circles using leg-yield

This exercise lays the foundation for more advanced types of spiral, and leads ultimately to the canter pirouette. It will help with the horse's turning, and to acquaint him with the outside aids.

How do I ride this exercise?
- ❏ Ride a 20m circle in walk.
- ❏ Spiral it down to a 10m, and then…
- ❏ …leg-yield out to 20m again.
- ❏ Repeat on the opposite rein.

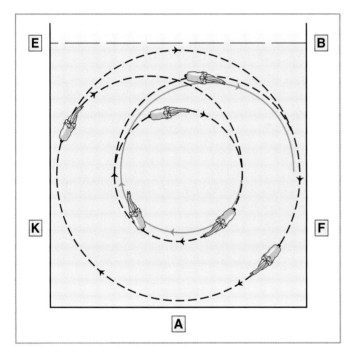

What should happen?
The horse should decrease his circle uniformly around its central point, becoming more collected as the circle decreases in size.

How do I ride the 'outside of the horse'?
Sitting in inside position, the horse must be trained to believe the outside leg and hand unite to form a wall that he must react to by moving – not falling — inwards.

Double check
On the leg-yield out, check that the horse isn't swinging his quarters out.

Moving on
Ride this exercise in trot.

What can go wrong?
Your horse will find it easy to fall out through the shoulder.
Ride on the outside aids to guard against this.

If it's not working...
Work on 20m, 15m and 10m circles (Exercise 26), and leg-yielding to the track (Exercise 50).

BEGINNERS ✪

PRELIMINARY ✪✪✪

NOVICE ✪✪✪✪✪

ELEMENTARY ✪✪✪✪

MEDIUM ✪✪✪✪

Leg-yield in haunches-in position

The wall makes it possible for you to ride this exercise without using too much restrictive hand, which might otherwise confuse your horse.

How do I ride this exercise?
❑ On the right rein, just before A, collect your horse's walk.
❑ Turn right in the direction of E.
❑ Just before E, almost halt and…
❑ …with the left leg, ask your horse to move sideways up the long side in a leg-yield.
❑ Just before H, straighten and ride forwards through the corner.
❑ Repeat from C.
❑ Repeat on the opposite rein.

What should happen?
This is a good way to teach leg-yield to a horse that tends to run from your leg, because the wall helps to collect him.

Double check
Check that he is only showing a slight bend to the outside. Too much will prove that he is falling on to the right shoulder (on the right rein).

Moving on
Combine this with leg-yield in the shoulder-in position (Exercise 54).

What can go wrong?
Your horse slows his rhythm.
This may be because he is intimidated by the wall. Reduce the angle and use more inside leg.

If it's not working...
Go back to leg-yield from the three-quarter line to the track (Exercise 50).

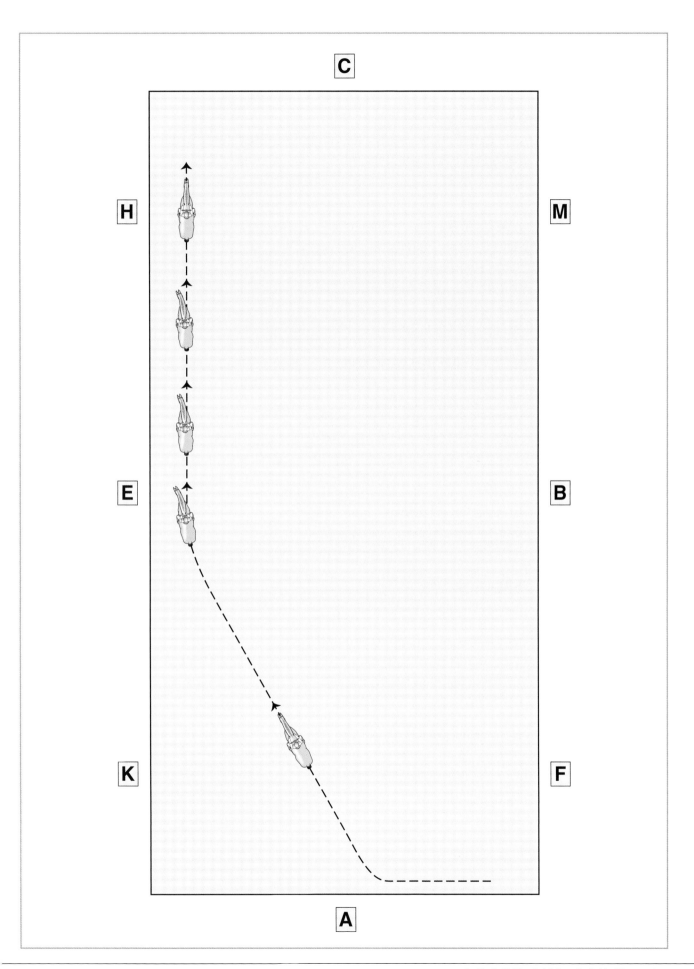

EXERCISE

59

BEGINNERS ✪✪✪

PRELIMINARY ✪✪✪✪✪

NOVICE ✪✪✪✪

ELEMENTARY ✪✪✪

MEDIUM ✪✪

Leg-yield zig-zags

Leg-yield exercises such as the following are fantastic for helping to develop a feel for your horse's movement, and control of his body.

How do I ride this exercise?

❏ On the right rein, establish walk and make a right-handed turn up the centre line.

❏ Ask for a change of bend, and leg-yield away from the left leg (to the right) for five or six steps.

❏ Now take your horse a few steps forwards, ask for the opposite bend, and leg-yield back across the centre line for six or eight steps.

❏ Straighten up for a few steps, then change his bend and leg-yield back.

❏ Repeat the exercise until you run out of space.

What should happen?

Your horse should leg-yield obediently, and without losing balance, in both directions, becoming more engaged and more channelled between your aids as the exercise progresses.

Double check

Be sure that you are sitting in position left to leg-yield to the right, and position right to leg-yield to the left.

Moving on

Ride this exercise in trot.

What can go wrong?

1 Your horse tends to swing his quarters, and tries to lead with his haunches.
   Find an easier exercise to teach him basic leg-yielding (such as Exercises 50, 51 and 52).

2 Your horse falls through his shoulder.
   Use a little more half-halt on the outside rein.

If it's not working...

Go back to leg-yielding away from the track (Exercise 55).

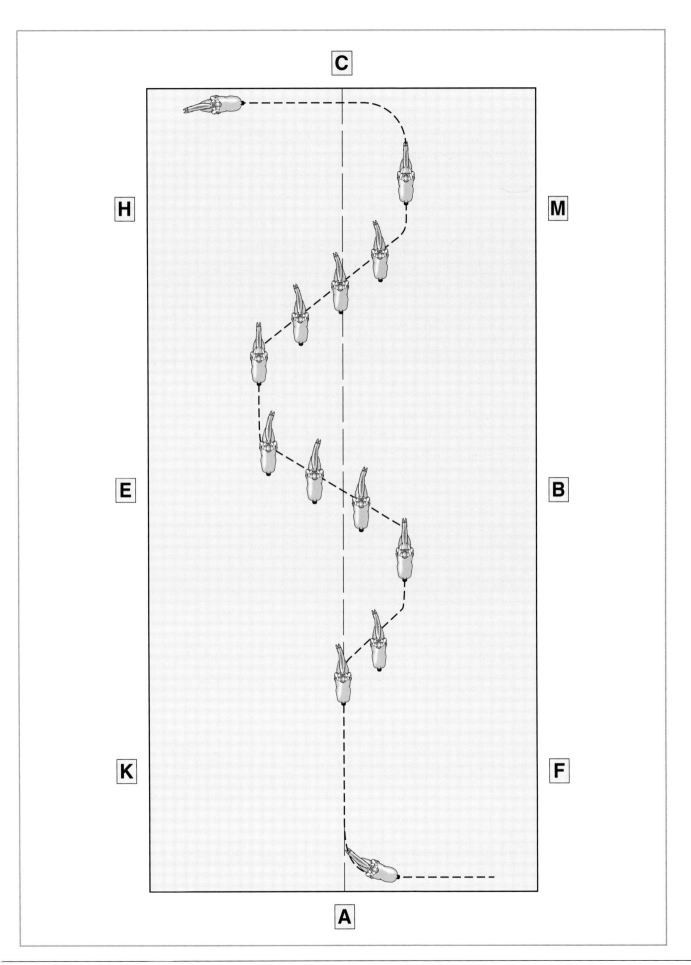

Leg-yielding on increasing angles

Once your horse understands the aids for leg-yielding, it is time to practise riding it at different angles.

BONUS

If you have an athletic horse approaching medium level, this is a good exercise for developing his ability to cross or step sideways.

How do I ride this exercise?

❏ On the right rein and in walk, ask for a left bend just before K, and leg-yield from K to M.

❏ Rejoin the track (you will now be on the left rein), straightening up until just before H.

❏ Now leg-yield from H to F.

❏ Rejoin the track at F, straighten, then leg-yield from K to half way between M and B.

❏ Rejoin the track, straighten, then leg-yield from H to half way between B and F.

❏ Rejoin the track, straighten, then leg-yield from K to B.

❏ Rejoin the track, straighten, then leg-yield from H to B.

❏ Repeat on the opposite rein, with the opposite bend.

What should happen?

The steeper the angle at which you leg-yield, the more difficult it is for your horse.

Double check

Be sure that, in striving for a greater angle, you are not compromising the balance and lightness of your horse.

Moving on

Try the exercise in trot.

What can go wrong?

Your horse becomes stiff, loses rhythm, or doesn't go forwards.

Reduce the angle, re-establish his balance, and build up his confidence before trying this exercise again.

If it's not working...

Go back to leg-yielding from the three-quarter line to the track (Exercise 50), then leg-yield on a diagonal from K to M, and H to F, before attempting this exercise again.

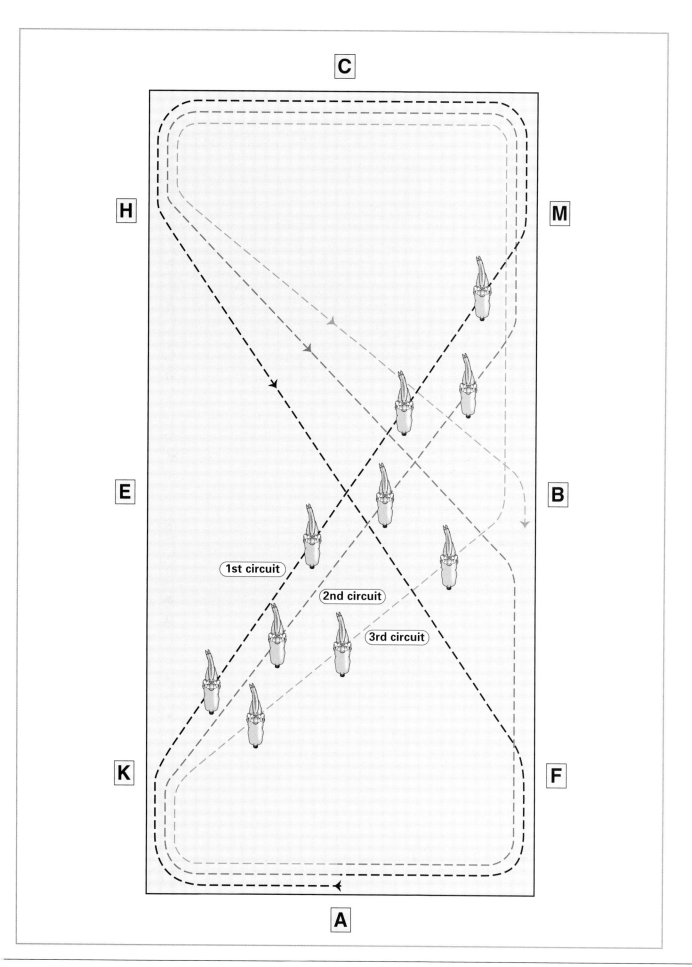

CONTROL AND COLLECTION

Shoulder-Fore and Shoulder-In

THE EXERCISES

Shoulder-fore and shoulder-in have many values, from improving collection and impulsion, to giving you more control over your horse's forehand, and a much better awareness of his sensitivity to your aids. They also allow you to perform the exercises to the best of your horse's abilities, because he can start with a small angle of bend and increase the angle as his suppleness and balance develop. What is important is the quality of the paces – their rhythm and activity – rather than the angle of bend.

Both shoulder-fore and shoulder-in are usually ridden in trot, as this generates initial impulsion; however, so that you can more easily learn the exercises, and appreciate what they are aiming to achieve, we have started most of them in walk. It is important that when riding shoulder-fore and shoulder-in the horse is balanced, and maintains both rhythm, activity and impulsion. If you are aware that your horse is losing any of these during the exercises, go back to riding him forwards and straight.

As a result of the benefits to the horse, almost any exercise is improved if preceded or followed by shoulder-in.

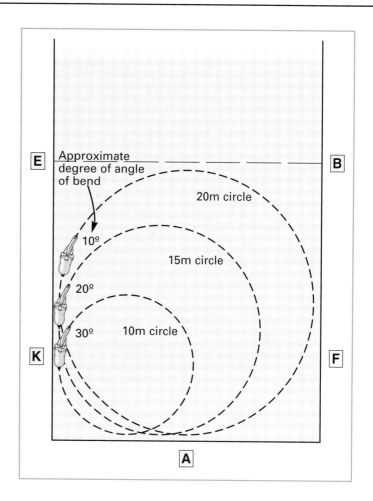

A first exercise in shoulder-in

Shoulder-in teaches the horse's inside hind leg to step under his centre of gravity, supporting his bodyweight with his hind legs and thereby lightening his forehand, more definitively than any other exercise.

RIDER'S TIP

As you work on shoulder-in, give and retake the reins to ensure that your horse is in self-carriage, and that your rein contact is elastic and 'giving'.

How do I ride this exercise?

❏ Establish a good walk. At any corner of the school, ride a 10m circle.
❏ As you retake the track, maintain the bend of the circle so that the forehand is slightly to the inside; use your outside rein to prevent your horse continuing on the circle.
❏ Ride forwards from the inside leg up the long side of the school, being careful not to push the horse sideways; if necessary use your outside leg to stop the quarters moving out.
❏ Your weight should be on the inside.
❏ Repeat on the opposite rein.

Why are we riding this?

Shoulder-in has a wide range of benefits to the horse:
❏ You encourage your horse's inside hind leg to step further under him and carry more weight. This helps improve collection.
❏ Taking his weight on to his hindquarters and increasing the flexion of his haunches gives your horse more freedom in his shoulders.
❏ His hip and stifle joints will be required to bend more than is usual.
❏ As you develop your horse's abilities in shoulder-in, by increasing the angle of the bend, you gain better control of his forehand, which in due course will help you to ride your horse 'straight'.

How do I ride this shoulder-in?

Your aim is to bring your horse's forehand to the inside of the line of the haunches.
❏ Begin the exercise with little half-halts.
❏ Your inside leg is on the girth encouraging your horse to move forwards and sideways, giving him some bend and asking him to take his weight on to his inside hind foot.
❏ Your outside leg is a little behind the girth, preventing the outside leg from swinging out.
❏ Your inside rein leads the forehand in from the track at the beginning of the exercise, and thereafter helps maintain the bend (see Rider's Tip).
❏ Your outside rein backs up your outside leg, guarding and supporting the bend, but with sufficient flexion to allow the horse to work forwards, through his outside shoulder.

What should happen?

If your horse by nature tends to rush, this is a particularly useful exercise as it helps to establish and maintain regularity of pace. It also frees up the shoulders and engages the hocks. As your horse is carrying most weight on his inside hind leg, he has to increase flexion in the joints of this leg.

Double check

Be sure that there is never more weight in the inside rein than the outside rein.

Moving on

Try the exercise in trot: it is of most benefit to the horse when performed in trot.

What can go wrong?

1 Your horse falls in on his inside shoulder and tries to leave the track.
Collect him more with the outside rein using half-halts, and be stronger with the inside leg.

2 Your horse's haunches fall out, giving you too much angle.
Be careful that your inside rein is not too strong, and make sure that your outside leg is back.

If it's not working...

Go back to shoulder-fore, where the horse's angle is less acute — 10°, equivalent to the bend and angle he would have on a 20m circle — or work on the particular fault in leg-yield exercises (see Section 4).

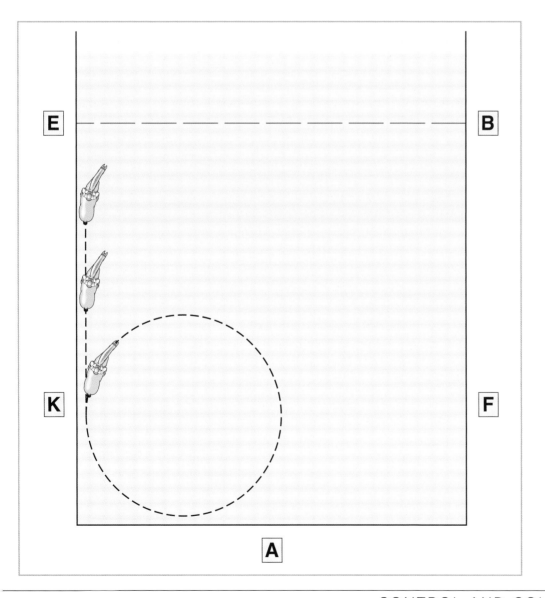

EXERCISE 62

BEGINNERS

PRELIMINARY

NOVICE ✪✪✪

ELEMENTARY ✪✪✪✪✪

MEDIUM ✪✪✪✪✪

Shoulder-in on both reins

This exercise works on changing the bend from one direction to another, and is therefore an excellent suppling exercise for your horse. This gives you a great opportunity to compare your horse's performance on each rein.

BONUS

There are movements like this in many of the elementary and medium level dressage tests.

How do I ride this exercise?

- ❑ Begin in walk. On the left rein, ride a left shoulder-in down the long side to the half-way marker.
- ❑ Ride a half 10m circle left to the centre line…
- ❑ …and then a half 10m circle right to the half-way marker on the opposite long side.
- ❑ Continue along the track on the opposite side in a right shoulder-in.
- ❑ Repeat the exercise, this time starting on the right rein.

What should happen?

The two shoulder-ins should be at an identical rhythm, angle and bend, and without a twist in the neck; the two half circles should be perfectly equal in size.

RIDER'S TIP

It is important that you remain in balance. Look through your horse's ears whilst riding shoulder-in so as to help you keep your weight evenly distributed.

Double check

Be sure that you are riding in a good balance, and that the horse maintains a perfectly even rhythm.

Moving on

This exercise can be done in walk and trot. Or, try

- ❑ …riding a left shoulder-in down the centre line…
- ❑ …into a l0m circle left in the direction of E, returning to X
- ❑ …followed by a 10m circle right in the same way.
- ❑ Then proceed down the centre line in shoulder-in right (see illustration for Advanced Exercise).

What can go wrong?

Your horse's haunches fall out in the second half circle.

As you come to the second shoulder-in, be prepared to support the haunches with your outside leg.

If it's not working…

Go back to walk.

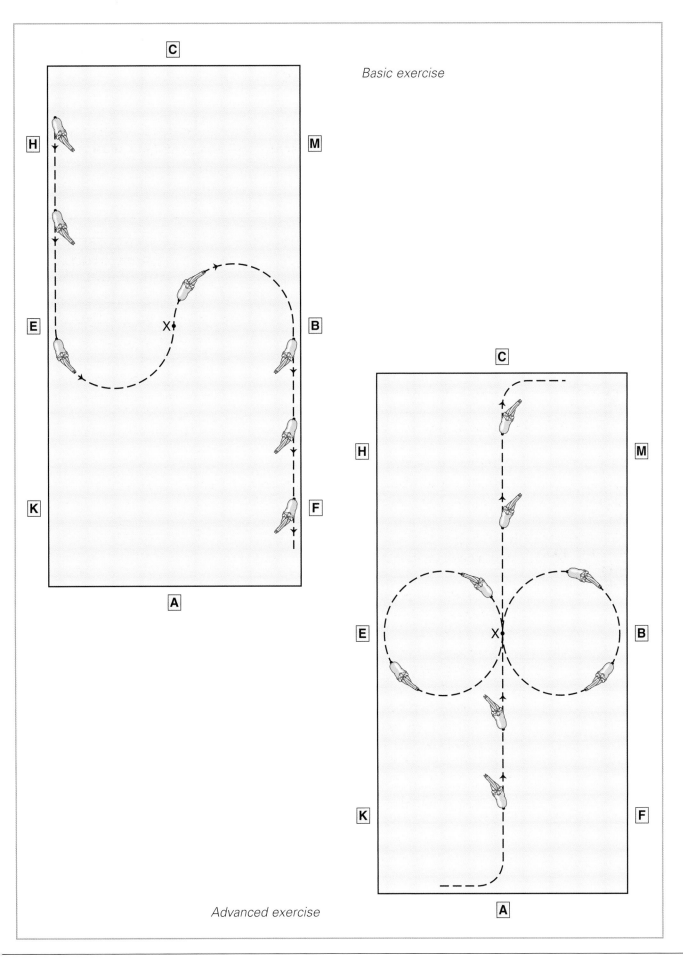

Basic exercise

Advanced exercise

EXERCISE

63

BEGINNERS

PRELIMINARY

NOVICE ✪✪✪

ELEMENTARY ✪✪✪✪✪

MEDIUM ✪✪✪✪✪

Alternating shoulder-in and shoulder-fore

This exercise will fine tune your horse's reaction to your aids, because to ride it accurately whilst all the while maintaining impulsion, your horse must be balanced and responsive.

How do I ride this exercise?

❏ In trot on the right rein, from K ride a few metres straight, and then…
❏ …approximately 8m in shoulder-fore,
❏ 8m in shoulder-in,
❏ another 8m in shoulder-fore,
❏ then straighten before the corner, and
❏ continue on the track.
❏ Repeat on the opposite side, and on the opposite rein.

What should happen?

This exercise will make your horse much more responsive to your aids, and in particular quicker away from your leg. It will improve his balance in his paces, and you will find that he becomes more easily manoeuvrable.

Double check

Take care that you don't have too much bend in your horse's neck.

Moving on

Try this on the three-quarter line without the support of the fence or the guidance of the track. Increase the angle of the routine, making it three-track shoulder-in, four-track shoulder-in, three-track shoulder-in.

What can go wrong?

When you ask for shoulder-fore, your horse gives you more angle than you want.
Make sure that your outside leg is controlling his quarters.

If it's not working…

Go back to working in shoulder-in on a single

THREE-TRACK AND FOUR-TRACK SHOULDER-IN

❏ Shoulder-in can be ridden on three or four tracks (see diagrams opposite), three-track being easier than four-track. Three-track is the normal starting point, while four-track is of greater gymnastic worth.

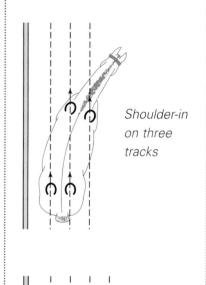

Shoulder-in on three tracks

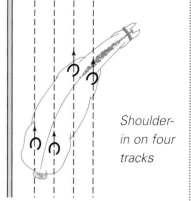

Shoulder-in on four tracks

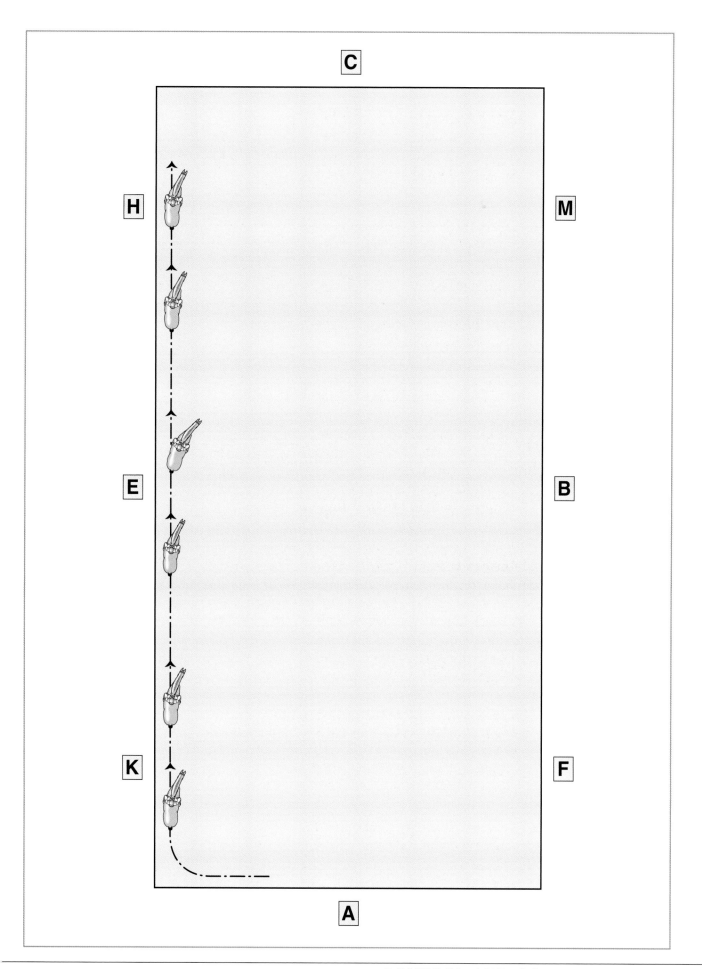

EXERCISE

64

BEGINNERS

PRELIMINARY ✪✪✪

NOVICE ✪✪✪✪

ELEMENTARY ✪✪✪✪✪

MEDIUM ✪✪✪✪✪

Shoulder-in to extended walk to the quarter and centre lines

This is an excellent exercise to use to improve impulsion and discourage the horse from falling through his outside shoulder.

How do I ride this exercise?

❏ From the corner of one long side of the school, in walk, ride shoulder-in for three to four strides...

❏ ...then go straight in extended walk to the quarter line.

❏ At the quarter line take up shoulder-in once again for three to four strides...

❏ ...then extended walk to the centre line.

❏ On reaching the centre line, take up shoulder-in once again until you reach the top of the school.

THE AIDS FOR EXTENDED WALK

❏ Use as much inside leg as is necessary in order to generate impulsion;

❏ a bolder swing to your seat;

❏ and by allowing more with the reins, allow the neck to lengthen – but take care that your horse doesn't disengage and poke his nose out.

What should happen?

The most important thing is that the horse's rhythm and balance should stay the same.

Double check

Guard against your horse's haunches escaping in the shoulder-in.

Moving on

This exercise can also be ridden in trot, though don't expect too much length of stride.

What can go wrong?

Your horse falls in on his shoulder.

If he falls through the right shoulder, return him to straightness with pressure from the right rein and right leg; if the left shoulder, use left rein and left leg.

If it's not working...

Go back to easier exercises for both shoulder-in (Exercises 61 and 63) and extended walk (Exercise 15).

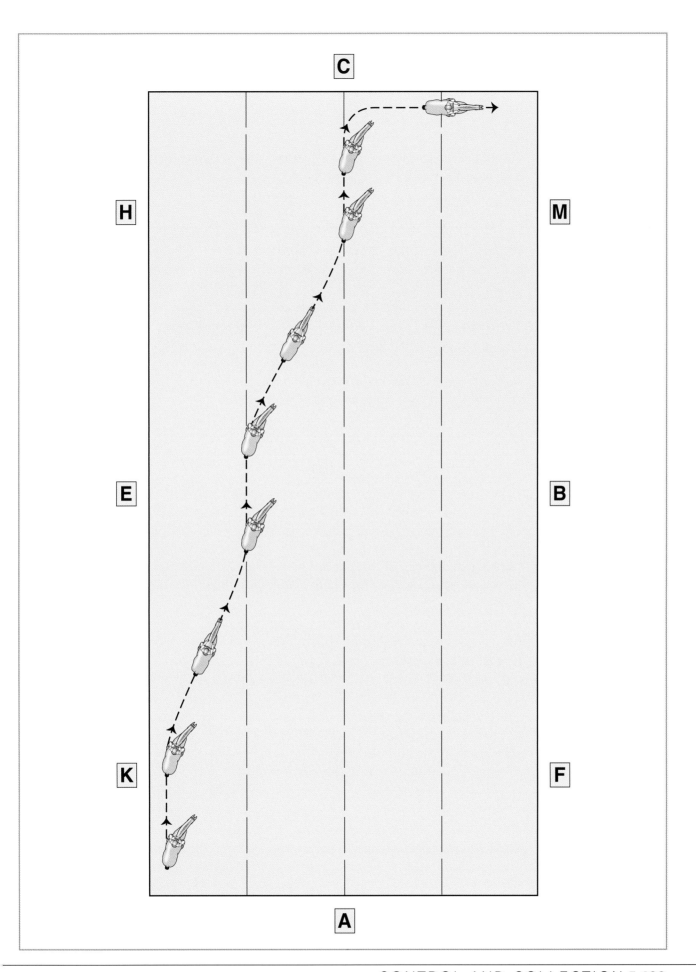

CELEBRITY
EXERCISE

65

BEGINNERS

PRELIMINARY

NOVICE ❂❂❂

ELEMENTARY ❂❂❂❂❂

MEDIUM ❂❂❂❂❂

Centre-line shoulder-in to extended walk
from Jennie Loriston-Clarke

'I find it useful to suggest riding shoulder-in down the centre line: getting a rider away from the wall is a better way of riding shoulder-in, and helps make the rider balance the horse.'

BONUS

Shoulder-in in walk is one of the best start routines to get a horse together and to put him on the aids – it is something he can do soon after arriving in the arena, providing you ride him forwards into trot fairly soon afterwards.

How do I ride this exercise?

❑ On the centre line in a forward walk, ride shoulder-in left from A to X.

❑ At X, proceed in extended walk on a diagonal line to H, allowing the horse plenty of freedom to move over his back. Rejoin the track.

❑ Turn down the centre line again from C, and ride shoulder-in right to X.

❑ At X proceed on a diagonal line to K in extended walk.

What are the benefits?

❑ To improve the horse's reactions to the leg aids;

❑ to work on getting the horse from the leg into a supple contact; and

❑ to allow the horse forwards into an extended walk.

What should happen?

The horse should go forwards with energy and impulsion from your inside leg to your outside rein so that you can control his shoulders. When riding forwards into the extended walk, this improves suppleness and extension through his back.

Double check

Be sure you are not succumbing to the following faults: first, is your inside leg creeping backwards? And then, are you pulling your horse's head to the inside, rather than riding the shoulder-in between your inside leg and outside rein?

Moving on

Ride the exercise in trot. If your horse is comfortable with shoulder-in, try riding it with the opposite bend (such as renvers): this will check whether your horse is supple and working through both reins.

What can go wrong?

1 You lose control of your horse's shoulders.
This is probably because you do not have the horse up to the outside rein, and in effect you are pulling his head in. His shoulder therefore falls out, and he is actually on one track and hasn't either brought the shoulder in, or engaged the hind leg.

2 Your horse loses balance in the extended walk and comes above the bit.
Be cautious, and try to increase the length of the walk step only gradually.

3 You become too strong with your rein aids, and effectively cramp the walk.
After achieving this exercise on both reins in walk, go forward to the same thing in trot – although think more medium trot, rather than extended, after the shoulder-in.

If it's not working...

Move your horse forward into trot and try to ride shoulder-fore in trot, using your stick to encourage your horse if necessary. Be careful not to have him on four tracks, as this will make him lose impulsion and his balance.

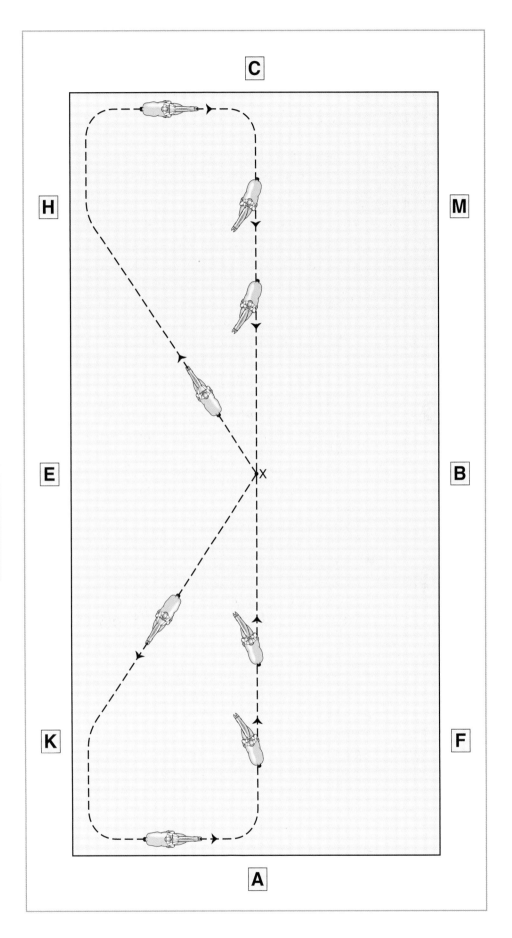

BEGINNERS ○

PRELIMINARY ○○○

NOVICE ○○○○○

ELEMENTARY ○○○

MEDIUM ○○

Shoulder-in combined with three 10m circles

This is an excellent exercise for improving the balance and suppleness of your horse; it will also teach him to be more attentive to your aids, in particular to be quicker off your leg.

BONUS

This movement is included in elementary and medium tests.

How do I ride this exercise?

❏ Proceed from the A marker on the right rein in walk, and ride a 10m circle in the corner of the school.

❏ Ask for shoulder-in out of the circle, and down the track to E.

❏ At E ride another 10m circle…

❏ …and then ask for shoulder-in to H.

❏ Ride a third 10m circle at H, then round the corner, and straighten to C.

❏ Turn up the centre line at C to change the rein.

❏ Repeat on the left rein.

What should happen?

It is part of a horse's education that he should be sufficiently balanced and attentive to be able to ride a correctly balanced shoulder-in out of a 10m circle, and back into a 10m circle.

Double check

Make sure that your weight is on your inside seatbone, and that your outside leg isn't too far forwards.

Moving on

Try this exercise in trot.

What can go wrong?

Your horse loses his balance in the shoulder-in and falls out through the outside shoulder.

Check that you achieve the turn into the 10m circle by using the outside rein against the horse's neck.

If it's not working…

Practise riding shoulder-in away from the track.

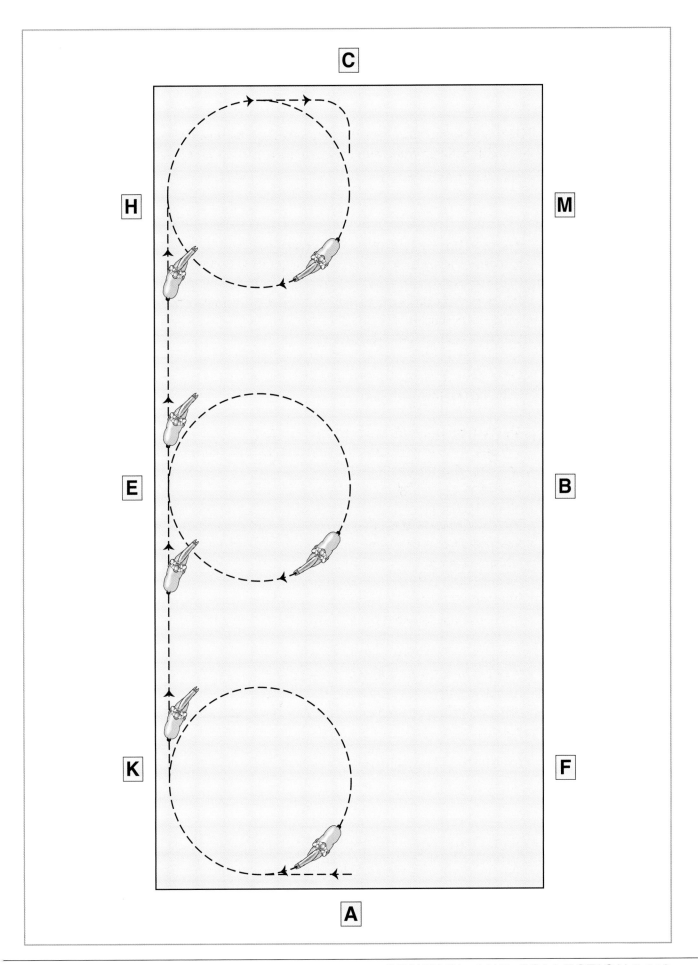

EXERCISE

67

BEGINNERS

PRELIMINARY ⊙

NOVICE ⊙⊙⊙

ELEMENTARY ⊙⊙⊙⊙⊙

MEDIUM ⊙⊙⊙⊙⊙

Shoulder-in to medium trot on a straight line

This exercise will help re-train a horse that persists in falling in on the inside shoulder during shoulder-in.

RIDER'S TIP

Take care to straighten the horse with your inside leg and the inside rein (don't use the outside rein).

How do I ride this exercise?

❑ In trot, ride shoulder-in on the first half of the long side of the school,...

❑ ...then take the forehand back to the track through shoulder-fore,...

❑ ...and coax a medium trot from the horse for the remainder of the long side.

What should happen?

For a horse that likes to fall on the inside shoulder, taking the forehand back to the track whilst retaining the inside bend will help him to come up off his inside shoulder, to set him up for the medium trot.

Double check

Make sure that your inside leg stays forward both during the shoulder-in and in the straightening process.

Moving on

This exercise can also be done in canter, but only in shoulder-fore, and not full shoulder-in.

What can go wrong?

Your horse's weight does not come up off his inside shoulder.

Are you pulling your horse's head back to the track with the outside rein and hoping that the forehand will follow?

If it's not working...

Try riding shoulder-in on the three-quarter line, then leg-yield from the three-quarter line back to the track for the last half of the long side.

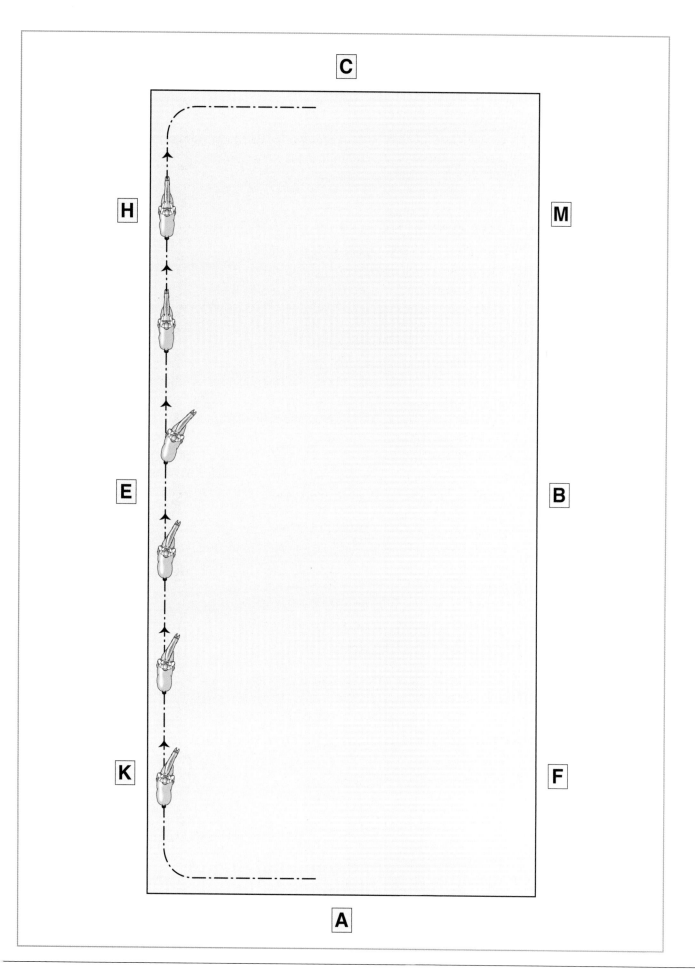

68

Shoulder-in to medium trot on a diagonal

This is similar to the preceding exercise, in that it helps retrain a horse that persists in falling in on the outside shoulder during shoulder-in.

BONUS

This movement is used in elementary and medium dressage tests.

How do I ride this exercise?

❏ On the left rein, in trot, ride a shoulder-in from F to B.

❏ From B, change the rein to H in medium trot.

❏ Rejoin the track, and repeat from M to B on the right rein, changing the rein to K.

What should happen?

In order to change from shoulder-in to medium trot on the diagonal the horse has to lift his weight up off his outside shoulder. Repetition of this exercise will help the horse to predict the possibility of being asked to make the diagonal in medium, and he will then be less likely to fall on the outside shoulder.

Double check

Make sure that the horse is obedient to your outside leg aids so that when you come to make the medium trot transition he doesn't swing his quarters out.

Moving on

This exercise can also be done in canter, but only in shoulder-fore, not in full shoulder-in.

What can go wrong?

Your horse can lose balance and break to canter.

Start the medium trot earlier, and make the transition more gradually.

If it's not working...

This is probably because your shoulder-in is not balanced. Go back to riding shoulder-in on the three-quarter line.

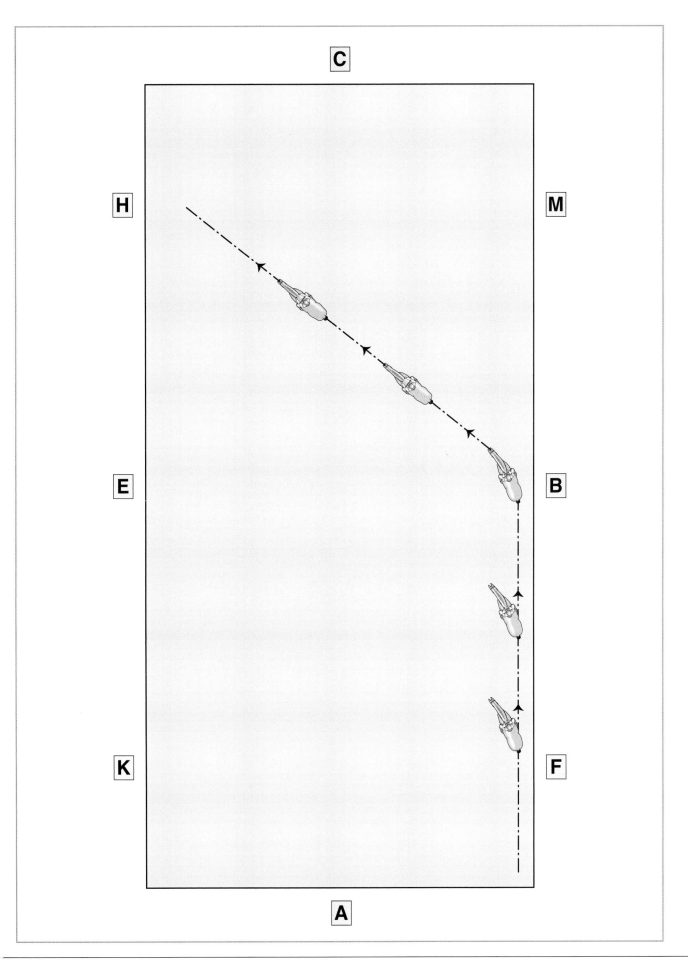

69

Shoulder-fore into canter

Whilst shoulder-fore is a good starting point for shoulder-in, it can also help to improve your canter transitions.

BONUS

This exercise will really improve the collection of your horse's canter.

How do I ride this exercise?
❏ On the left rein, in trot, ride shoulder-fore down the long side of the school.
❏ Half way along, ask for left canter and ride forwards on to a 20m circle.
❏ On completing your circle, ride a transition back to trot…
❏ …and resume shoulder-fore left.

What should happen?
From performing shoulder-fore, your body position should already be in the correct position for the canter strike-off.

RIDER'S TIP

Horses like to canter with their haunches to the inside because like this they avoid using their hock and stifle, and make more use of the stronger hip joint; this is why much of the work we do in canter is about straightening your horse.

Double check
Be sure to use the outside rein to prevent the horse falling out through the shoulder, and the outside leg to support the canter.

Moving on
Ride this exercise without the circle, asking for the canter transition and maintaining the canter along the long side.

What can go wrong?
Your horse's shoulders escape to the outside.
This is almost certainly caused by your horse trying to strike off on the wrong leg. Make sure that you have not forgotten to use your outside leg to support the canter, and that your inside leg is not too far back.

If it's not working…
Go back to working on your trot/canter transitions on a circle (Exercise 10).

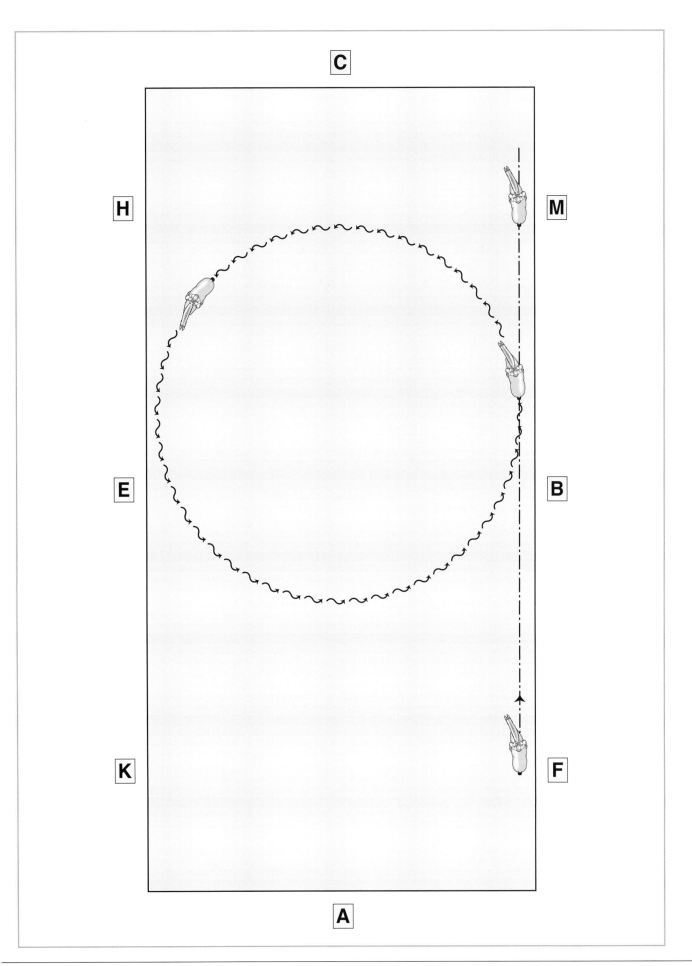

EXERCISE

70

BEGINNERS

PRELIMINARY ✪

NOVICE ✪✪✪

ELEMENTARY ✪✪✪✪✪

MEDIUM ✪✪✪✪

Shoulder-in to prepare a turn

You can tell whether you're doing this exercise correctly because your horse's hind feet should remain on the centre line; so if you're planning to work on this exercise, draw a line in the school to mark out the centre line before you begin (or get someone to do it for you, if you forget!).

BONUS

This is a particularly good exercise for balancing your horse. There are two or three medium-level dressage tests that contain a similar exercise to this, but with only one period of shoulder-in.

How do I ride this exercise?

❏ In walk, turn up the centre line in shoulder-in left.

❏ After six or eight steps, make a 10m circle to the left returning to the centre line at the point at which you began the circle.

❏ Continue along the centre line, changing your bend to shoulder-in right.

❏ After a further six or eight steps, ride a 10m circle to the right, returning to the centre line again.

❏ Repeat this pattern until you reach the other end of the school.

What should happen?

Having preceded each of the 10m circles with a certain period of shoulder-in, your horse should execute each one with perfect attention to the aids: this is because, in order to have performed a correct shoulder-in, he will have been responding to the inside leg by not falling on the inside shoulder, and to the outside leg by not falling out through his haunches.

Double check

Check that you are riding on the outside aids.

Moving on

This is a nice exercise to ride in trot.

What can go wrong?

When you change the bend your horse falls off the centre line.

Change your bend more gradually, taking care to change your legs and seat at the same time.

If it's not working...

Go back to practising longer periods of shoulder-in (Exercises 61 and 63) without the confusion of the circles.

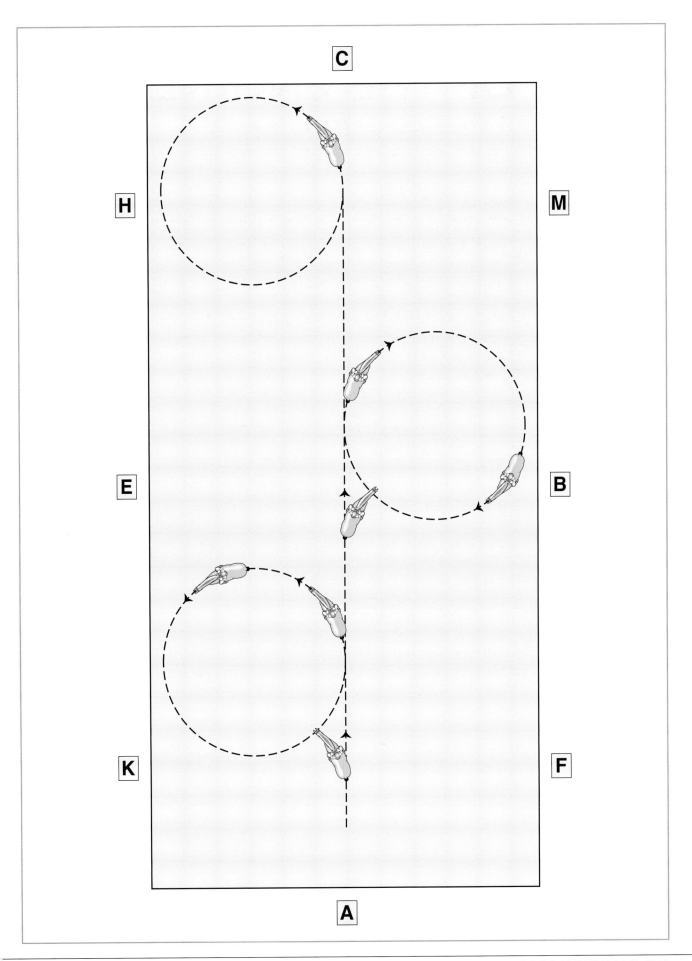

BETTER CONTROL OF THE ENGINE

Travers and Renvers

THE EXERCISES

Travers (quarters-in) and renvers (quarters-out) work on the performance of your horse's hindquarters, thus helping with collection and at the same time setting him up for half-pass. The optimum angle for either is 30 degrees, but this can be adjusted depending on your horse's abilities. Once again, most of these exercises begin in walk, but once you and your horse have mastered the movement, progress to trot.

TRAVERS, RENVERS AND SHOULDER-IN EXPLAINED

❑ **Travers**

In travers, the horse looks straight down the track, and is bent in the direction of travel, with a bend through the head and neck to the forelegs: the forehand remains on the track, and the hindquarters are to the inside. He moves on four tracks.

❑ **Renvers**

In renvers, the hindquarters remain on the track and the forehand is to the inside; the horse looks, and is bent, in the direction of travel (unlike shoulder-in), and moves on four tracks.

❑ **Shoulder-in**

In shoulder-in the horse generally moves on three tracks, and only occasionally on four; the hindquarters remain on the track, and the forehand is moved to the inside so the forelegs cross as the horse progresses up the school. He looks, and is bent, away from the direction of travel.

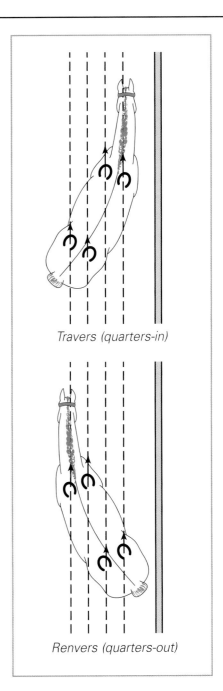

Travers (quarters-in)

Renvers (quarters-out)

A first exercise in travers

Travers is also known as 'haunches in'. It is a useful suppling exercise that will help to increase the flexibility of your horse's hind-leg joints and lumber region.

BONUS

Both travers and renvers test your horse's obedience to your legs, and prepare him for half-pass.

How do I ride this exercise?

❑ On the right rein, in walk, ride a 10m circle in the corner at the beginning of one long side of the school.

❑ Half-halt, maintaining the bend, and just as you rejoin the track, apply the left leg behind the girth to push the hindquarters over so they travel up the inside of the long side in travers right.

❑ Before reaching the corner, straighten up.

❑ Now repeat on the other rein.

RIDER'S TIP

Imagine that you are approaching the track about to complete the last step of a circle before the horse straightens up. This is the correct position for travers.

What should happen?

In travers, your horse should move along a given line with his forehand on the track and his haunches in. This will create a bend through his body, with his forehead facing the direction of travel. Your upper body position controls the angle of his shoulders, which should be about 35 degrees towards the track. Viewed from the front, all four legs are visible. As your horse lowers his hocks and takes more weight on to his hind legs, he will learn to collect.

How do I ride travers?

❑ In walk on the right rein, ride a correct bend through the corner at the beginning of one of the long sides of the school.

❑ Keep your weight on your inside seatbone, with your upper body turning with the horse's body. Keep your inside leg near the girth so that the horse has a support around which to bend.

❑ Your outside leg should be behind the girth controlling the haunches: your outside thigh and knee prevent him from losing the bend through his body, and your outside lower leg asks for the horse's outside hind leg to step across the inside hind leg, underneath his body.

❑ Allow your lower back to move with your horse as he walks.

❑ Your inside rein maintains an elastic contact with the bit to keep the horse soft and relaxed in his jaw, and your outside rein controls the outside shoulder while allowing him to travel forwards along the track.

❑ To end the travers, ride the hindquarters back on to the track.

Double check

Be sure that your inside leg is near the girth and your outside leg is behind it, to maintain the forward and lateral movement, and that your rein contact is not stopping the horse from moving actively forwards.

Moving on

This exercise can be ridden in trot.

What can go wrong?

1 Your horse swings his haunches away to the outside, losing bend and not allowing his outside hind leg to step across in front of his inside hind.

Your inside leg may be too far back. Keep your inside leg on the girth to support him in the bend.

2 Your horse's haunches are drifting too much to the inside.

You are probably sitting on the wrong seatbone, which is affecting his ability to bend around your inside leg. You should try to keep your weight on your inside seatbone.

If it's not working...

Go back to working on leg-yields (Section 4), and try turn on the forehand (Exercise 49) on the wrong bend.

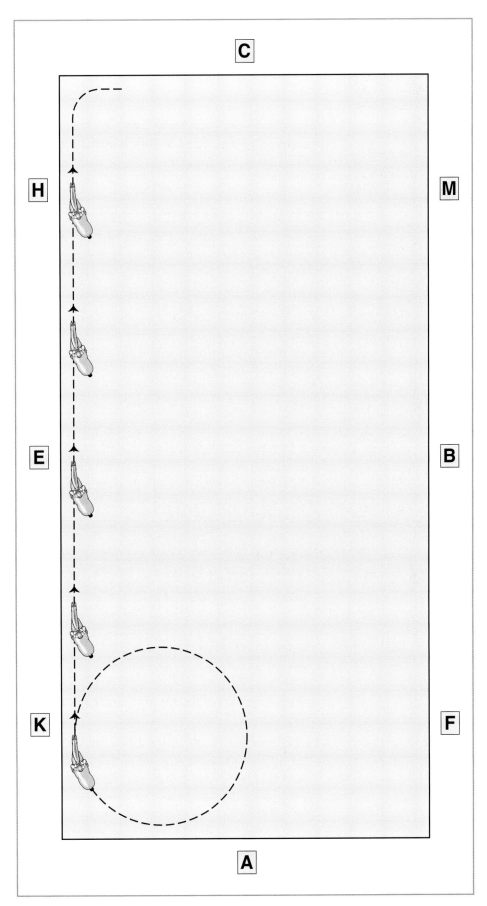

EXERCISE

72

BEGINNERS

PRELIMINARY

NOVICE ✪✪

ELEMENTARY ✪✪✪✪

MEDIUM ✪✪✪✪✪

Travers on a circle

As well as being an excellent suppling exercise, travers and renvers on a circle are also good for testing your horse's obedience to your leg. It can be used as a start exercise for canter pirouette.

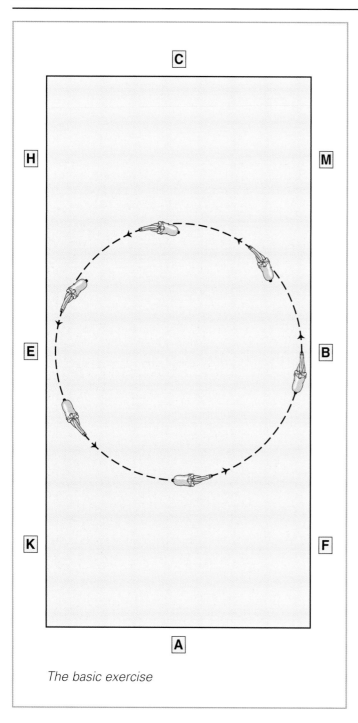

The basic exercise

How do I ride this exercise?

❑ On the left rein, in walk, ride a 20m circle.

❑ On reaching your starting point, ride into travers for half a circle.

❑ Straighten the horse, and ride the remaining half circle in a bold medium walk.

❑ Repeat on the other rein.

What should happen?

In travers your horse should keep his front feet on the original circle path, and carry his haunches a little to the inside of the circle path (on four tracks). He should be evenly bent through his body in front of and behind the saddle, and he should be bent enough to put his outside cheek exactly in parallel with the arc of the circle.

Double check

Make sure that you are not sitting to the outside.

Moving on

❑ This exercise can be ridden in trot and in canter.

❑ Repeat the exercise, riding into renvers instead of travers (see diagram opposite top).

❑ Repeat on the other rein, or try riding a figure-of-eight, with one circle in travers and the other in renvers (see diagram opposite below).

What can go wrong?

Your horse's front feet leave the path and your circle becomes smaller and smaller.

Make sure that whilst your outside leg is back asking for haunches-in, your inside leg is at the girth, preventing the forehand from sliding in.

If it's not working...

Go back to travers on a straight line (Exercise 71).

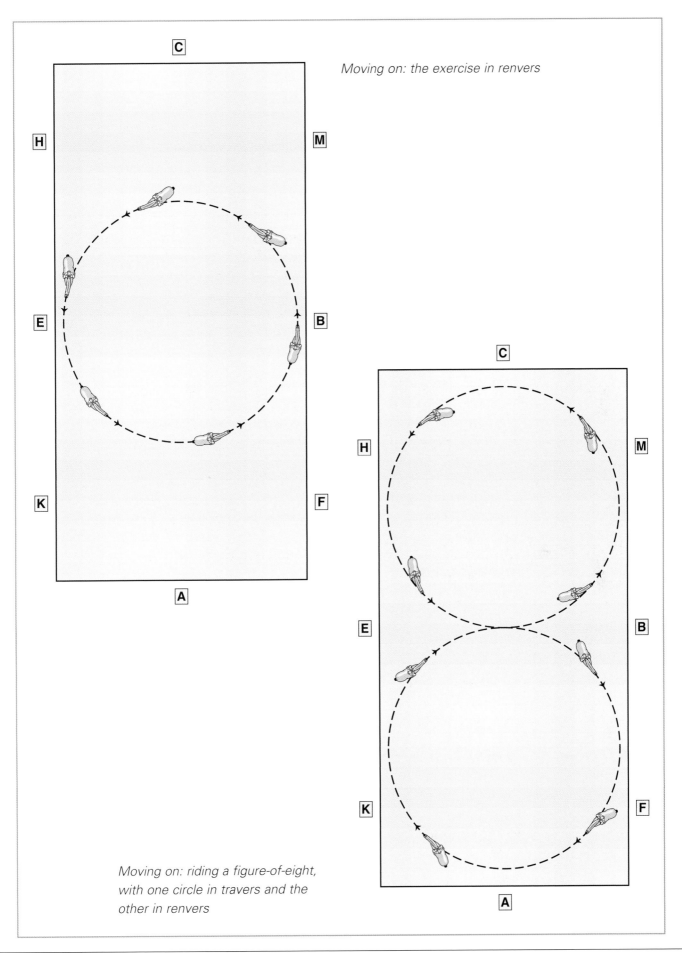

Moving on: the exercise in renvers

Moving on: riding a figure-of-eight, with one circle in travers and the other in renvers

Travers on an oval

This exercise will help to make your horse's back more supple, and should also help him to understand the outside leg better. It is a good building block for the walk pirouette.

RIDER'S TIP

Make sure it is the outside leg and rein that turn the horse into the half circles.

How do I ride this exercise?

❑ Ride travers right along the centre line from A.

❑ At X, ride a half 10m circle right also in travers, rejoining the track at B;

❑ ...continue in travers to the F marker.

❑ Maintaining this position, make another half 10m circle.

❑ Continue in the movement for a few steps...

❑ ...then march forwards straight in the direction of M, to change the rein.

What should happen?

To make a good travers the horse has to step his outside hind hoof across and in front of the inside hoof; in doing so he will stretch the muscles of the outside of his back and neck, and he will also have to bend the outside stifle more, which will help to increase the suppleness of this joint.

Double check

Make sure you are not sitting to the outside and pushing the horse sideways with your inside leg.

Moving on

Try riding this exercise in trot using 15m circles, but do not continue riding it for too long, as it is very demanding in trot.

What can go wrong?

Your horse falls in through the inside shoulder and loses the bend.

He needs to be collected with little half-halts on the inside rein used in conjunction with the inside leg until he understands to remain upright in the shoulder, and so maintains his balance.

If it's not working...

Go back to straight travers on the long side (Exercise 71).

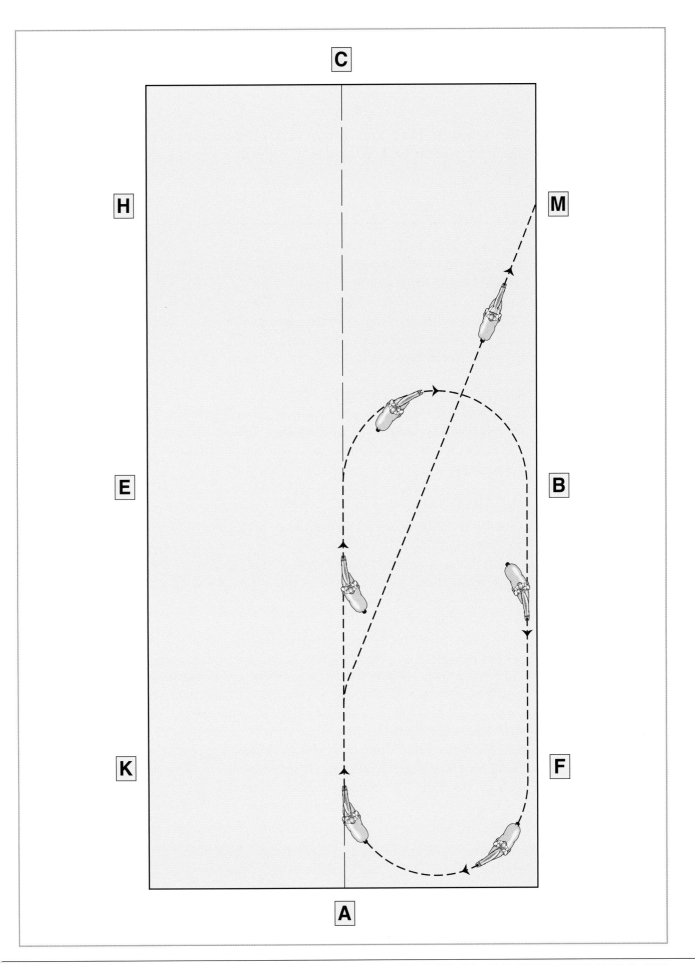

EXERCISE

74

BEGINNERS

PRELIMINARY

NOVICE ✪✪

ELEMENTARY ✪✪✪✪

MEDIUM ✪✪✪✪✪

Leg-yield into travers

In this exercise, preceding the travers with a leg-yield can help to make your horse better balanced and more engaged.

How do I ride this exercise?

❏ Passing K on the right rein, ask your horse to bend a little to the left, and make a leg-yield inwards to the centre line.

❏ As you reach the centre line, make a half 10m circle left;

❏ just before reaching the track, pick up a travers position, and…

❏ …proceed up the long side in travers.

❏ Repeat on the other rein.

What should happen?

The horse, having been obedient to the left leg in the leg-yield, should be more receptive to the travers aid in the second part of the exercise.

Double check

Make sure your weight is on the correct seatbone, and that your inside leg in each circumstance is forward.

Moving on

This exercise can also be ridden in trot, and the leg-yield can then be replaced with half-pass.

What can go wrong?

Your horse is losing flexion.

In the travers you are probably not facing the direction in which you are moving. Be sure you are looking in the direction in which you are travelling whilst riding travers, and in the opposite direction for leg-yield.

If it's not working...

Go back to working on leg-yield (Section 4) and travers (Exercise 71) separately before attempting to ride both in one exercise again.

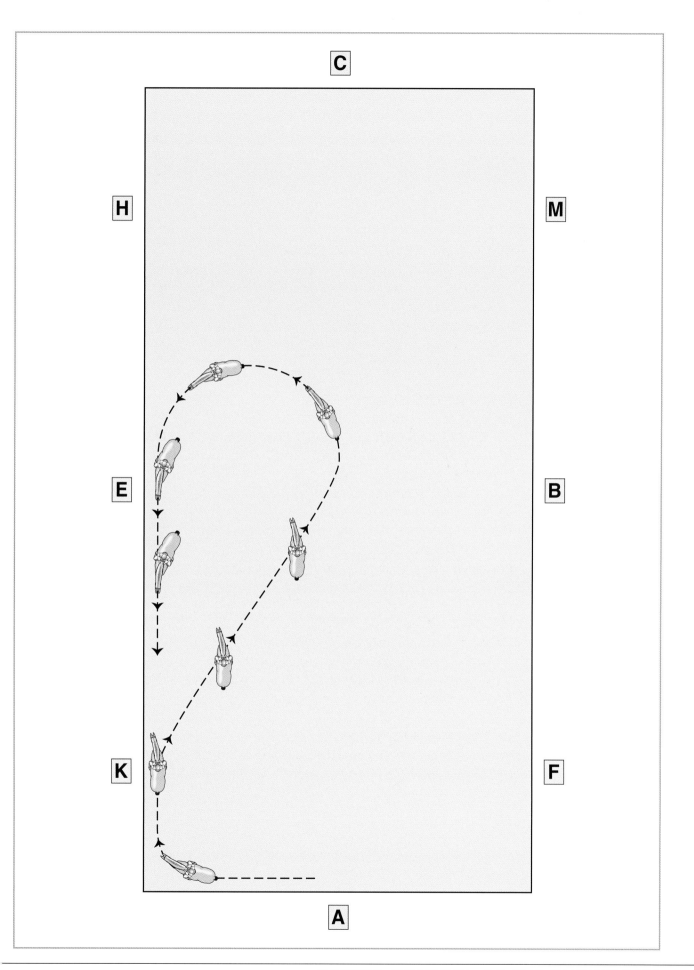

EXERCISE

75

BEGINNERS

PRELIMINARY

NOVICE

ELEMENTARY ✪✪✪✪

MEDIUM ✪✪✪✪✪

Quarter pirouettes into travers

This is a good exercise for a horse that tends to fall forwards or on to the shoulder in quarter pirouettes. However, it is not suitable for a horse that lacks impulsion in the pirouette, because the presence of the wall will tend to stop him going forwards.

BONUS

Using the corners helps your pirouettes.

How do I ride this exercise?

❑ On the left rein, in walk, ride up the quarter line of the school.

❑ At the end, make a quarter pirouette left towards the wall and, maintaining the bend to the left, …

❑ …proceed in travers left up the long side.

❑ Straighten up and repeat up the other quarter line on the other rein, starting with a quarter pirouette right…

❑ …to take you into travers right.

What should happen?

The presence of the wall should help your horse to collect.

Double check

Make sure that you are sitting on the inside seatbone, and that the inside leg is against the horse's rib-cage to support the inside shoulder.

Moving on

Try riding up the quarter line in trot, walking a few steps before the second quarter pirouette, and then riding the travers in trot.

What can go wrong?

1 Your horse is bending his neck too much.

He should be bending through his body and round your inside leg. You are probably using too much inside rein. Try to re-establish an even contact.

2 Your horse backs off the wall and stops or twists.

Instead of riding this exercise from the quarter line, try riding it from the centre line.

If it's not working...

Practise riding half pirouettes on the centre line between K and F, and H and M.

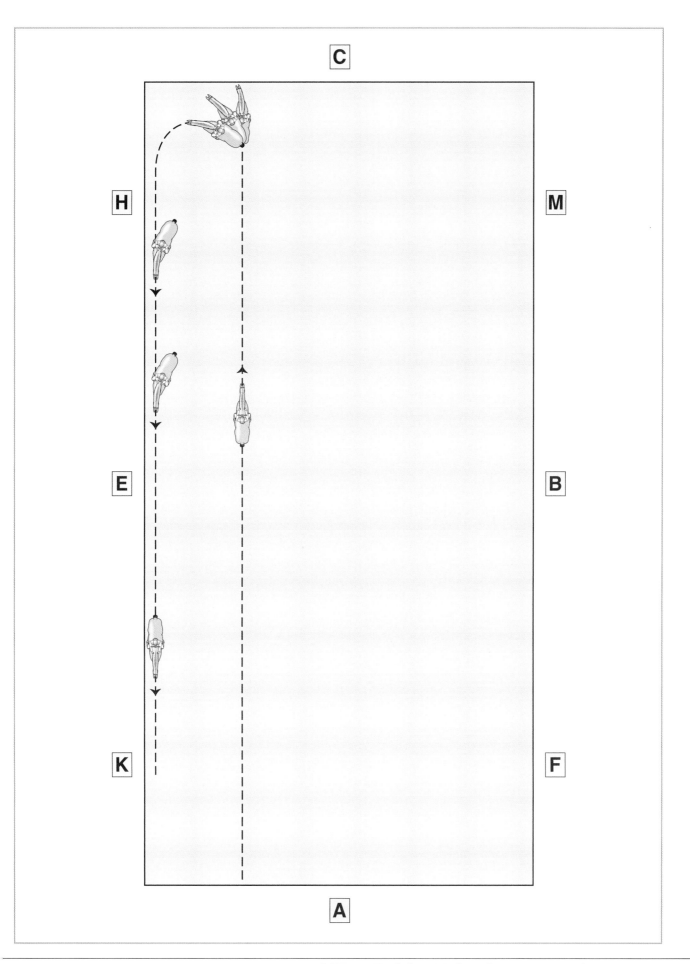

76

A first exercise in renvers

Renvers – or haunches-out – is a mirror image of travers, and has the same bio-mechanical benefits. However, there are fewer opportunities to practise it.

BONUS

This exercise really helps to improve your shoulder-in, and is also a building block for flying changes.

How do I ride this exercise?

❏ On the left rein in walk, leave the track just after K, join the inner track (1m from the main track), and crossing the short side of the school, collect the horse.

❏ With your body in position right, ask the horse to bend to the right, and with your left leg (now the outside leg), press the haunches over so that they join the main track.

❏ The right leg and right rein combine to support the horse's forehand, and enable you to retain the forehand position on the inner track, with a right bend.

❏ Your outside (left) rein maintains an elastic contact with the bit to keep the horse soft and relaxed in his jaw, and your inside rein controls the inside shoulder while allowing him to travel forwards.

❏ To end the renvers, bring the forehand back on to the track and straighten the horse.

❏ Repeat on the opposite rein.

What should happen?

The gymnastic demands of renvers are the same as for travers. Its real use is in enhancing the rider's control over the position and bend of the forehand and the haunches.

Double check

Make sure you are not sitting to the wrong side.

Moving on

Try riding renvers on the circle.

What can go wrong?

Your horse becomes tense.

This exercise can be obscure and quite confusing for a horse (and sometimes a rider!). Make sure you are not holding the reins too tight.

If it's not working...

Go back to the exercises in shoulder-in (Section 5) and travers (Exercise 71).

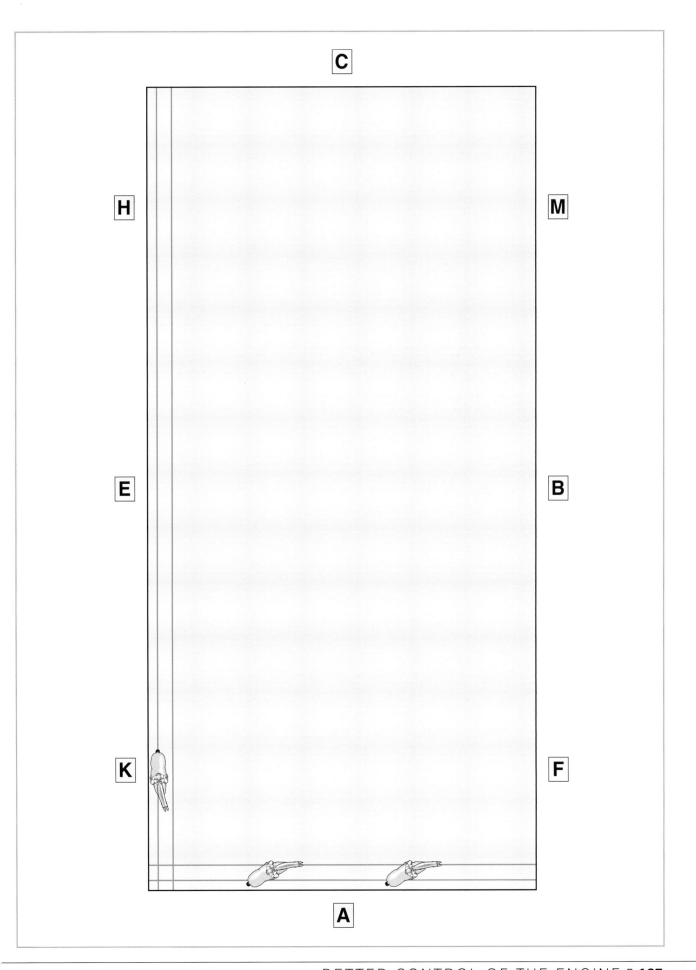

EXERCISE

77

BEGINNERS

PRELIMINARY

NOVICE

ELEMENTARY ✪✪

MEDIUM   ✪✪✪✪✪

Half pirouette into renvers

If your horse can come out of a half pirouette into renvers, it shows that he is obedient to your inside aids.

How do I ride this exercise?

❏ On the left rein, in walk, ride up the long side of the school.

❏ At the corner, perform a half pirouette to the left...

❏ ...and continue in renvers left along the new inside track.

❏ After 10 or 12 steps, straighten up and extend a little...

❏ ...before collecting and repeating the exercise on the other rein, beginning with a half pirouette to the right and continuing in renvers left.

What should happen?

This exercise is particularly beneficial to a horse that tends to disregard the outside leg in the walk pirouette, and to step out with the haunches, because just before the walk pirouette is concluded, while the forehand is still one small step in from the track, the rider can ask the horse to make a separate give to the outside leg (in the case of the left pirouette, this is the right leg) and then proceed back up the track in renvers.

It is also very beneficial for a horse that tends to fall on the inside shoulder in a walk pirouette. In order to stop the walk pirouette in the last steps so that you can proceed in renvers, the horse has to be obedient to the combined effect of the inside leg and inside rein.

Double check

Make sure you are sitting to the inside.

Moving on

Try adding a half 10m circle in renvers at B.

What can go wrong?

Your horse disregards your outside leg, and instead of proceeding in renvers, goes straight.

Ask for a halt, and in the halt ask for the haunches to move one step left while keeping the left bend; then try again to proceed in renvers.

If it's not working...

Return to travers exercises on the long side.

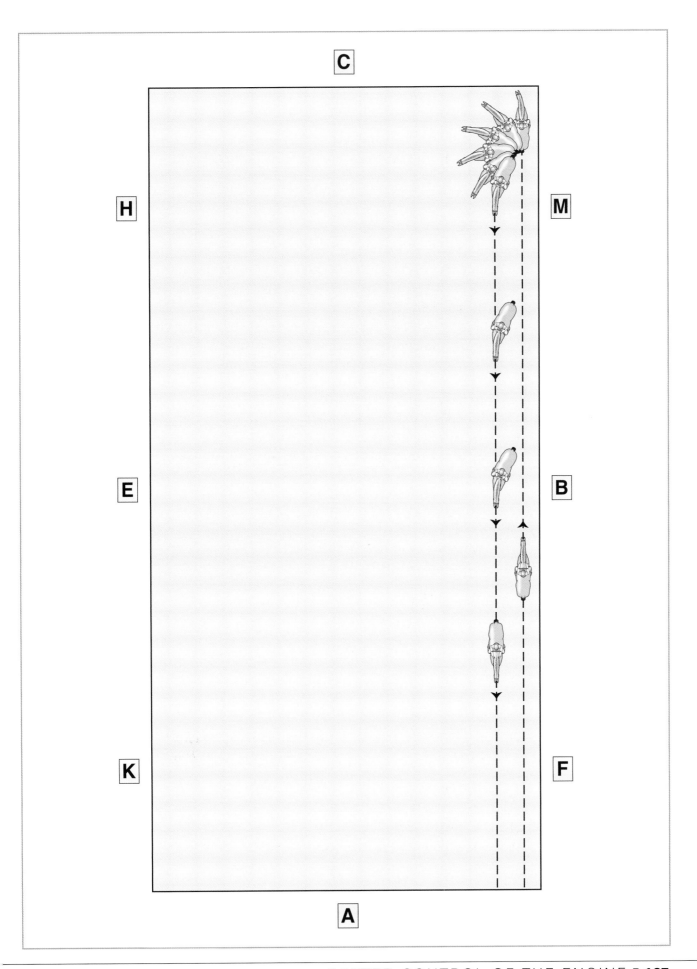

EXERCISE

78

BEGINNERS

PRELIMINARY

NOVICE ✪

ELEMENTARY ✪✪

MEDIUM ✪✪✪✪✪

Shoulder-in to renvers

This exercise will show whether the horse is sufficiently supple and balanced, and quick and obedient to your leg, to maintain impulsion whilst changing the bend and flexion through his body.

How do I ride this exercise?

- ❏ In walk, on the left rein, ride shoulder-in up the long side of the school.
- ❏ Before the half-way marker, half-halt, using your shoulders to maintain the angle away from the wall, and change your lower body into a right bend position.
- ❏ Turn your head to face up the track, change the flexion of your horse to the right, and proceed in renvers to the right until just before the corner.
- ❏ Change bend and ride forward.
- ❏ Repeat on the opposite rein.

What should happen?

Your horse should demonstrate that he is pliable, supple and able to maintain a consistent angle and rhythm in the side step whilst bending to the left and bending to the right.

Double check

Make sure that you are not leaning to the left or the right. It helps to have someone on the ground to check this for you.

Moving on

On the left rein and in walk, begin in shoulder-out up the long side of the school. Before the half-way marker, half-halt, maintain the angle towards the wall with your shoulders, and change your lower body into a left bend position. Now proceed in travers to the left. Repeat the exercise on the other rein.

What can go wrong?

Your horse ignores your future outside leg, and slips his quarters in from the track.

Be prepared! Ask him to halt, and in the halt make a one-step turn on the forehand away from the left leg in order to remind him that he is to be obedient to the left leg.

If it's not working...

Go back to leg-yield zig-zags (Exercise 59).

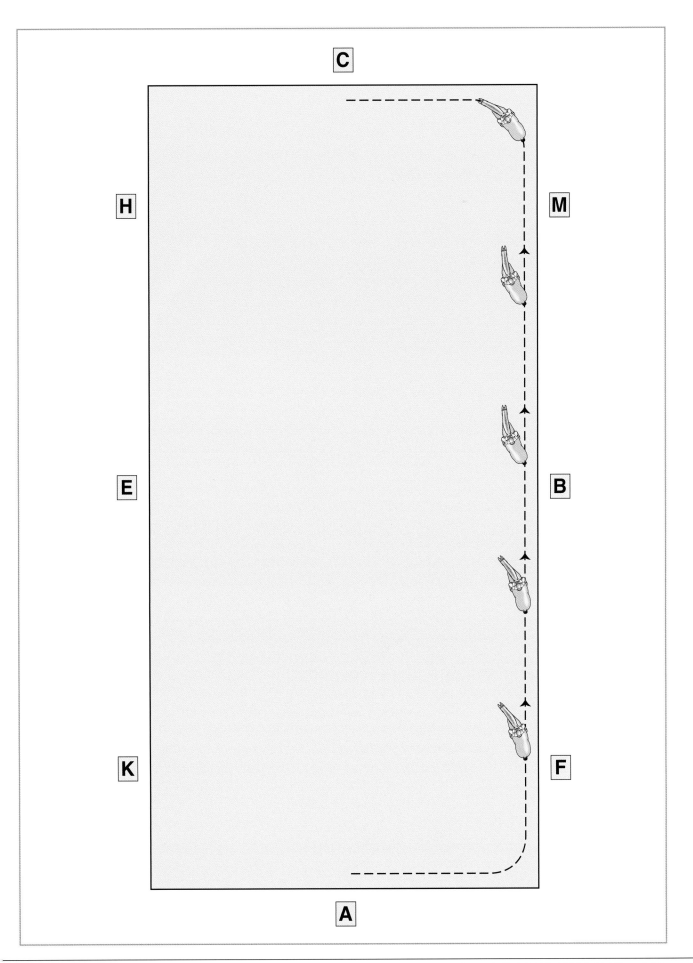

EXERCISE
79

BEGINNERS

PRELIMINARY

NOVICE   ✪

ELEMENTARY ✪✪

MEDIUM   ✪✪✪✪

Travers to pirouette to half-pass

The most important point of this exercise is that your horse understands what is required of him and maintains the quality of his steps throughout.

BONUS

This is a great collecting exercise, in particular for the horse that is inclined to swing his quarters out on the walk pirouette.

How do I ride this exercise?

❑ In walk on the left rein, ride travers along the centre line to X.

❑ At this point, ride a half walk pirouette, and then…

❑ …half-pass back to the track by F.

❑ Straighten up and rejoin the track…

❑ …turn up the centre line, and…

❑ …repeat the exercise riding travers right.

What should happen?

❑ In travers the horse's outside hind leg crosses in front of his inside leg, in pirouette his outside front leg crosses in front of his inside front leg, and in half-pass both his outside hind leg and his outside foreleg cross in front of the inside legs: so in this exercise each stage of the movement should flow quite easily into the next.

❑ In travers, your horse's quarters should be about 30 degrees to the inside.

❑ In the half-pass make sure the shoulders lead, and not the hindquarters.

Double check

Your body position and hand and leg aids should be the same throughout this exercise.

Moving on

As long as your horse is not inclined to lose energy in the half pirouette, try doing a full walk pirouette and half-pass back to the track by H.

What can go wrong?

Your horse crosses his hind leg too much to the inside.

It is likely that your horse is bringing his haunches too much to the inside. This exercise would encourage him to do this, and is therefore not recommended for horses with this tendency.

If it's not working…

Go back to travers on the long side (Exercise 71).

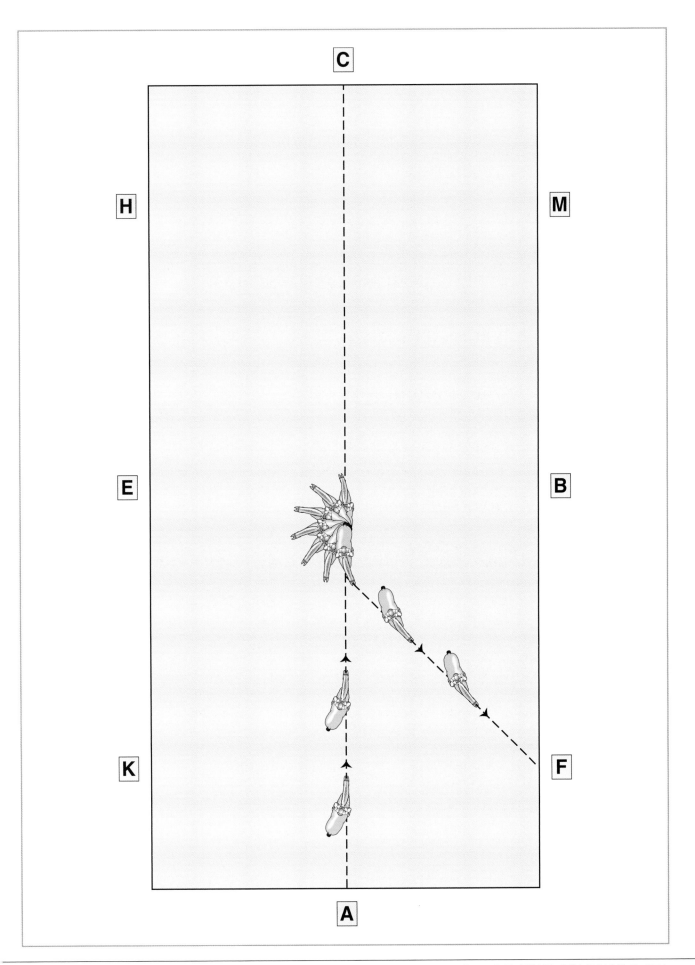

80

Lassetter's Hokey-kokey
from John Lassetter

BEGINNERS

PRELIMINARY

NOVICE

ELEMENTARY ✪✪

MEDIUM ✪✪✪✪✪

'When working in, once the horse has worked a period in walk doing loops and serpentines, bending and stretching, I like to take him up and work on something gymnastic to loosen the whole horse.'

How do I ride this exercise?

❑ On the right rein in walk, at B ride a 20m circle.

❑ On returning to B, ride a 10m circle.

❑ Rejoin the larger circle, and ride the next quarter segment in shoulder-in right.

❑ As you cross the centre line, ride another 10m circle to the inside.

❑ Rejoin the main circle, and ride head-to-wall (a less curved travers) for the next quarter segment.

❑ Just past E, change flexion and ride counter shoulder-in (see illustration) for the next section of the circle.

❑ Upon reaching the centre line opposite C, ride a 10m circle to the outside of the main circle.

❑ Rejoin the main circle, and ride the final quarter segment in tail-to-wall (a less curved renvers).

❑ When you get back to B, half-pass or leg-yield inwards, decreasing the size of the circle.

❑ Ride a 10m circle in the middle of your 20m circle.

❑ On this smaller circle, ride a few strides of travers, a few strides of shoulder-in, then leg-yield outwards to the track.

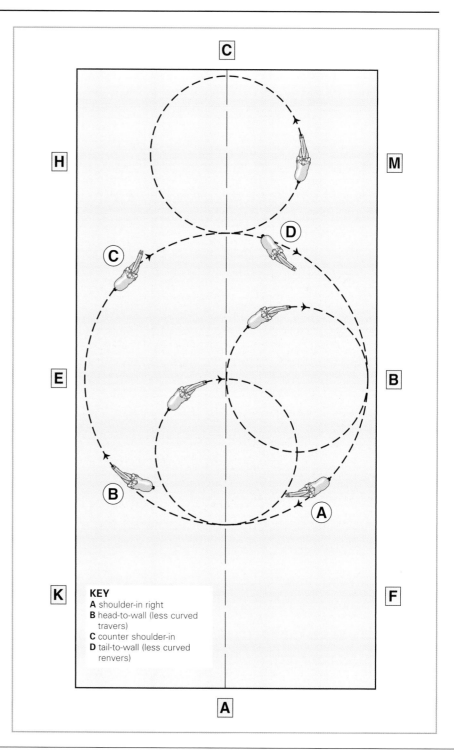

KEY
A shoulder-in right
B head-to-wall (less curved travers)
C counter shoulder-in
D tail-to-wall (less curved renvers)

❑ Now ask your horse to stretch down, and you should receive a reasonable extension in the walk!

What should happen?
In being party to this complex sequence of lateral steps and careful control of bend, the horse should become not only supple and engaged, but totally absorbed with the rider's aids.

Double check
All your circles must be absolutely accurate and you must be quite clear in your mind about each of the different movements before you begin this exercise.

Moving on
Try the exercise in trot.

What can go wrong?
You end up sitting in the wrong position.
This exercise requires total concentration from both you and your horse, and the likelihood is that in following the movement you have lost focus on your position. Rejoin the track, re-establish your position, and ride the exercise in walk, to establish where you should be as you go through the more complex format. Then try the exercise again.

If it's not working...
Break down the exercise into its component parts, and work on the particular problems.

> **BONUS**
>
> This exercise probably works every single muscle in the horse's body and most of his brain, too! (And the rider's!) It is also a very attractive exercise to ride.

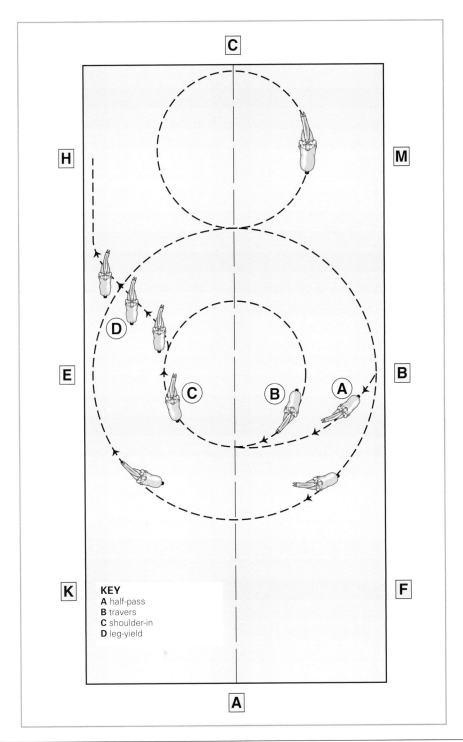

KEY
A half-pass
B travers
C shoulder-in
D leg-yield

THE GYMNASTIC HORSE

The Half-Pass

THE EXERCISES

A well ridden half-pass is a joy to watch. Your aim is to keep the same rhythm and balance throughout the exercise, and to keep your horse bent round your inside leg. The aids are the same as for travers, and in the words of Lizzie Murray: 'Half-pass is simply travers on a diagonal line.' In half-pass, the forward movement should always take priority over the sideways movement. The impulsion necessary for a collected trot or canter is more suited to this exercise. However, once again we have commenced in walk in order to establish the routine.

HOW TO RIDE HALF-PASS

- ❏ Begin your half-pass in the second corner of a short side of the school. Ask for a half-halt just before the corner.
- ❏ Using your inside leg on the girth, ride right into the corner, asking for a good bend and inside flexion with your inside hand. Use your outside hand to control the pace and bend.
- ❏ Look in the direction in which you intend to travel. When your horse's shoulders are on the diagonal, drop your weight on to your inside hip, squeeze your horse forwards with your inside leg on the girth, and ask for sideways movement with the outside leg behind the girth.

81

A simple exercise in half-pass on both reins

Half-pass is a lateral movement that, as regards difficulty, is on a par with renvers and travers. The horse moves forwards and sideways, bent through his body in the direction in which he is travelling, with the forward movement always taking priority over the sideways movement. His shoulders lead his hindquarters, and the outside legs cross in front of the inside legs. This exercise is a good first exercise in half-pass.

BONUS

Once your horse understands half-pass, it becomes much easier to ride a good circle.

How do I ride this exercise?

❏ In walk on the left rein, ride down the H/K long side on the track.

❏ Just before K, ride a half-circle to the centre line.

❏ Half-pass left towards H.

❏ Rejoin the track, and ride a half 10m circle to the centre line…

❏ …then half-pass right to K.

❏ Repeat on the opposite rein.

What should happen?

The half-circles should prepare your horse for the half-pass, and because you are starting from the middle of the school, he won't be inclined to rely on the fence or the track.

RIDER'S TIP

When beginning half-pass, it is most important to establish rhythm and impulsion, therefore do not expect too sharp an angle to begin with. Only increase the angle when your half-pass is rhythmical and flowing.

Where appropriate, ride well into the corners of the arena.

Double check

Be sure that your inside leg doesn't come away from the horse's side.

Moving on

This exercise can be ridden in any pace.

Increase the angle of half-pass from the centre line to E rather than H, rejoining the centre line for the second part of the exercise between B and E.

What can go wrong?

1 Your horse swings his quarters over too soon.

The chances are that you are using your outside leg too quickly. Take one or two steps in shoulder-in before asking for the half-pass.

2 Your horse is 'tipping his nose'.

The likelihood is that he is moving at too much of an angle for his capabilities. Firstly be sure you are not asking for too much flexion. If this is not so, ride your horse into the left rein to reduce the angle of bend, lightening both reins to help him balance.

If it's not working…

Go back to 'a first exercise in travers' (Exercise 71), using the fence or wall to assist.

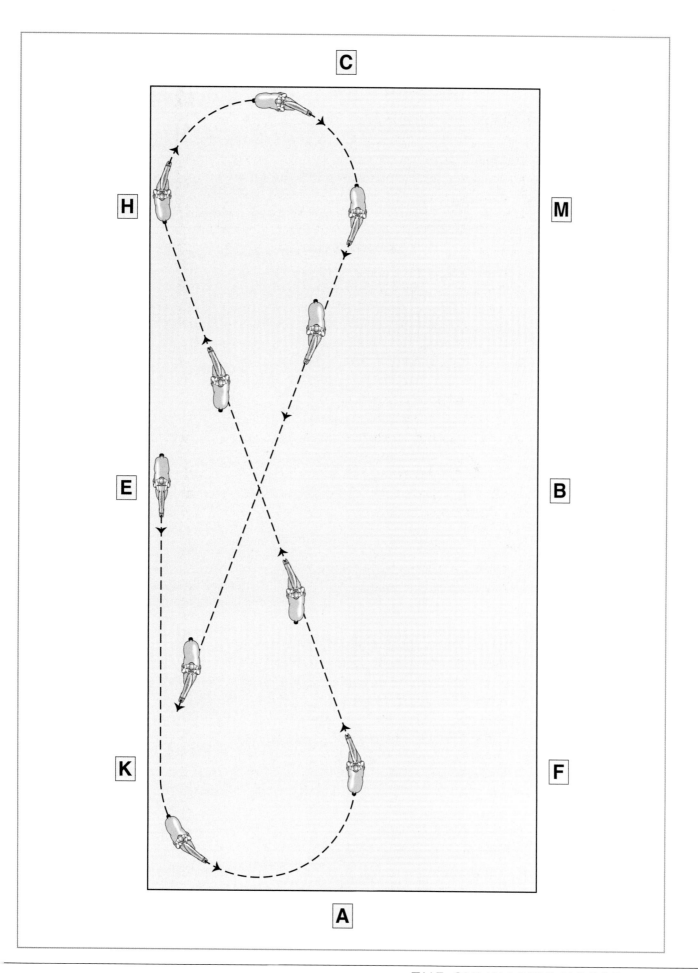

82

Teaching half-pass from travers
from Lizzie Murray

'Half-pass is simply travers on a diagonal line. I find a lot of people understand that as a much easier way of thinking about half-pass.'

RIDER'S TIPS

If your horse's quarters are leading, he will not be looking at the marker he is going towards.

You must keep your weight central, or inclining towards the movement. It is important not to lean away from the movement.

If you are having trouble staying on line, you can lay a line of poles along the track you want to ride.

How do I ride this exercise?

❏ On the right rein in walk, ride travers from the beginning of one long side of the school to the B or E marker.

❏ Straighten, and repeat on the opposite long side of the school.

❏ Only when you are satisfied with your horse's understanding of the movement, on the right rein from the centre line, ride travers on a diagonal line to half way between M and B.

❏ On reaching the track, straighten, and repeat on the opposite rein.

What should happen?

Your horse should make a lively, forward half-pass with good impulsion.

Double check

The eyes and ears, and the head, neck and shoulders must stay on the line looking to the marker.

Moving on

You could try riding this in trot and canter; or you could increase the angle of the diagonal. Lizzie says: 'In the Grand Prix test we are asked to go from F to E and back to M!'

What can go wrong?

Your horse falls in on his inside shoulder.
Ride straight parallel to the track, and then rebalance and take a new line to M instead. You could also try riding shoulder-in, or try leg-yielding away from the inside leg, then re-aligning to another marker so that you don't make the line steeper than travers on a diagonal line again.

If it's not working...

Go back to working on 'a first exercise in travers' (Exercise 71), or make the line less steep on the diagonal.

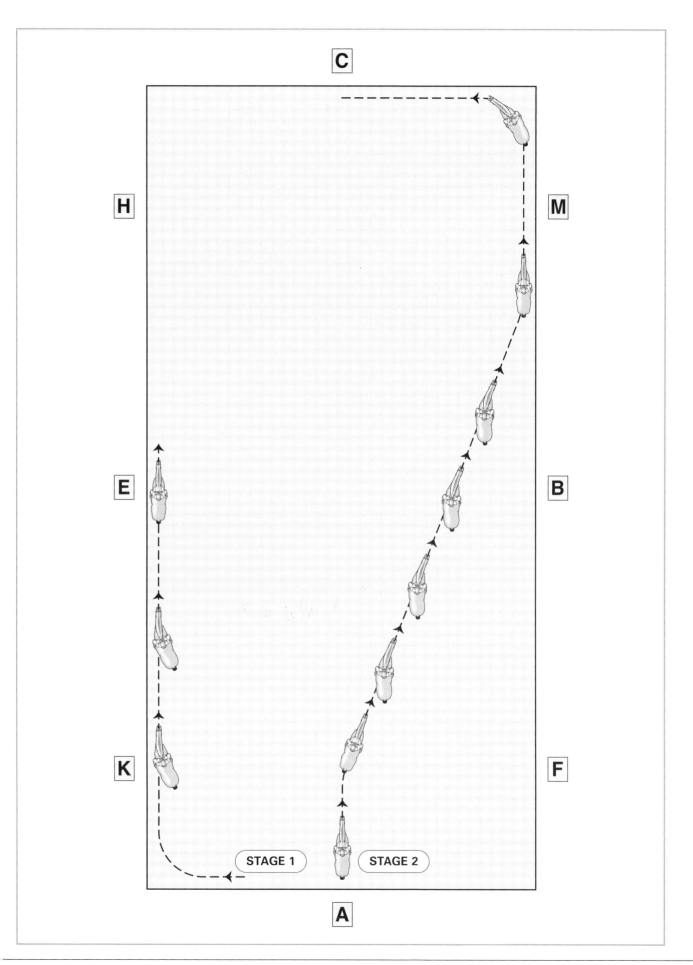

BEGINNERS

PRELIMINARY

NOVICE

ELEMENTARY ❍❍❍

MEDIUM ❍❍❍❍❍

Getting the quarters working correctly

This exercise is divided into two parts: the first part will correct the performance of a horse that leads with his quarters; the second is useful for a horse that trails his quarters.

BONUS

This is a great exercise for improving your skills in applying the aids.

How do I ride this exercise?

❏ On the right rein, establish walk across the short side of the school, and from K make a half-pass right to X.

❏ At X proceed in medium walk to the diagonally opposite corner of the school.

❏ Turn left and repeat the exercise, riding half-pass left.

❏ Now come around the school, and from K ride straight across the diagonal to X;

❏ from X finish the diagonal in a half-pass, picking up the horse with the outside leg, and collecting with the inside rein to control the forehand.

What should happen?

The first part of this exercise enables the rider to rally the horse up during the half-pass, and to march him actively forwards from the half-pass. As you approach X, take the forehand well ahead in order to position the horse on the diagonal.

The second part of the exercise is a good collecting procedure that requires your horse to understand not to fall in on the inside shoulder as the outside leg asks for half-pass.

Double check

In the half-pass, check that you are sitting centrally, with your weight on your inside seatbone and into the inside stirrup.

Moving on

Now try it in trot!

What can go wrong?

Your horse's haunches may lead, or they may trail.

If his haunches lead in the first part of the exercise, bring your inside shoulder further back and your outside shoulder further forward. If his haunches trail in the second part of the exercise, use more half-halt to collect the inside shoulder, or work through the renvers exercises (Section 6).

If it's not working...

Go back to riding the first part of teaching half-pass from travers (Exercise 82).

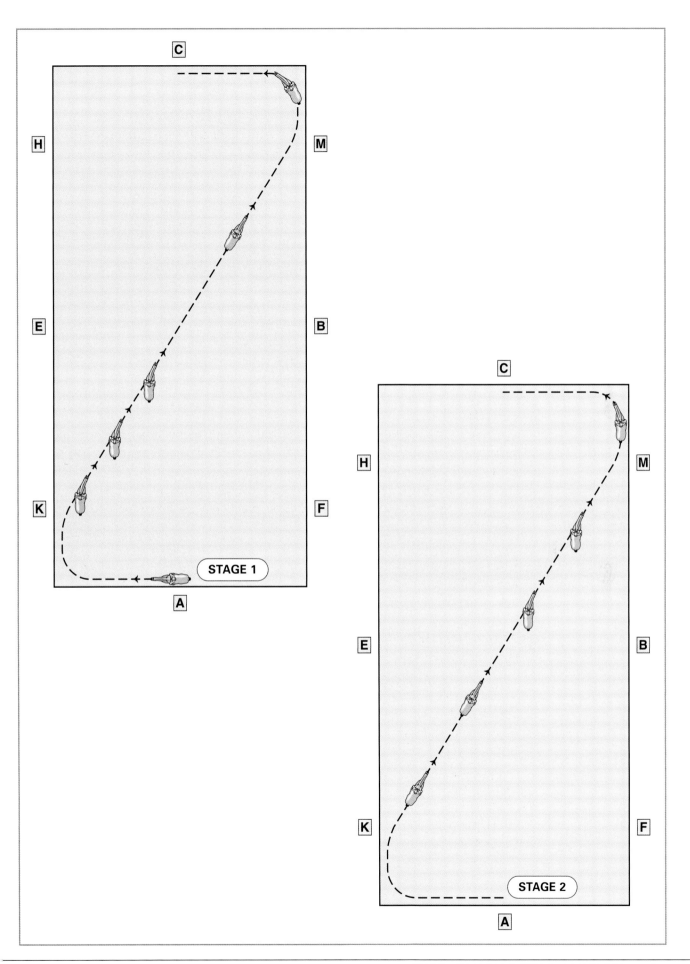

STAGE 1

STAGE 2

Bending and straightening in half-pass
from Jennie Loriston-Clarke

'Think mostly about your horse's balance in the half-pass. He should be bent in the direction he's going. Then take the bend out, make him absolutely straight, and then put the bend back in again. This will encourage your horse to carry himself a bit more, and he'll be better balanced in the end.'

BONUS

This is a great exercise for practising the use of the inside leg during half-pass.

RIDER'S TIP

'Straight' means no flexion and no bend.

How do I ride this exercise?

❑ On the right rein in collected trot, at K ride a few steps in half-pass,
❑ followed by a few steps straight...
❑ ...and then back to a few steps in half-pass again, ensuring that your horse's body is parallel to the arena walls throughout.
❑ Repeat until you arrive at the other side of the arena.
❑ Try to finish straight, then change the rein in collected trot, and repeat.

What should happen?

If a horse loses balance in half-pass and starts to fall sideways, especially through the shoulder, asking him to step forwards straight out of half-pass ensures that he doesn't have a chance to do this. By alternating between half-pass and straight strides, you can improve your horse's balance in half-pass as well as making sure that he maintains a lively impulsion.

Double check

Be sure that the rhythm remains the same throughout this exercise.

Moving on

Try to ride the exercise in canter, or try making the angle of the diagonal more oblique, ie riding from M to B..

What can go wrong?

Your horse tries to fall on to his inside shoulder.
Use more inside leg and maintain the inside bend, with your horse yielding away from the left or right leg, depending on which way you are going.

If it's not working...

Work on leg-yield zig-zags (Exercise 59)

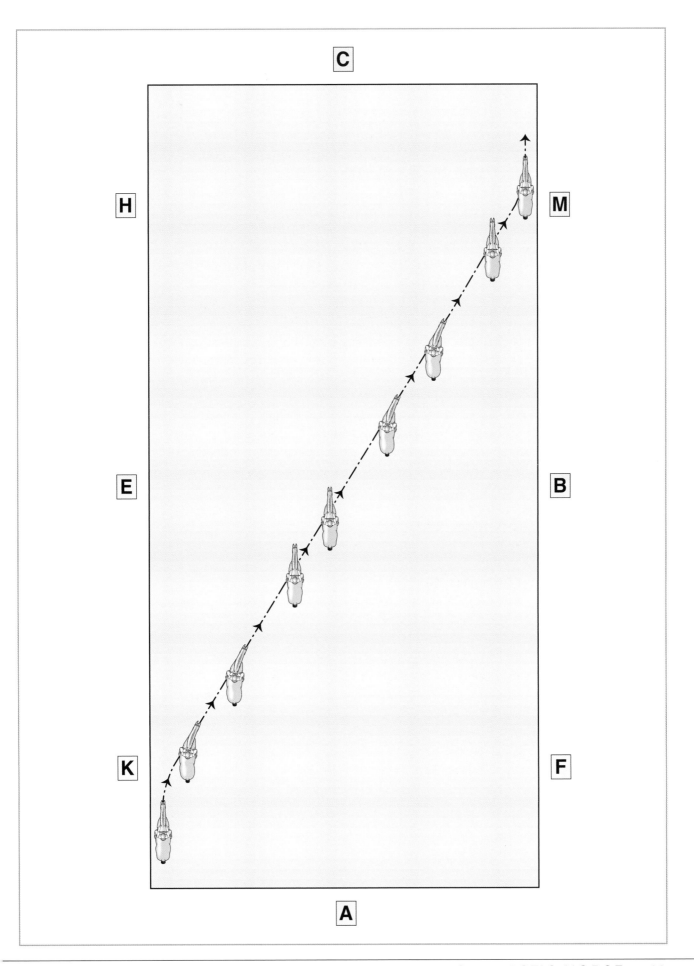

EXERCISE

85

BEGINNERS

PRELIMINARY

NOVICE

ELEMENTARY ✪✪

MEDIUM ✪✪✪✪✪

Using a figure-of-eight to improve your half-pass

This is a good exercise for a horse that leads with the haunches; there is also time within the exercise that the rider can use to relax the horse and improve the quality of the paces (walk, trot and/or canter).

BONUS

This is a great sequence to use in a freestyle test.

How do I ride this exercise?

❏ In collected walk on the right rein, establish shoulder-fore in the corner of the school;

❏ from K or M, ride half-pass to the half-way line, just before X.

❏ Straighten and ride a 10m circle to the right...

❏ ...followed by a 10m circle to the left.

❏ Rejoin the centre line at X, and ride half-pass back to the original long side of the school.

❏ Repeat on the other rein.

RIDER'S TIP

Only continue in half-pass as long as you can maintain your horse's rhythm and looseness. As soon as you feel your horse beginning to become tense, ride either a small circle, shoulder-in, or a transition.

What should happen?

The figure-of-eight is a good 'repair and prepare' interlude between the half-passes, because the rider can take the opportunity to relax the horse, and improve the bend, rhythm and submission.

Double check

Be sure that you change your leg, seat and hand aids as you change the bend at X.

Moving on

This exercise can be ridden in canter with a simple or a flying change at X.

What can go wrong?

This is a good exercise if your horse tries to lead with his haunches, but do be careful with a horse that likes to fall on his inside shoulder. In this case you are best to ride half-pass to straight lines.

If it's not working...

Start and finish the exercise on the three-quarter line so that you don't have to go quite so far in half-pass.

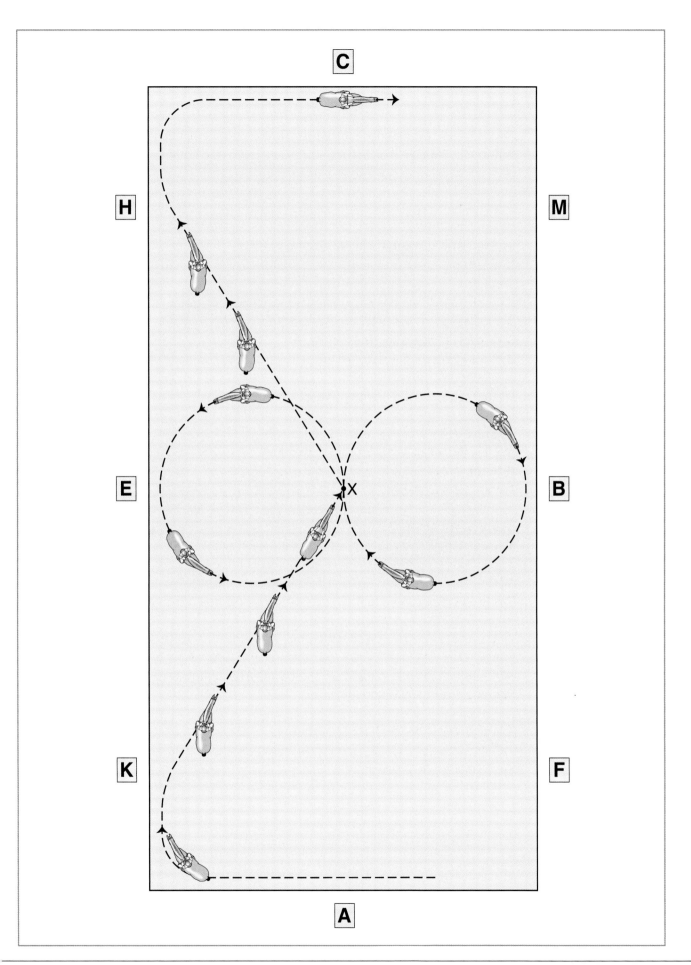

EXERCISE

86

BEGINNERS

PRELIMINARY

NOVICE ✪

ELEMENTARY ✪✪✪✪

MEDIUM ✪✪✪✪✪

Putting your half-pass to the test

This exercise will establish the horse's obedience to the rider's aids, and will help to improve his balance in half-pass.

How do I ride this exercise?

❏ Establish collected trot on the right rein. Passing K, ride a few steps in shoulder-fore…

❏ …and then immediately go into half-pass right to the first quarter line.

❏ On the quarter line, ride a few more steps in shoulder-fore…

❏ before continuing the half-pass to the centre line.

❏ If you have space, ride a few more steps in shoulder-fore towards C…

❏ …and turn right.

❏ Ride along the long side straight, to re-establish the balance and comfort of the horse.

❏ Repeat on the other rein.

What should happen?

Maintaining a good rhythm, the horse should stay consistently curved around your inside leg, and should alternate between shoulder-fore and half-pass without loss of balance.

Double check

Be sure that your weight is correctly distributed.

Moving on

Try the same exercise in collected canter, or try riding shoulder-in rather than shoulder-fore.

What can go wrong?

1 You give the wrong aids.

In the early stages of learning half-pass it is easy to use the inside rein or the outside leg too strongly, and not to use enough inside leg.

2 Your horse loses his rhythm.

Go back to establishing impulsion in trot and canter on the straight or on a circle.

3 Your horse falls out through his hindquarters.

In this case only ride half-pass from a shoulder-in until the exercise is better established.

If it's not working...

Go back to shoulder-fore, then ride a diagonal line for a few steps, before resuming shoulder-fore on the quarter line.

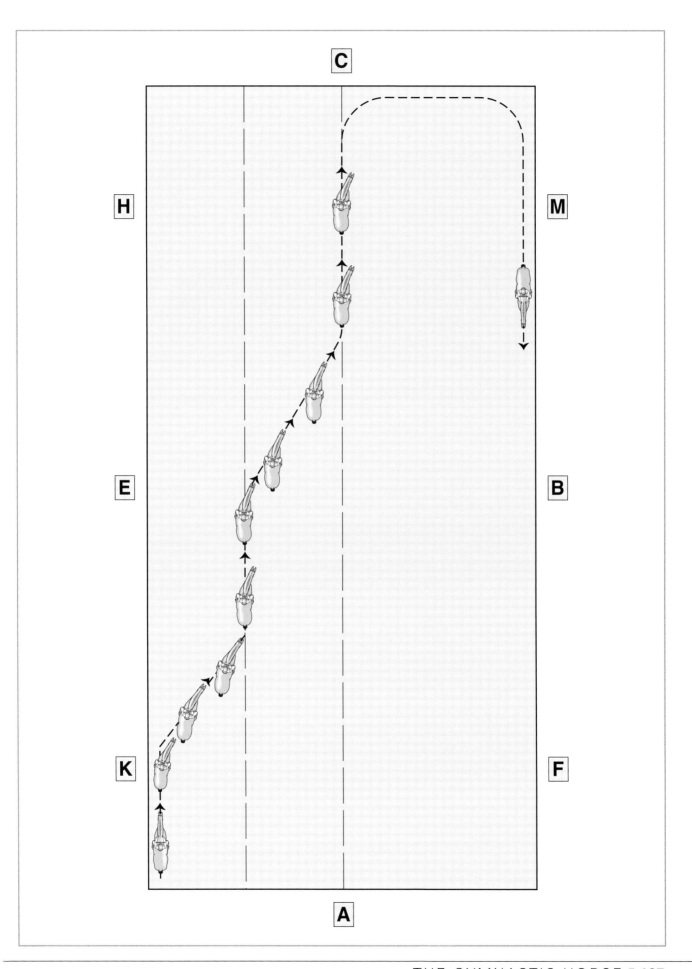

87

PRELIMINARY	✪
NOVICE	✪✪✪✪
ELEMENTARY	✪✪✪✪✪
MEDIUM	✪✪✪✪✪

Making the change from half-pass right to half-pass left

This movement is somewhat confusingly known as 'counter change of hand'. As you change the flexion from right to left, your horse should continue to willingly accept your aids, and the rhythm of the exercise should not change. It should not be attempted until your horse is adept at half-pass.

BONUS

This is a really interesting exercise for the horse to do, and keeps him on his toes and alert.

How do I ride this exercise?

❑ On the right rein, come up the centre line from A or C in walk.
❑ Ride half-pass right, joining the track at B or E, and then …
❑ …ask for half-pass left and rejoin the centre line at either A or C.
❑ Repeat on the other rein.

What should happen?

This exercise helps your horse to understand how to adapt his bend to correspond with your position, and how to move forwards and sideways away from a particular leg.

RIDER'S TIPS

When you teach counter changes to your horse, begin with just a slight bend and a gradual changeover, and build up the angles as your horse's confidence and experience grows.

When you ride the change from half-pass right to half-pass left, ride one or two straight steps before asking for a change of bend and flexion.

Double check

Be sure that on each occasion you are sitting on the inside, and that your weight is more in the inside stirrup than the outside stirrup.

Moving on

Try half-pass zig-zag: make a right turn up the centre line. Ride half-pass right for three metres, half-pass left for six metres, half-pass right six metres and half-pass left three metres. This exercise is good in walk and trot.

What can go wrong?

Your horse's haunches lead in the second half-pass.
This is because you haven't straightened your horse sufficiently before changing your bend from the first half-pass when his forehand was leading. Try again, concentrating on straightening up first.

If it's not working...

Try half-pass from the centre line to the three-quarter line, and changing the bend before half-pass back to the centre line.

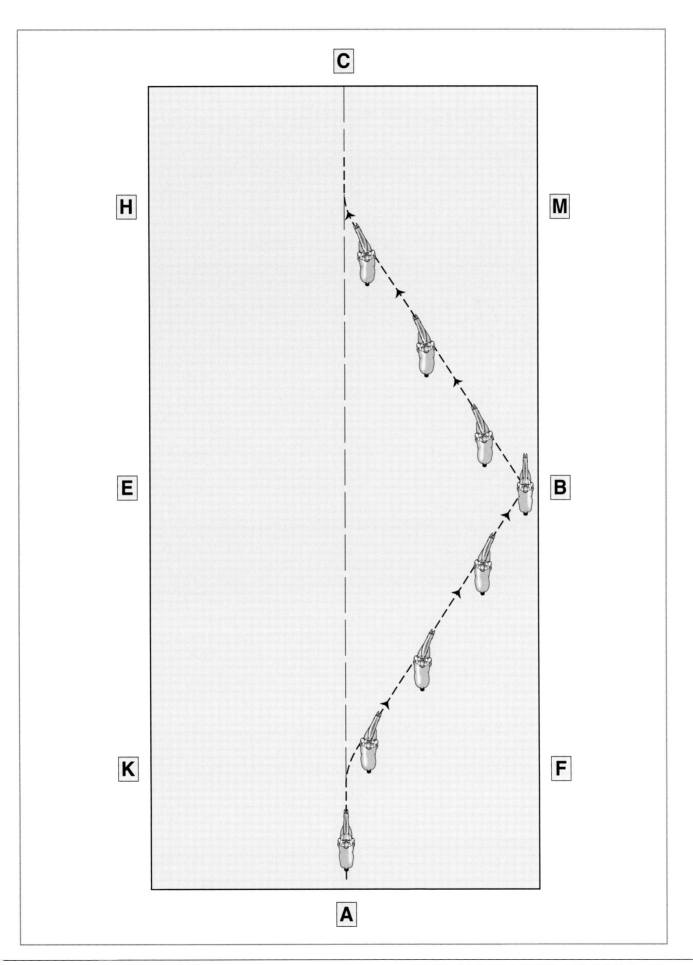

EXERCISE

88

BEGINNERS

PRELIMINARY

NOVICE

ELEMENTARY ✪✪

MEDIUM ✪✪✪✪✪

Using half-pass on a circle to improve balance
from Karen Dixon

'This exercise takes the pressure off the half-pass, as the half circles are the most difficult bit for your horse. Half-pass becomes a relief!'

How do I ride this exercise?

❏ In trot on the right rein, ride half-pass from the K marker across the diagonal to M.

❏ Just before M, ride a half 10m circle left to the centre line, maintaining the same aids.

❏ Once the half circle is complete, strike off in half-pass right from the centre line to the E marker.

❏ At E straighten up, and continue to F;

❏ from the F marker, ride half-pass left to the H marker…

❏ …and repeat the above exercise on the other rein.

What should happen?

This exercise will massively improve your horse's half-pass. It will get him crossing his legs over much better, and he will become more confident in your aids. Also, when ridden successfully, this is a good exercise for a horse that tends to be rather 'shoulder-heavy' in half-pass, because rather than tipping on to his shoulder, he will work more from behind and so will stay lighter and 'up', because he is expecting to be turning at the end of the diagonal.

Double check

You will need to keep turning the horse on the half circle with just your legs – too much hand will cause him to lose the counter bend, and he will altogether lose impulsion.

Moving on

Increase the angle of the half-pass, riding from K to B, or try moving up a gear.

What can go wrong?

1 Your horse finds the half circle very difficult.

It is very difficult for your horse to turn with an outside bend on the half circle. On the right rein he will be pushing on to your right leg, and you've got to push him off it. The tendency is to 'help' him with the counter bend by crossing your right rein over his neck; this will be contra-indicative, however, and it is better to keep your hands wide, either side of your horse's neck, and try just using your legs to turn, even if the circle starts off larger than you would like.

2 Your horse may lose impulsion, particularly on the half-circle.

Because the exercise is new and different, your horse may tend to lose impulsion. So watch that you maintain the rhythm throughout the exercise. Once the horse gets the hang of it, you can make the half-circle smaller again.

If it's not working...

Ride the exercise in walk to help your horse understand what is being asked of him. Begin with a larger circle, still keeping the counter bend, and go for less half-pass. Once the horse gains in confidence, go for quality, not quantity.

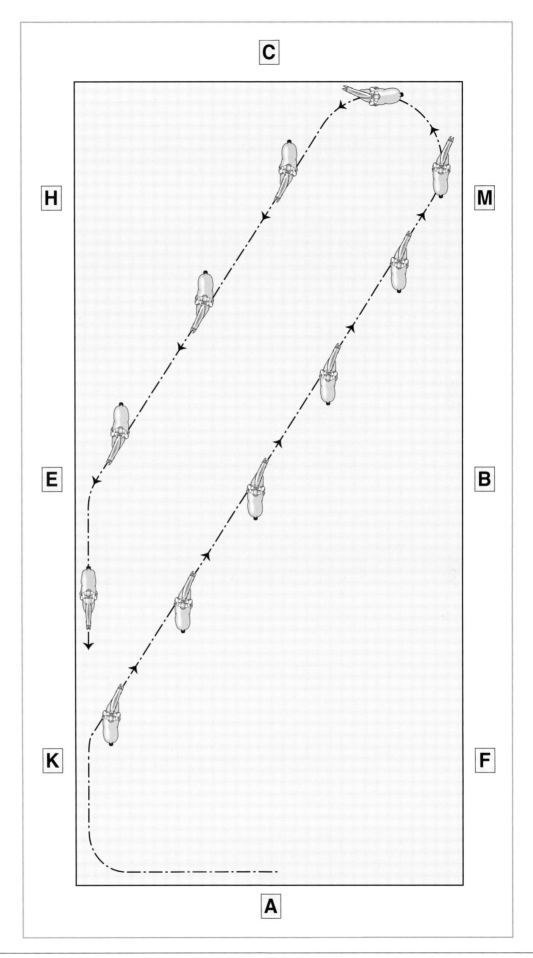

STRENGTHENING THE CANTER

Counter Canter

THE EXERCISES

Counter canter is a great straightening, strengthening and collecting exercise. In effect, you will be cantering with the outside leg leading – so, for example, if you are on the left rein, your horse will lead with his right leg. Keep a very slight flexion to the side of the leading leg so your horse understands that counter canter is required, and keep your weight in the stirrup and seatbone on the same side. Your horse should master counter canter before he moves on to flying changes.

Some horses can become quite worried and tense when learning counter canter, so it is important to introduce it gradually – practise only shallow canter loops to begin with, and be sympathetic, but consistent and accurate, with your seat and leg aids so as to keep the horse calm and help him understand what you want. If he is tense he will very readily break back into trot, or put in a flying change.

SIX GOOD REASONS WHY YOU SHOULD WORK YOUR HORSE IN COUNTER CANTER:

1 It has a good suppling effect, increasing athletic ability.
2 It teaches obedience to the rider's aids.
3 It can help to straighten a crooked horse.
4 The horse's balance improves, and the hindquarters show greater engagement.
5 It is an important step towards flying changes.
6 It is a good forehand lightening exercise.

THE AIDS TO COUNTER CANTER

Counter canter aids are:
- ❏ inside leg on the girth;
- ❏ outside leg behind the girth;
- ❏ weight on the inside seatbone and the inside stirrup;
- ❏ inside shoulder back;
- ❏ outside shoulder forward;
- ❏ inside hand leading;
- ❏ outside hand to wither.

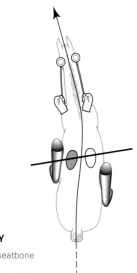

KEY

◯ seatbone

⬤ weight in seatbone

A first exercise in counter canter

Horses often find counter canter confusing and quite difficult. Be sure you are not doing half-pass off the track, and leg-yielding back, which they find easier. To get the angle of your loop correct, aim for A or C, according to which end of the school you begin the exercise at.

RIDER'S TIPS

Pay particular note to your weight being on the inside stirrup and inside seatbone. Return your horse to the track by means of pressure from the inside leg, and using both hands to help him lift his forehand back to the track.

How do I ride this exercise?

❏ Having established a well balanced canter, along the next long side ride a 3m loop out from the track.
❏ Return to the track.
❏ Repeat on the opposite side of the school. The loop is ridden in counter canter.
❏ Repeat on the other rein.

What should happen?

If you have left the track in balance, the horse should stay vertical on the forehand, without swinging the haunches in or falling through the shoulder. He should change his direction a little with each step through the loop, until he is facing in the direction of M to return to the track.

Double check

Check that you have the feeling of being in balance, and of not falling prematurely back into,or back out of the loop.

Moving on

Increase the loops to 5m and 10m; and try shallow loops up the three-quarter line.

What can go wrong?

1 Your horse falls through his outside shoulder and returns to the track prematurely.
   Show him what you are asking for, using more outside rein and outside leg: try riding the following exercise:
   Commence a shallow loop from just past K, as in the original exercise. However, when you arrive at the 3m mark, ride straight up the school parallel to the fence or boundary. Rejoin the track at the short end of the school, and once your horse is happy with this, repeat on the opposite rein. This can also be ridden as a 5m shallow loop to the quarter line.
2 Your horse could swing his quarters to the inside and avoid the demands of the exercise.
   Work on your horse's straightness on the three-quarter line before attempting any further counter canter.

If it's not working...

Try riding the half loop where you turn in from the track, say from F on the left rein, riding on a line towards C. Then gradually turn right to join and ride up the quarter line. This decreases the demands of the counter canter.

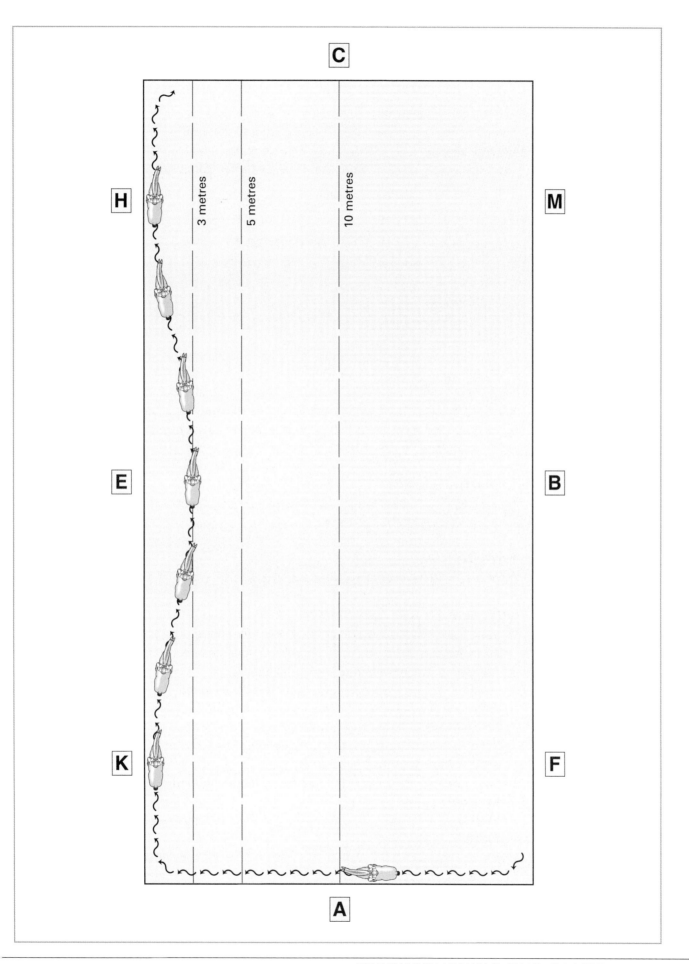

C

H

M

3 metres

5 metres

10 metres

E

B

K

F

A

EXERCISE
90

BEGINNERS

PRELIMINARY

NOVICE   ✪✪✪✪

ELEMENTARY ✪✪✪

MEDIUM   ✪✪

Counter-canter loops

This is an important exercise to test the level of training of yourself and your horse, because keeping a good balanced canter up to the corner before making a correct trot transition features in most dressage tests from novice to medium level.

How do I ride this exercise?
- ❏ On the right rein and just before F, ride a half 15m circle in canter…
- ❏ …then incline back to the track, and rejoin it in counter canter, in the first instance aiming for M.
- ❏ As your horse becomes better balanced, rejoin the track nearer to B, asking for more strides along the track.
- ❏ Be content with straight lines at first, before trying to tackle corners or bends, as this can be very hard work for the inexperienced horse.

What should happen?
Your horse should collect and learn counter canter with an upright torso, and should stay on one track (forehand and haunches).

Double check
Be sure that your horse keeps the bend that accords to the canter lead. Also check that you are sitting with your body in the correct position according to the lead.

Moving on
Decrease the half-circle to 10m.

What can go wrong?
1 Your horse may break into trot.
Don't let him!
2 He may try to change legs in front or behind.
In this case, go back to the easier version.

If it's not working...
Try working the three-quarter lines in canter.

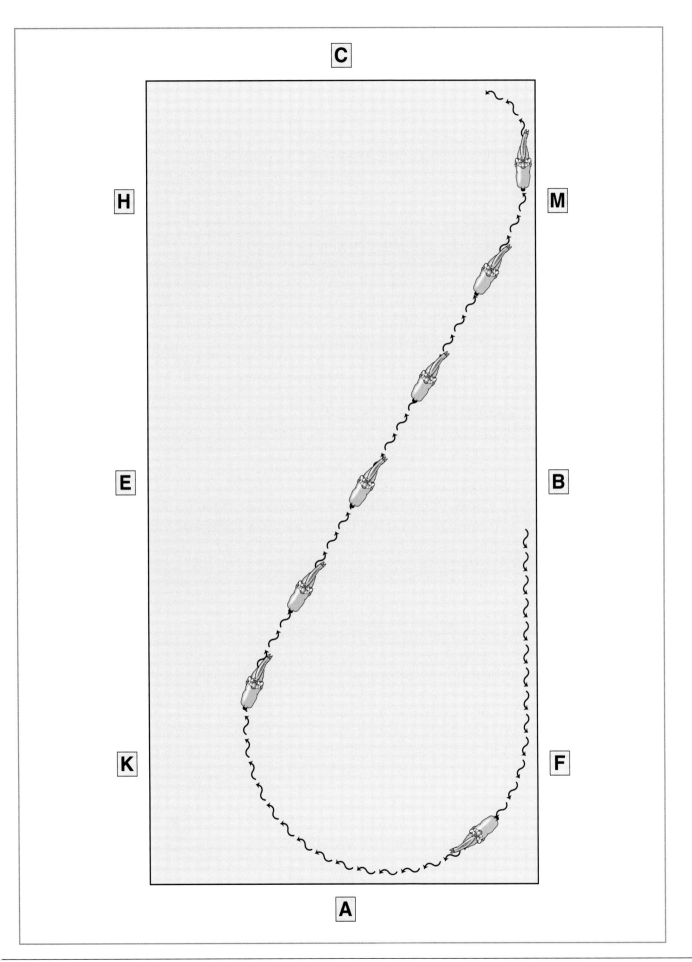

EXERCISE

91

BEGINNERS

PRELIMINARY

NOVICE

ELEMENTARY ✪✪

MEDIUM ✪✪✪✪

Counter-canter 'box'

This exercise demands a 90-degree turn in counter canter, which requires your horse to be capable of a high degree of collection.

How do I ride this exercise?
❏ On the right rein, ask for counter canter along one long side of the school.
❏ Turn straight across the school from B or E in counter canter.
❏ If your horse feels balanced, turn right at the opposite track, keeping counter canter…
❏ …but if he feels at all insecure, or loses rhythm or suppleness, turn left in true canter.
❏ As long as he feels calm and in balance, continue in counter canter, riding a corner at F and K.
❏ Repeat on the other rein.

What should happen?
The 90-degree turns are very demanding for a horse, so it is important that the rider helps him maintain a calm, regular rhythm by sitting in the correct position (right or left according to the canter lead). It is important to maintain the quality of the canter: make the turns shallower if it starts to feel stilted, and use true canter to re-establish 'jump' and rhythm.

Double check
Make sure that your position – your seat and your weight distribution – is correct for the movement you are performing.

Moving on
Try riding a flying change over X so you can turn left again in counter canter.

What can go wrong?
Your horse goes crooked or breaks to trot.
Turn left into true canter. Work on counter canter along the long side of the school, and use an easier turning exercise, such as Exercise 39 or 41.

If it's not working...
This is a very demanding exercise. It is best to 'feel' your way into it so that your horse doesn't make a mistake and get worried.

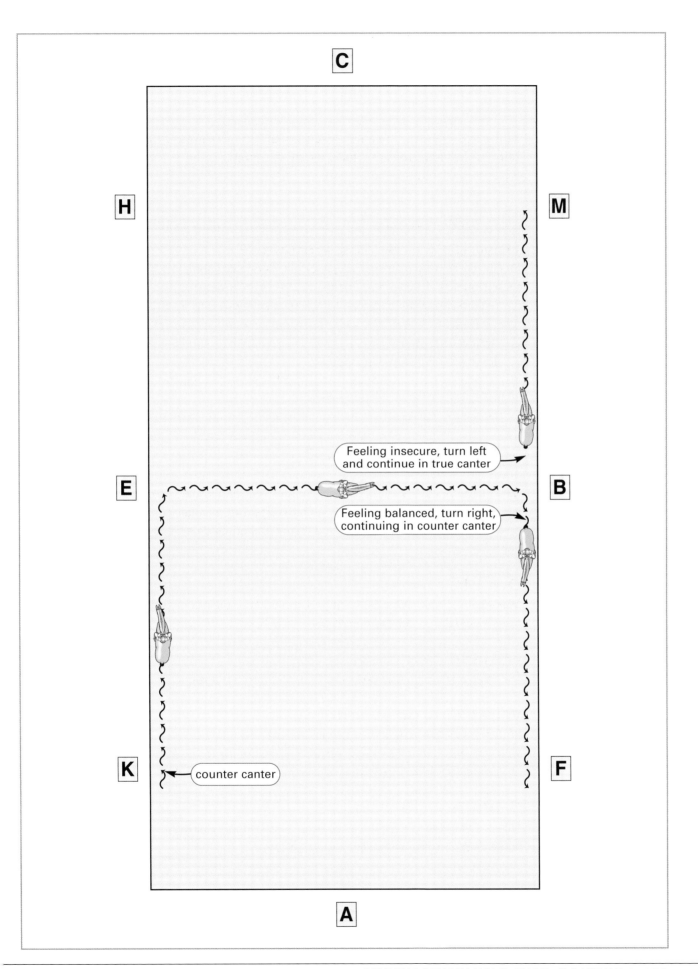

Feeling insecure, turn left and continue in true canter

Feeling balanced, turn right, continuing in counter canter

counter canter

BEGINNERS

PRELIMINARY

NOVICE

ELEMENTARY ✪✪✪

MEDIUM ✪✪✪✪✪

Counter-canter serpentine

Riding a serpentine in canter involves riding counter-canter loops, which can be difficult. To make it easier for horses that are not coping, make the counter-canter circle bigger – up to 25m.

How do I ride this exercise?

❏ On the left rein in canter, begin a three-loop serpentine at C.

❏ As you cross the centre line for the first time, ride a 10–12m circle in canter. As you come out of the circle, stay in counter canter for the loop.

❏ Continue on the serpentine at B. As you next cross the centre line ride a 10–12m circle in true canter.

❏ Then repeat on the opposite rein.

What should happen?

Riding the loop of a serpentine can be difficult for the inexperienced horse. By setting him up with a 10m circle before each loop you will help him to establish his rhythm and balance.

Double check

Make sure that your rhythm stays the same throughout the exercise.

Moving on

Try riding the exercise with four loops.

What can go wrong?

Your horse can lose balance between the 10m circle and the counter-canter arc.
Go back to simple counter-canter loops (Exercise 90).

If it's not working...

Go back to working on looping into a half serpentine (Exercise 47).

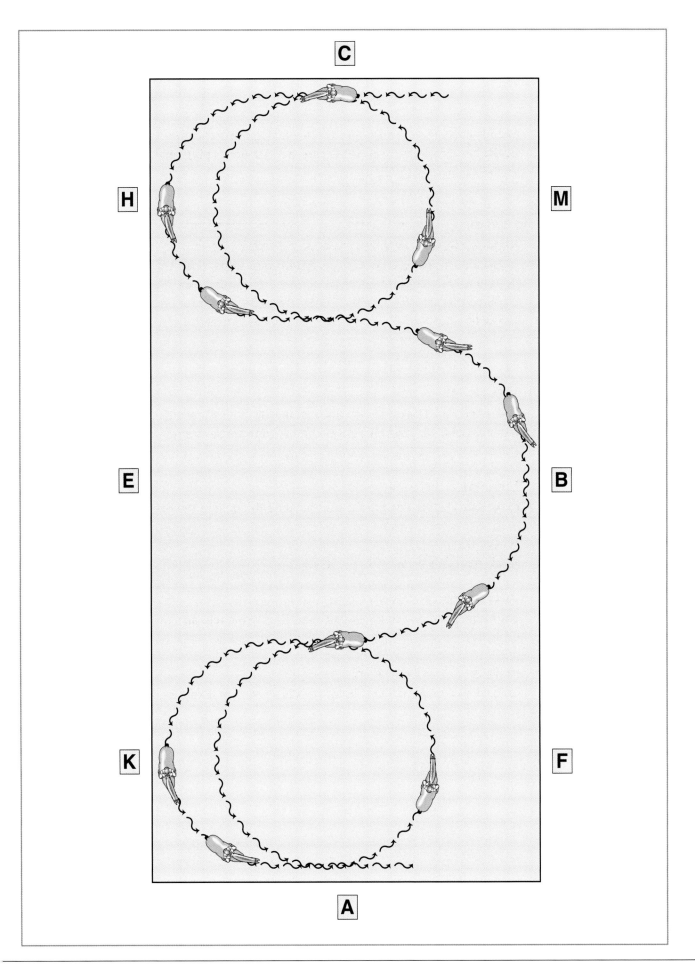

Counter-canter curves

In this exercise remember that the terms 'inside' and 'outside' refer to the bend of the horse, so in right canter the inside leg is the right leg, and the outside leg is the left leg.

BONUS

This is one of the best exercises for collecting the canter.

How do I ride this exercise?

❑ Remain in right canter throughout this exercise.

❑ Establish a right lead canter and from F, ride a half-circle right to the centre line…

❑ …and rejoin the track at B in counter canter.

❑ From halfway between B and M, make a three-quarter circle (20m), using the entire school width and circling back to X.

❑ Now curve right to rejoin the track.

What should happen?

In a correct counter canter the horse should stay perpendicular through the shoulders, and should stay on one track, with the hind and the front feet sharing the same path. He should stay slightly curved in the direction of his lead, and the rider should be sitting in position right or left according to the canter lead.

Double check

Be sure that your weight is in the inside stirrup, and on the inside seatbone.

Moving on

Try riding counter canter on the oval: ride one half-circle in counter canter, and then proceed up the long side; just before K repeat your half-circle. Go up the next long side and repeat the half-circle for a third time.

What can go wrong?

1 Your horse swings his quarters to the inside of his bend, and goes crooked.
Try to keep the forehand in front of the haunches, using your outside rein against the neck.

2 The counter canter fails, he falls on to his shoulder and changes legs in front or behind.
Be careful that you are not turning too suddenly.

If it's not working...

Work on shallow loops. Begin a shallow loop from just past K, as in Exercise 89. However, when you arrive at the 3m mark, ride straight up the school parallel to the fence or boundary. Rejoin the track at the short end of the school, and repeat on the opposite long side. Once your horse is happy with this, repeat on the other rein. Then include a little counter canter by riding a 5m shallow loop but returning to the 3m line.

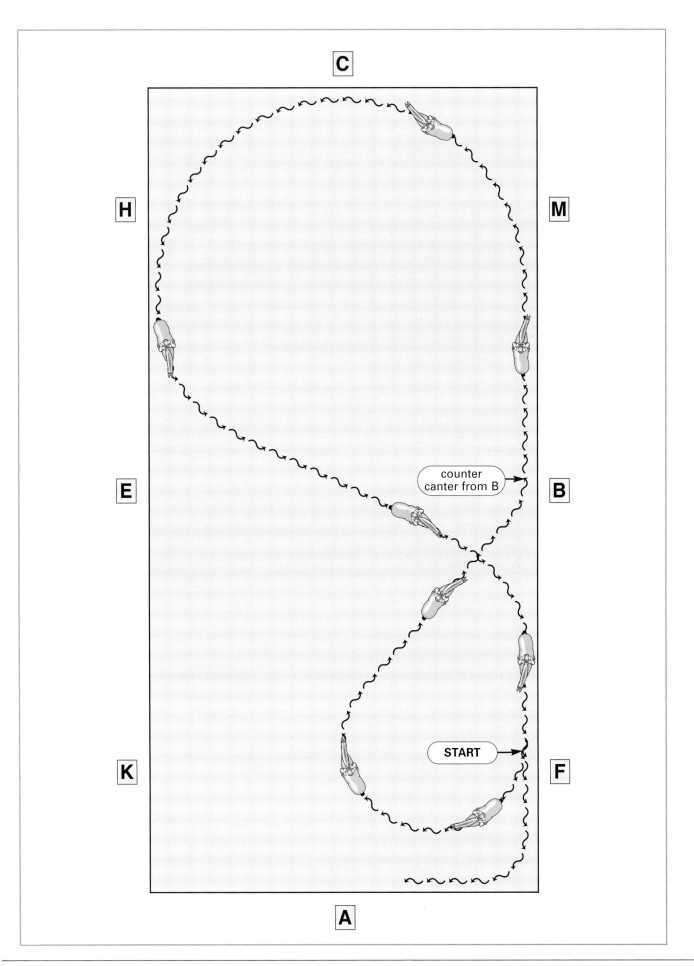

C

H

M

B

counter
canter from B

E

START

K

F

A

EXERCISE

94

BEGINNERS

PRELIMINARY

NOVICE ✪✪✪

ELEMENTARY ✪✪✪✪

MEDIUM ✪✪✪✪✪

Counter-canter circles

This is a good exercise for the less experienced horse because the 10m circles in true canter encourage and rebalance him, and the counter canter is only for a half 20m circle. For the more experienced horse it can be combined with flying changes, to keep him really on his toes.

How do I ride this exercise?

❏ On the right rein, ask for counter canter (left lead), and at B or E start to ride a 20m circle.

❏ As you cross the centre line, either the first or the second time, ride a 10m circle to the left, maintaining the lead leg.

❏ Rejoin the 20m circle, in counter canter;

❏ …when you get to the centre line after a half 20m circle, ride another 10m circle.

❏ Repeat on the opposite rein.

What should happen?

The 10m circles are a good opportunity to relax and rebalance the canter before returning to the 20m counter-canter circle.

Double check

Be sure that your rhythm stays the same between the two parts of the exercise.

Moving on

Ask the horse to perform a flying change as he goes from the 20m circle to the 10m circle: this would be a difficult exercise, because he would be going from counter canter to counter canter.

What can go wrong?

1 Loss of balance can occur between the circles.
Go back to an easier format, such as the half serpentine.

If it's not working…

Go back to an easier exercise, such as the half serpentine (Exercise 47).

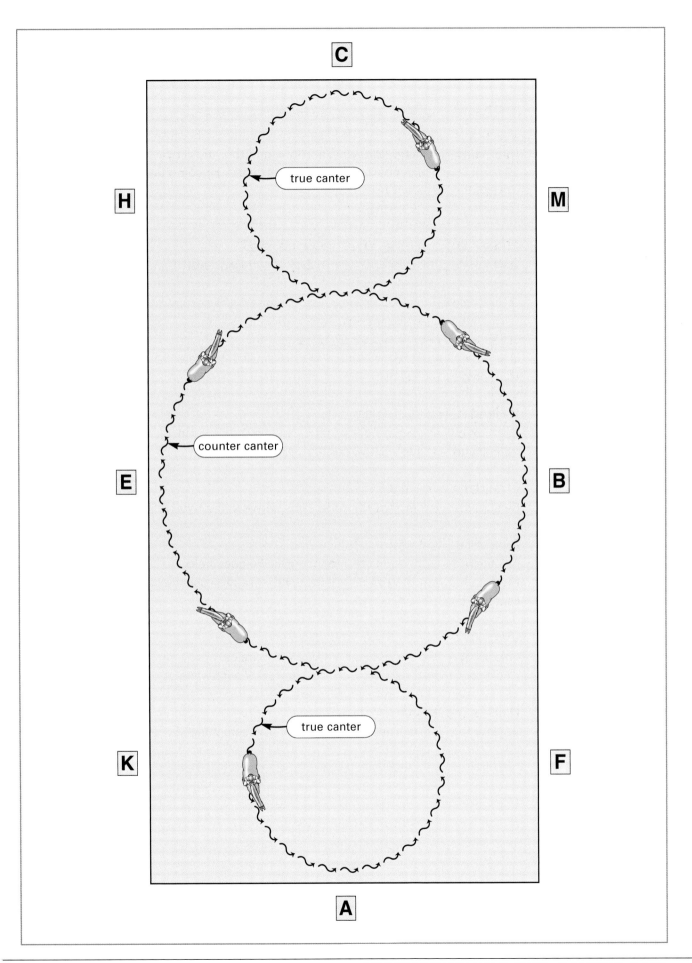

EXERCISE

95

BEGINNERS

PRELIMINARY

NOVICE ✪✪

ELEMENTARY ✪✪✪✪

MEDIUM ✪✪✪✪✪

Building up counter canter using satellite circles
from John Lassetter

'This exercise is a modern-day interpretation of an exercise used at Vienna in the Spanish Riding School. The idea is firstly to build up your counter canter in small increments. However, it also helps the horse that finds holding the counter canter difficult.'

RIDER'S TIP

If you or your horse are in the early stages of counter-canter training, make the arc of the 20m circle shallower (it could be almost a straight line, but with a very slight curve) to make this distance in counter canter easier.

How do I ride this exercise?

❑ On the left rein, having established canter, begin the exercise by riding a 10m circle, commencing on the quarter line, in one corner of the school.

❑ Imagine that this circle is attached to a 20m circle in the centre of the school: as you re-cross the quarter line, join this 20m circle. This will take you across the centre line in three or four strides of counter canter.

❑ At the three-quarter line, ride a second satellite circle (in true canter).

❑ Rejoin the 20m circle: you now have a longer way to go in counter canter before riding the third (true canter) satellite circle (see Rider's Tip box).

❑ Now ride your third, and then your fourth (true canter) satellite circles.

What should happen?

The initial counter-canter period and 10m circles should engage and collect your horse; eventually it will prepare him for flying changes.

Double check

Be sure that your horse's counter-canter movements are on one track, and that he is not travelling in a renvers position.

Moving on

Once you have established the exercise you can try putting in a change from counter canter through trot into true canter; and with practice, a simple change: that is, from walk into true canter.

You can gradually dispense with the satellite circles: only include them should you feel that the quality of the canter is failing, if the canter is losing its 'jump', or if you wish to make the horse more attentive. If you wish to make more energy, use true canter rather than counter canter.

Once all this is established, you can work towards including a flying change. The important thing about flying change is to learn to feel when your horse is ready to make the transition.

Thus you could make a change to the inside lead at E and B, and a change to the outside lead as you cross the centre line, riding forwards and using the satellite circles as necessary.

What can go wrong?

1 Your horse falls on the inside shoulder when he changes from one circle to another.

Make the arc of the 20m circle shallower, so the counter canter is easier for him to achieve; use a stronger inside leg.

2 **You lose your way!** *Go back to using the satellite circles in true canter, as was the initial aim of the exercise, in order to re-establish your goals.*

If it's not working...
Go back to the simpler exercises in counter canter (Exercises 89–94).

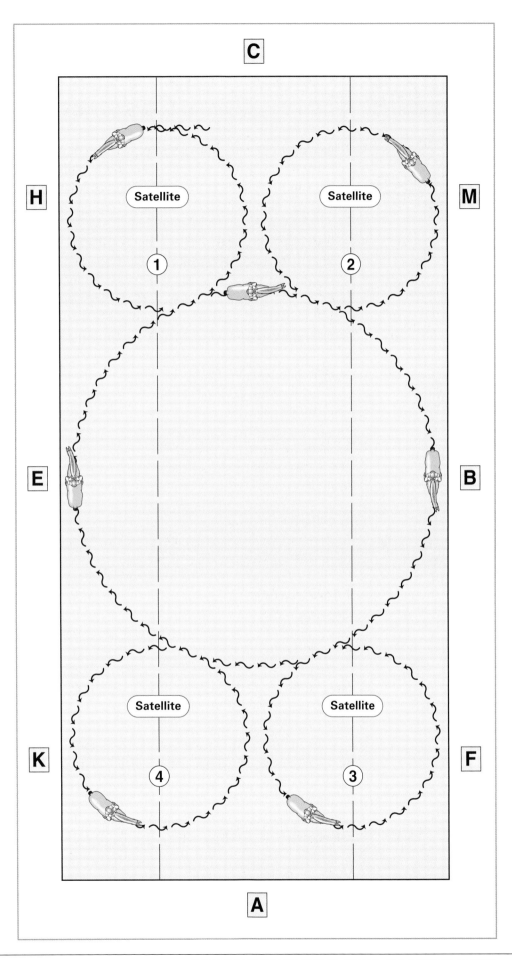

GETTING OFF THE GROUND
Flying Change

THE EXERCISES

Watch a horse cantering round a field, and you'll see that he will put in a flying change – that is, he will change from one lead leg to the other — just when he needs to, quite spontaneously. The aids for flying change are the same as those for canter from trot, so any rider capable of that transition, and with a horse of sufficient collection and training, can aspire to this movement. What is important is that either you or your horse has some experience of accomplishing a flying change, and that your horse can canter correctly on a straight line, and is happy and balanced in counter canter. Begin with simple changes before moving on to a first exercise in flying change.

The change of legs should take place during the moment of suspension in the canter, and the exact moment at which the change needs to be asked for by the rider varies from horse to horse, depending on how quickly he responds, his stage of training, and his athletic ability.

TIPS FOR ACHIEVING FLYING CHANGE

❏ You will know which leg your horse prefers in canter. Start teaching flying change from the difficult lead leg to the favoured lead leg, and only change to the other way once he understands the exercise.

❏ Use repetition to help with your training (see Exercise 13), and in the initial stages always ask for the change at the same spot in the arena.

❏ Be satisfied with one or two changes in the early stages of training, and do not punish your horse if he doesn't understand what you are asking for. He is your pupil, and it's your job to teach him.

SIMPLE CHANGE AND ITS RELATION TO FLYING CHANGE

❏ A simple change is a transition from canter direct to walk, and then from walk direct to canter on the opposite lead. In a dressage test the horse should show between three and five clear walk steps — although the more advanced the horse, the fewer the walk steps. The essence of the simple change is that it should be direct from canter to walk and then walk to canter with no trot steps; in elementary level you are allowed to make a few trot steps in the downward transition, but it wouldn't earn you a good mark. Your aim is to get a direct transition from canter to walk and ensure your horse takes his weight on his hind legs, and that from the canter, the very first step of walk is a clean step, and not a jog.

❏ The simple change prepares your horse for flying change in three ways:

• Alternating between left and right leads initially shows which lead your horse finds more difficult: the simple change, when ridden correctly, with repetition will redress this imbalance.

• To make the transition from canter to walk requires in the horse a fairly high degree of collection, and it is this degree of collection that is necessary to perform flying change.

• A change from left lead to right lead in the canter requires the rider to switch from position left to position right. Your horse's recognition of the change of lead that is required of him when you make this position change is developed via simple changes.

BEGINNERS

PRELIMINARY

NOVICE

ELEMENTARY ✪✪✪

MEDIUM ✪✪✪✪✪

Preparing for flying change using simple change

The horse becomes familiar with your leg and seat position to dictate which lead he is to pick up, and this opens the door for flying change, and teaches him to associate left lead with position left in the rider's legs, and vice versa.

How do I ride this exercise?
- ❏ On the left rein, in walk, ride across the diagonal from H to F.
- ❏ On reaching F, ask for right canter.
- ❏ Just after K, turn on the short diagonal to B: ask for a few steps in walk…
- ❏ …and then change to left canter.
- ❏ Ride a turn at B, and on the short diagonal to H, ask for a few strides in walk…
- ❏ …and then change to the right lead once more.
- ❏ Repeat on the opposite rein.

What should happen?
Your horse should become confident and competent in making clean and accurate simple changes.

Double check
Make sure your horse is straight during the simple changes: generally this means, when you take your leg back to give the aid for the new canter lead, make sure he doesn't bring his quarters to the inside.

Moving on
Try a three-loop serpentine with simple changes.

What can go wrong?
Your horse breaks to trot when you collect him for the simple change.
Practise collecting him, but then quickly ride on again without the walk transition until he understands what is being asked of him.

If it's not working…
Go back to working on a 20m circle and ride canter/walk, walk/canter on the circle. This means you can address the transitions without having the complication of left lead and right lead.

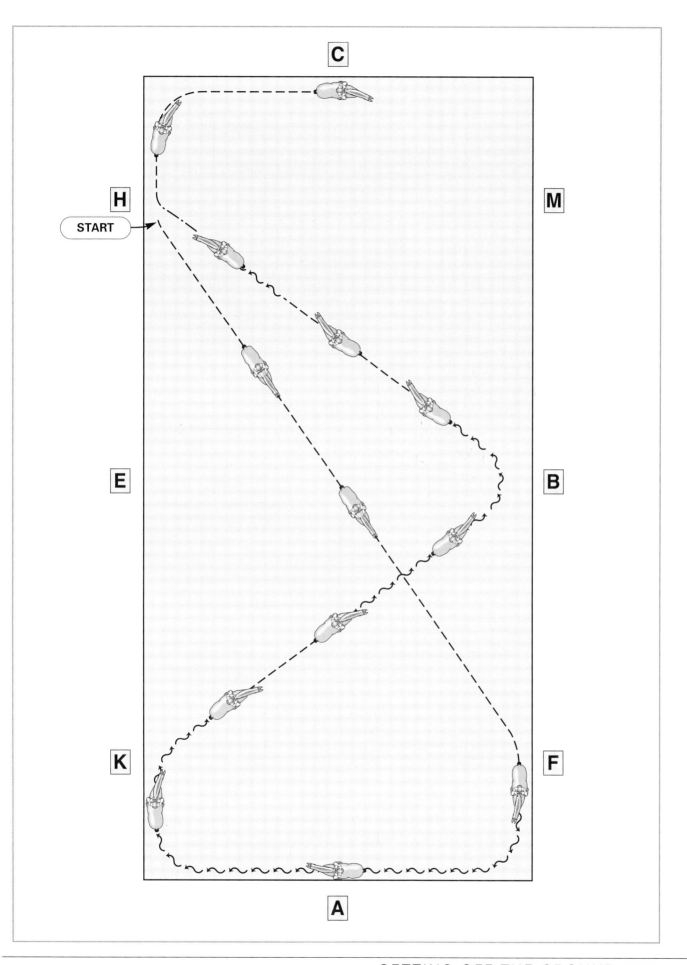

A first exercise in flying change

Of all the movements that we ride, a flying change has the most potential for upsetting your horse if it is not ridden correctly. Balance and straightness are crucial, and it should not be attempted until you are in absolute control of both. There are several different ways to teach flying change; however, this exercise is one of the best.

BONUS

After teaching a horse to accept the bridle, flying change is one of the biggest steps you can take in your joint training.

How do I ride this exercise?
- ❏ On the right rein, establish canter along the long side of the arena.
- ❏ At the end of the long side, ride a half 10m circle to the centre line, and…
- ❏ …change the rein back to E or B.
- ❏ Now ride a few steps of counter canter, and…
- ❏ …attempt a flying change just before the corner.

How do I ride a flying change?
- ❏ Establish canter.
- ❏ Get your horse's attention with a half-halt.
- ❏ Move what was your outside leg forward to the girth.
- ❏ Almost simultaneously move your other leg – was inside leg, now 'new' outside leg — back with a stronger contact behind the girth.
- ❏ Just before the change, flex your horse slightly in the new direction but allow your 'new' inside hand to give slightly, whilst retaining a light contact. Your reins should control shoulders, balance and speed.
- ❏ Use your seat to drive your horse forwards – though you must remain light enough in the saddle to allow your horse to make the jump from one leg to the next. Your new inside seatbone should be pushed slightly forward.
- ❏ Now use your legs to ride the horse forwards and straight, keeping your 'new' inside leg on the girth to keep the rhythm.

RIDER'S TIP

Try not to throw your weight from one seatbone to the next as this disturbs the horse's balance.

What should happen?
The half 10m circles help to collect your horse. The return to the track enables you to straighten the horse in counter canter so that when you ask for a flying change he is straight before he has to negotiate the corner.

Double check
Stay calm, do not put too much pressure on your horse, if it doesn't work, keep trying.

What can go wrong?
Your horse may increase his speed in anticipation of the change.
If this happens it is likely that the change will be late behind. Try working on a circle with transitions from counter canter to true canter via simple changes to slow him.

If it's not working...
Go back to simple changes (Exercise 96).

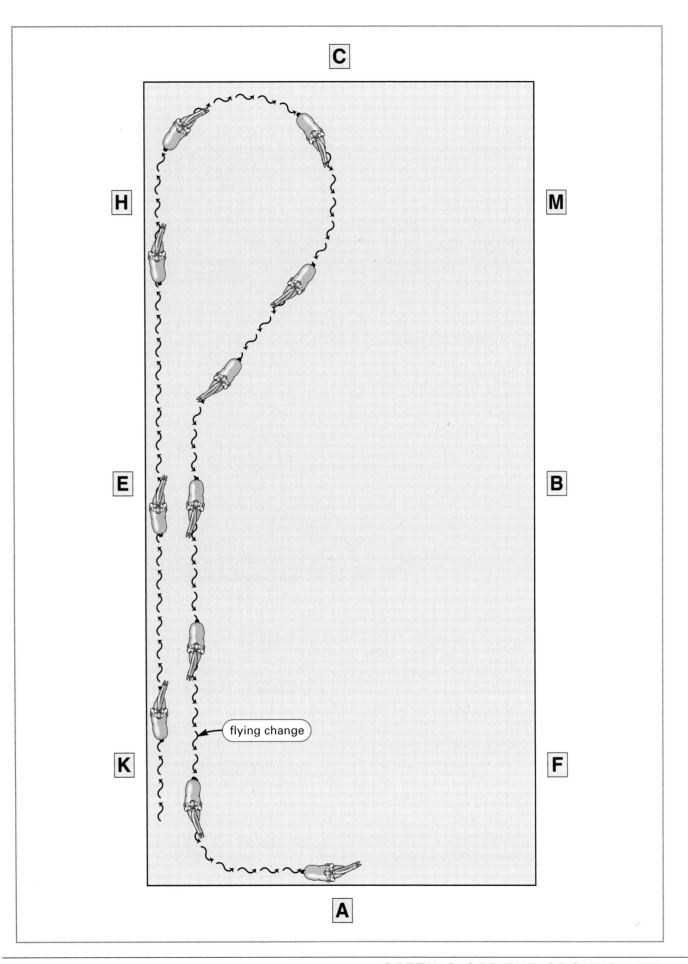

flying change

Half-pass into flying change

This exercise calls for a high degree of collection and obedience from the horse. Moreover, half-pass in canter is a good preparation for canter pirouette. This is because it improves lateral bend, helps to make the horse more connected and 'coming through', and encourages him to take more weight on to his inside hind leg – all of which will give the flying change more 'jump' and quality.

How do I ride this exercise?

❏ Along the M to F side of the school, establish canter on the right rein.
❏ Turn on to the centre line from A, and half-pass right back to the track, arriving at the track between B and M.
❏ Canter straight for a few steps, and then ask for a flying change just before M.
❏ Use the track round the outside of the school to rebalance the horse so that he is ready again to turn up the centre line on the left lead at A;
❏ ...then half-pass back to the track between H and E.
❏ Straighten the horse for a few steps for a flying change at H.
❏ Continue around the track a little before walking and resting.

What should happen?

The half-pass before the flying change collects the horse, and focuses his attention on the rider's outside leg – in this case his left leg in half-pass right; then when the rider changes the aids and brings the right leg back in the aid for a flying change, it stands out in the horse's attention.

RIDER'S TIP

Riding a few straight strides of counter canter will give your horse time to familiarize himself with the sequence of movements.

Double check

Be sure the horse allows you to straighten him between the half-pass and the change.

Moving on

Try the counter change of hand as described in Exercise 87.

What can go wrong?

Your horse changes lead in front or behind.
This is called becoming disunited. You have two choices:
1 Halt, and strike off again in canter on the original leg, and then ask again for the flying change. By doing this your horse will learn only the correct way of responding to your aids for a flying change: that is, springing through in front and behind.
2 Continuing in canter, you can try to persuade the horse to change back on to the original lead and then ask for a flying change a second time. This works well with stubborn horses that are not going forward or responding to your forward aids.

If it's not working...

Sometimes a horse will use the flying change to escape the demands of collection in the half-pass. If this happens, work on half-pass from the track to the centre line, and then straight with no flying change, until your horse is totally comfortable with that exercise; only then try again.

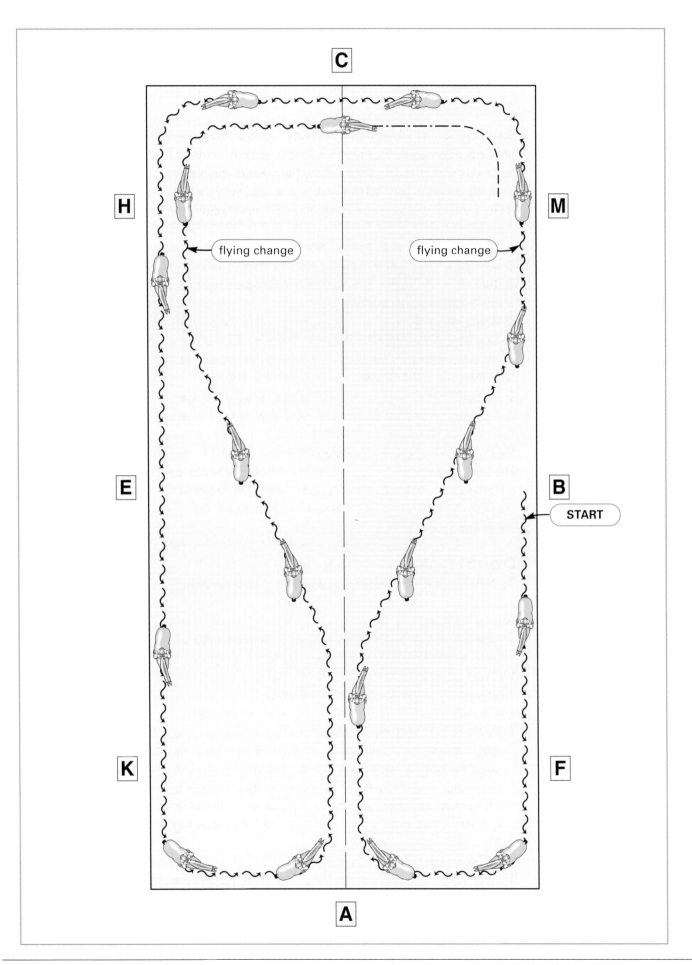

C

H

M

flying change

flying change

E

B

START

K

F

A

EXERCISE

99

BEGINNERS

PRELIMINARY

NOVICE

ELEMENTARY

MEDIUM ✪✪✪✪✪

Preparing for flying changes on a serpentine

The preparation and presentation time for flying change on a serpentine is shorter than anywhere else in the school: the challenge is therefore in turning the horse from the track across the school on the appropriate curve, and within two steps straightening and presenting him for the flying change. To help a horse become accomplished at flying changes on a serpentine, it is good to practise on the E/B (half school) line.

BONUS

This is the best way of preparing your horse for flying change on the serpentine.

How do I ride this exercise?

❏ On the left rein, canter up the long side from F and turn left at B.

❏ Straighten the horse for a couple of steps, and...

❏ ...ride a flying change over X.

❏ At E, turn right.

❏ Continue round the school and turn right at B...

❏ straighten the horse and...

❏ ...ride a flying change at X.

❏ At E, turn left.

What should happen?

Your horse should turn correctly, in balance, from the outside rein and outside leg, and arrive on the half school line still with 5m to spare before X. In those 5m he can be presented for the flying change and the correct aids given.

Double check

Be sure that your horse is being turned from the outside leg and outside rein, and not being pulled around by the inside rein, in which case the quarters will slip out during the turn.

Moving on

When your horse is confident in this exercise on the half school line, make the turn on two occasions: turn left half way between F and B for your first turn across the school, and then turn right half way between E and H for your second line across the school. In effect, this becomes a square serpentine.

What can go wrong?

Your horse loses balance and doesn't turn correctly at B, falling on to his right shoulder so that you cannot present him for the flying change.

In these circumstances you can take the width of the school to straighten and align your horse as if for a flying change, but then turn left at E, and come round and present him again.

If it's not working...

Take the width of the school to straighten as if for a flying change, but don't ride the flying change, simply turn left at E and come round again for another attempt.

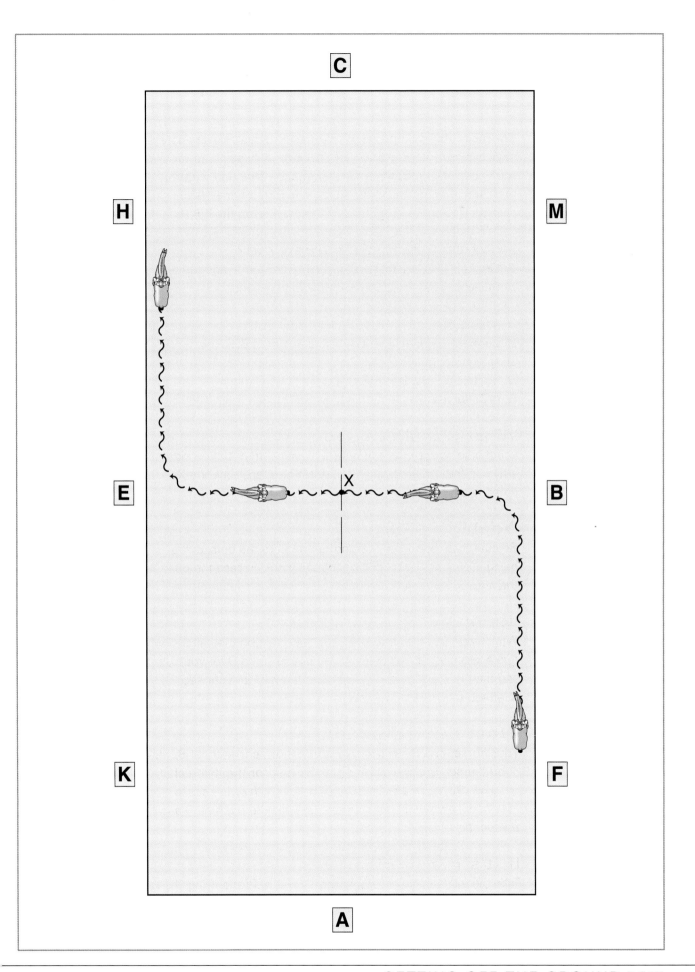

Flying change on a serpentine

To perform flying change on a serpentine is really quite difficult as you have so little time to prepare the horse for the change. It requires a very well balanced horse, but in the words of consultant editor, Andrew Day, it is 'extremely good fun to ride!'

BONUS

This is a great straightening exercise, as it gives you a chance to compare the left and the right rein in your horse's canter. It is also featured in most of the advanced medium standard British Dressage tests, and some of the advanced tests.

How do I ride this exercise?

❏ Ride a three-loop serpentine commencing at A in right canter, and ask for a flying change as you cross the centre line.

❏ Keep the loops of the serpentine in a shape that is comfortable for your horse, but ride a couple of strides straight before, and after, asking for the flying change.

❏ At the opposite end of the school rejoin the track, and ride large to repeat.

What should happen?

Your horse should conclude each arc of the loop, and allow you to straighten and prepare him for the flying change. He should make a neat, co-ordinated flying change over the centre line, and then take one-and-a-half or two steps straight before starting to make the arc of the next loop.

Double check

Make sure your horse is straight before making the change.

Moving on

It is possible to ride a three-loop serpentine in counter canter with a flying change over the centre line. This is a good exercise for Freestyle Kür.

What can go wrong?

Your horse is too early in front or too late behind, and makes what is known as a 'broken' or 'split' change.

This is most commonly due to a loss of balance on the part of your horse, which prevents you from being able to straighten him before the change. If this happens, go back to an easier flying-change exercise where you have more preparation time.

If it's not working...

Go back to an easier, simpler flying-change exercise, where you have a longer period on a straight line to prepare for the flying change.

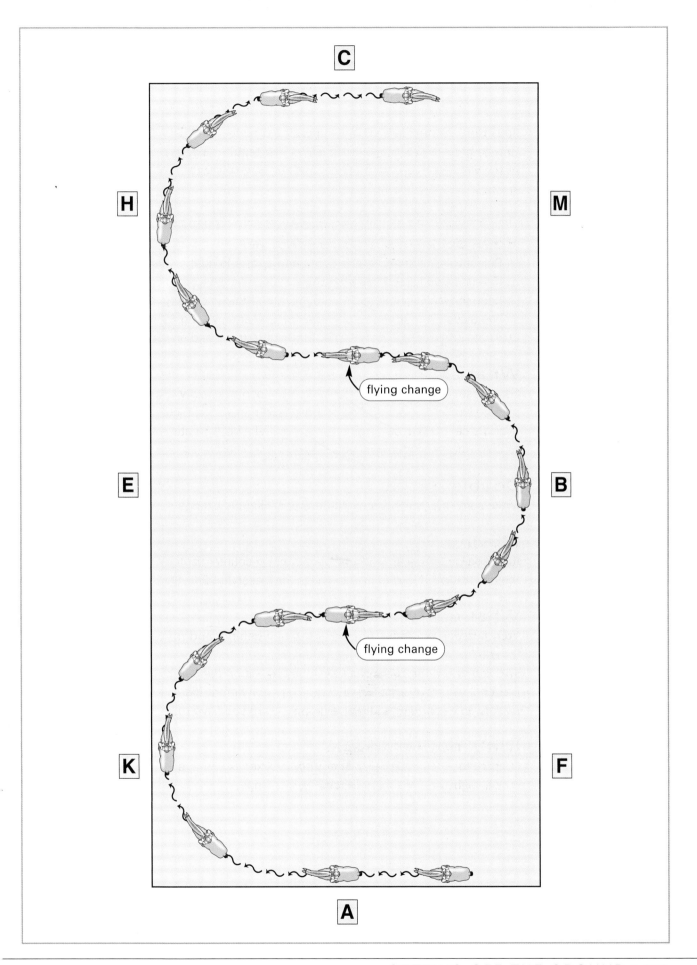

flying change

flying change

EXERCISE

101

BEGINNERS

PRELIMINARY

NOVICE

ELEMENTARY

MEDIUM ✪✪✪✪✪

Flying change on a circle

Teaching the horse to make changes on the circle is a great way to strengthen his technique, and important for the advanced freestyle dressage competition. This exercise is really good for improving forward movement, getting your horse to lift up, and making your flying changes more expressive.

How do I ride this exercise?
❏ At the E or B marker on the right rein in canter, ride a 20m circle.
❏ As you pass E, ride a flying change to the outside lead;
❏ then make another as you pass B, to return to the inside lead.

What should happen?
In this exercise your horse will really have to step forward with his new inside hind leg, so he will need to be sufficiently balanced in counter canter before you attempt this exercise.

Double check
Be sure that the rhythm stays the same in both the counter canter and the true canter.

Moving on
Try riding four flying changes: at E and at B, and each time you cross the centre line.

What can go wrong?
Your horse jumps sideways.
Most problems in the flying change are caused by incorrect preparation or inaccurate aids. Swinging or jumping sideways is usually the result of leg aids used too strongly: in effect you are pushing your horse sideways, when he needs to be straight through the flying change. Concentrate on keeping your horse straight with your aids, and riding him forwards with plenty of impulsion.

If it's not working...
Go back to working on flying change on a straight line.

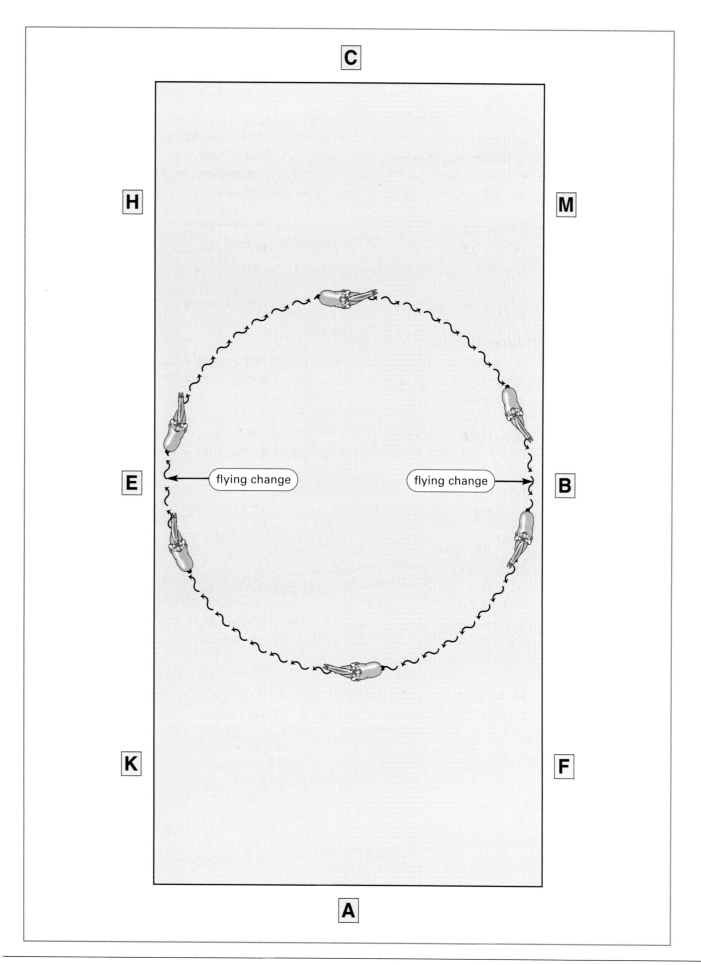

Celebrity biographies

I'd like to say a big thank you to all the celebrity riders who kindly contributed their favourite schooling exercises for inclusion in this book. Despite hectic schedules and international commitments they believe sufficiently in the value of schooling to want to pass on their expertise and experiences. I'm sure you're familiar with all of the names but here's a round up of what they've achieved up to the point of publication of this book, May 2005.

RICHARD DAVISON

Richard Davison, British Dressage National Champion 2003, has represented Great Britain at three Olympic Games, two World Equestrian Games, three European Championships and four World Cup Finals. Competing throughout Europe and the rest of the world, this experienced dressage rider from Uttoxeter in Staffordshire can truly be described as an international competitor.

When not competing, Richard, trained himself by Conrad Schumacher, is a much sought-after trainer and clinician. He is a member of the FEI Dressage Committee, and vice president of the International Dressage Riders Club. He has been voted *Dressage* magazine's 'Trainer of the Year', and *Horse & Hound's* 'Rider of the Year'.

KAREN DIXON

Karen began competing in the international arena at the age of 18, and has more than 20 years of competitive experience behind her: this includes having represented Great Britain in four Olympic Games during her eventing career. Regularly placed at all the major international eventing competitions held in the UK, she is a popular and well respected rider; when not competing, she trains horses and riders at her yard in County Durham.

PIPPA FUNNELL

In 2003 Pippa Funnell, at the age of 34, became the rider ranked number one in the world. She had just completed the Rolex Grand Slam of Eventing, winning Burghley, Lexington and Badminton in the same year, and in 2004 represented the United Kingdom at the Olympics in Athens. This was the second time she had represented her country at the Olympics, having won individual silver and team bronze at Sydney in 2000.

Pippa had struggled to make the breakthrough into senior international competitions, held back, by her own admission, by nerves. Help from a sports psychologist turned this around, and she has not looked back since.

MARY KING

Ask most non-equestrians to name an international rider and they will say 'Mary King'. During her eventing career, which has spanned 20 years, Mary has represented her country in four Olympic Games, including Athens in 2004. She has received four team gold medals at World and European Championships, and has won the title of British Champion four times.

Throughout all this fame and excitement, Mary remains remarkably down-to-earth and dedicated to her sport; when not competing she works hard at home in Sidmouth in Devon, training her horses and those of other riders.

JOHN LASSETTER

John Lassetter's abilities with horses became apparent at a really young age, and distracted him from his original ambition to become an actor. He has used his love of theatre to bring the skills of a dressage rider to a wide audience via his entertaining finales to demonstrations and clinics across the country.

John won a rare scholarship to the Spanish Riding School in Vienna, and then went on to train with the Cadre Noir in Saumur. A successful international competitor himself, he conducts clinics throughout Europe, and trains horses and riders in the UK, with the assistance of his wife Charlotte at their home in Goodwood in Sussex.

Sylvia Loch is a rider and trainer of classical equitation whose international career has spanned four decades. Best known for her books, videos and clinics, Sylvia has helped thousands of riders achieve a greater understanding with their horses. Originally trained in Portugal and influenced by maestros such as Nuno Oliveira, Sylvia bases her work on an understanding of the biomechanics of both horse and rider. In 1996 she founded The Classical Riding Club to spread the principle of 'Harmony in Horsemanship' and to provide a stimulating forum for education and discussion. For further information about her work, visit www.classical-dressage.net

SYLVIA LOCH

Jennie Loriston-Clarke has competed for Britain at every Olympic Games from 1972 to 1988 (1980 Alternative Olympics at Goodwood). Regularly placed in the World Equestrian Championships and the equestrian World Cup Finals, she retired from international competition in 1995 after winning her tenth Addington National Championship Grand Prix; however, she still competes in the UK.

Jennie continues to work as a breeder and trainer, and judges both in the UK and internationally. The influence of her training, and of the horses of the Catherstone Stud, run by Jennie, is evident throughout the equestrian world.

JENNIE LORISTON-CLARKE

The list of Lizzie Murray's notable competitive successes begins when she was 17 years old. The daughter of Jennie Loriston-Clarke, she began riding when she was two, and now rides and trains horses and riders from the very successful Catherstone Stud, still working alongside her mother.

Whilst Lizzie, now 33, is best known for her dressage skills – she was on the longlist for the 1996 Olympic games – her other equestrian activities have included eventing and showjumping. Lizzie cites her mother and Henk Van Bergan as the main influences in her riding career: 'I was lucky enough to travel as groom for my mother as a child, and saw many top riders and trainers in action.'

LIZZIE MURRAY

At the Olympics in Athens in 2004, 31-year-old Lee Pearson represented his country for the second time as a member of the Paralympic team. Lee also competes in able-bodied competition, and came second in the Medium Restricted class at the Winter Dressage Championships in 2004.

Lee loves training almost more than competition, and still refers to schoolwork as 'playing'. 'Although we call it playing, we have work time in the arena and then we have mad time!' Lee tends to school for between one hour to one hour and 20 minutes – a little longer than average – 'because I am not as strong as other riders, and so on, I like to get through to the horse exactly what I mean. I've never, ever sat on horse and it's just happened: my horses can read my mind, and still decide they don't want to do it! You need to be more flexible when schooling, rather than have too many rules.'

LEE PEARSON

At the time of writing Tim Stockdale is ranked eighth in the British Show Jumping Association listings. He has represented Great Britain on 33 occasions in Nations Cup teams, and was also on the World Equestrian Games team in 2002, and winner of the Horse of the Year Show Grand Prix. He started riding at the age of seven, coming up through the Pony Club ranks and training with Mike Saywell and Graham Fletcher. He competes regularly, and trains professionally at his yard in Northamptonshire, mainly showjumpers.

TIM STOCKDALE

Exercise index

All references are to exercise numbers and not pages